Legali...

Editorial Advisors:
Gloria A. Aluise
Attorney at Law
Jonathan Neville
Attorney at Law
Robert A. Wyler
Attorney at Law

Authors:
Gloria A. Aluise
Attorney at Law
David H. Barber
Attorney at Law
Daniel O. Bernstine
Attorney at Law
D. Steven Brewster
C.P.A.
Roy L. Brooks
Professor of Law
Frank L. Bruno
Attorney at Law
Scott M. Burbank
C.P.A.
Jonathan C. Carlson
Professor of Law
Charles N. Carnes
Professor of Law
Paul S. Dempsey
Professor of Law
Jerome A. Hoffman
Professor of Law
Mark R. Lee
Professor of Law
Jonathan Neville
Attorney at Law
Laurence C. Nolan
Professor of Law
Arpiar Saunders
Attorney at Law
Robert A. Wyler
Attorney at Law

CORPORATIONS

Adaptable to Sixth Edition*
of Choper Casebook

By Mark R. Lee
Professor of Law

and

Noel L. Smith
Attorney at Law

*If your casebook is a newer edition, go to www.gilbertlaw.com
to see if a supplement is available for this title.

THOMSON

BAR/BRI

EDITORIAL OFFICES: 111 W. Jackson Blvd., 7th Floor, Chicago, IL 60604
REGIONAL OFFICES: Chicago, Dallas, Los Angeles, New York, Washington, D.C.

SERIES EDITOR
Gail O'Gradney, J.D.
Attorney at Law

PRODUCTION MANAGER
Elizabeth G. Duke

FIRST PRINTING—2005

Legalines®

SHORT SUMMARY OF CONTENTS

TABLE OF CONTENTS AND SHORT REVIEW OUTLINE

I. INTRODUCTION

A. THE LEGAL CHARACTER OF THE CORPORATION: FACTORS INFLUENCING CHOICE OF CORPORATE FORM

1. **Major Features of the Corporate Form.** Several features make the corporate form more attractive for organizing large-scale businesses than other forms, such as the sole proprietorship and the partnership.

   a. **Limited liability.** Absent an agreement to the contrary, investors in an incorporated business bear no business-related liability beyond their investment—except in limited circumstances where courts "pierce the corporate veil" or apply related doctrines discussed later. In contrast, sole proprietors and partners risk all of the attachable assets that they own.

   b. **Perpetual existence.** Absent an agreement to the contrary, an incorporated business formally endures indefinitely, *i.e.,* the death, withdrawal, or insolvency of a principal has no formal effect on an incorporated business. In contrast, such an event would formally dissolve a proprietorship or partnership (absent an agreement to the contrary).

   c. **Easy transferability of investors' interests.** Absent an agreement to the contrary, an investor may transfer his interest in an incorporated business at will. A partner, in contrast, may transfer only a limited interest in partnership distributions, and may not transfer his partnership status (absent an agreement to the contrary). Free transferability makes possible secondary markets, *e.g.,* stock exchanges, in which the interests of corporate investors are traded.

   d. **Centralized management.** Absent an agreement to the contrary, investors in an incorporated business (acting in that role) do not make the day-to-day business decisions made by sole proprietors and partners. In fact, with respect to all but a handful of business decisions, these investors hold no formal decisionmaking power. The "equity" investors (*i.e.,* shareholders) elect a board of directors, and the directors collectively, along with the officers that they appoint, formally hold most of the decisionmaking power.

2. **Tax Treatment.** The choice of organizational form may have significant tax consequences, particularly income tax consequences. Generally, if an incorporated enterprise generates net revenue, this revenue is taxed (rates and brackets for corporate income tax differ from those for personal income tax) *in addition to* any personal income that the key actors derive from it. This would result in "double taxation" but for the fact that an enterprise may deduct one dollar from its revenue for each dollar distributed as personal income (except for dividends). (*Note:* If the IRS deems the other personal income, such as salaries, interest,

and rent "excessive," the IRS will treat the "excess" as "dividends" for the purpose of the income tax.) If the incorporated enterprise yields a loss—which many, if not most, start-ups do initially—the loss would not reduce any person's tax bill, although it might reduce the enterprise's tax bill for past or future years. In contrast, the revenues of an unincorporated business are subject only to personal income tax unless the principals choose two-tier taxation. They are subject to this tax whether or not the revenues are actually distributed; revenues and losses are "flowed through" to the sole proprietor, partners, or limited liability company ("LLC"). The principals of a closely held incorporated business may obtain partnership-like tax treatment by choosing "S" status if they, their business activities, and the organization of their enterprise qualify for this status.

3.   **Entity vs. Aggregate Treatment.** The income tax laws generally treat incorporated businesses as entities but unincorporated ones as aggregates of the individuals involved. This distinction abounds in the law. For example, consider property to which title is held in the name of a business. If the business is organized as a corporation, the principals have no formal legal interest in the property. If the business is organized as a partnership, each partner has a formal legal interest called a tenancy in co-partnership. An increasing number of state statutes, however, treat partnerships and LLCs as entities for a variety of purposes, including suing and being sued.

B.   A PRINCIPAL THEME OF CORPORATION LAW

Centralized management and perpetual existence could put the investment of passive shareholders at considerable risk from the actions of officers and directors. (Of course, limited liability and easy transferability would mitigate this risk.) Constraining the behavior of officers and directors, however, could result in a lower return to the shareholders. Much of the law of corporations addresses this trade-off.

C.   A SCORECARD OF THE PLAYERS: PUBLIC CORPORATIONS, DIRECTORS, AND SHAREHOLDERS

Corporation law provides for the roles of managers, directors, and shareholders, but it permits one person to play any combination of these roles. In a typical closely held corporation, the directors come from the ranks of the principal shareholders, and some of them, at least, also serve as managers. In a typical publicly held corporation, on the other hand, a majority of the board will consist of "outside" directors, *i.e.,* nonemployees owning relatively few shares.

1.   **Outside Directors and Their Influence.** Most outside directors are chief executive officers ("CEOs") and chief financial officers ("CFOs") of other corporations. Some outside directors, however, may have business relationships with the corporations on whose boards they serve—such as outside counsel or investment banker—which may somewhat align their interests with those of

the CEO. In any event, the part-time nature of their position and lack of staff constrain their influence. So, too, does the control of the board's agenda exercised by the CEO by virtue of his customary board chairmanship. In crises, however, outside directors have time and again removed CEOs or otherwise intervened decisively in corporate affairs.

Boards of public corporations typically operate through committees, among the most important of which are the nominating, compensation, and audit committees. Audit committees for corporations listed on the New York Stock Exchange ("NYSE") consist solely of outside directors (as required by NYSE rules first adopted in the late 1970s). So, too, do the nominating and compensation committees of many large corporations.

2. **Institutional Shareholders.** Investors in institutions such as pension funds and insurance companies now own more than one-half of the outstanding stock of publicly held United States corporations. Many of these institutions, however, hold relatively small quantities of any one corporation's stock. This facilitates diversification and permits the institutions to more readily sell their stake in a corporation without affecting its stock price. Even institutions with relatively large stakes in a single corporation, however, may remain passive investors. Monitoring and influencing a corporation's management can prove costly, and because of competition for pension and mutual fund accounts, fund managers cannot easily raise their fees to cover these costs. Moreover, a fund manager may not wish to confront (at least openly) a corporation's management for fear that he, or the investment banking firm with which he is affiliated, will lose a client or fail to attract a new one.

D. HISTORY AND EVOLUTION OF THE BUSINESS CORPORATION

1. **English Ancestors of the Modern Business Corporation.** From the late 1500s, the English Crown chartered incorporated businesses to develop foreign trade and colonies. The revenues generated by these businesses served as the payment for carrying out national policy. To consolidate power, the Crown insisted that only it—later, the Crown in Parliament—could create an incorporated business. As trading operations became more important than public functions for these royally chartered businesses, competitors and others used legal self-help to obtain some of the advantages of the corporate form. They organized their businesses using a combination of the law of trusts and either the law of principal/agent or the law of partnership.

2. **Developments in the United States.**

   a. **The law.** After the Revolution, the states succeeded to the position of the Crown with respect to incorporation. Given technological conditions and the consequent size of business, there was little demand for corporate charters until the late 1700s when much larger businesses—many of them franchised monopolies—began to operate. Political support for regulating these franchised monopolies through their charters tended to reinforce the claim of politicians to the sole power to create incorporated businesses. But the demand for charters grew so large that it swamped the legislative process. Some legislatures adopted enabling statutes that, although highly restrictive, did permit many people to organize businesses in the corporate form without obtaining a legislative charter. Organizing businesses under these statutes proved so beneficial that people in other states paid extra fees and taxes for the opportunity to do so. In response, some legislatures competed for these fees and taxes by adopting less restrictive enabling statutes. Critics of this competition called it the "race to the bottom." Proponents hailed it as a mechanism for prompting government to free people to organize their business and financial affairs to mutual advantage.

b. **Business organization.** Technological developments held out the potential that business could profitably undertake activities of increasingly greater scope, some of which involved vertical integration. Large-scale activities, however, posed large-scale coordination and financing challenges. Business responded to the coordination challenges with managerial hierarchies and specialization. The professional manager began to emerge. The response to financing challenges reinforced this trend. Entrepreneurial families turned first to financial institutions and then to the larger capital market. To compete for investment funds, the families had to cede increasing control to professional managers. Thus, "family capitalism" gave way to "financial capitalism," which in turn gave way to "managerial capitalism." In many large modern businesses, so many people supplied investment capital that no cohesive group of them had the "influence, knowledge, experience, or commitment to take part in the high command. Salaried managers determined long-term policy as well as managed short-term operating activities." [Chandler, The Visible Hand: The Managerial Revolution in American Business (1977)] In *The Modern Corporation and Private Property* (1932), Berle and Means called this development a "separation of ownership and control." They advanced the theory, contested by many economists, that this separation gave top managers substantial discretion to pursue their own interests, even at the expense of shareholders.

E. ECONOMIC ANALYSIS OF THE CORPORATION

1. **A Perspective.** Economics views the incorporated business as a group of individuals, each pursuing her own self-interest, constrained by a variety of market forces. This perspective sheds considerable light on the issues raised by the law of corporations.

2. **The Nature of the Firm and the Rise of the M-Form Corporation.** A joint enterprise may be organized across a market or hierarchically ("within a firm"),

or by combining the two in one of a wide variety of ways. Economics suggests that people will tend to choose the most cost-effective method of organization. They will try to economize on "transaction costs." Putting top managers in a position to pursue their own interests at the expense of shareholders is a transaction cost. Many economists, notably Oliver Williamson, argue that the multidivisional or "M-form" corporation—in which senior management engages in long-term planning, allocates capital to independently operated divisions, and monitors the managers of each—evolved as a cost-effective device for coping with this transaction cost.

3. **Managerial Discretion: The Debate Over the Berle/Means Thesis.** A variety of market forces and self-interest (*i.e.,* the compensation and wealth of top management may depend to a considerable extent on the value of the shares of the businesses it manages) constrain top management's discretion to pursue its own interests at the expense of shareholders. Advocates of additional legal constraints on top management have argued that top management does not try to profit maximize but to "profit satisfice"—to obtain a level of profits sufficient to assure interference-free operation of the firm. According to this argument, sometimes called the "behavioral model," top management diverts some potential profits to pay for growth-maximizing acquisitions, bigger staffs, or other "goods" that benefit itself—for example, by increasing job security— less visibly than direct compensation.

4. **The "Agency Cost" Model.** Principals always face some challenge controlling the actions of their agents. Many economists, notably Jensen and Meckling, view the possibility that top management of large businesses may enjoy discretion to pursue its own interests at the expense of shareholders as one example of this common phenomenon. Principals meet this challenge by offering incentives (*e.g.,* stock options as part of the compensation package), monitoring (*e.g.,* engaging independent auditors), and obtaining bonds or bond-like undertakings (*e.g.,* salary dependent on profits). To take these actions, however, principals must incur costs, so they will only go so far to control their agents. At some point, principals would rather just accept the costs of self-interested behavior on the part of agents. These costs are "agency costs." Economics suggests that people will tend to organize their business and financial activities to economize on agency costs. For example, they may finance the business with substantial debt if creditors enjoy a comparative advantage vis-a-vis shareholders in monitoring top management. In this model, top management suffers if it fails to adopt mechanisms designed to economize on agency costs because it will have to pay more to hire investors' capital. Advocates of additional legal constraints on top management argue that investors lack sufficient information to take into account the prospect of self-interested management behavior. In particular, according to this argument, investors cannot predict if or when a new top management team will make changes that better accommodate self-interested behavior. Because of the resulting uncertainty, the argument continues, shareholders may make investment decisions based on perceptions about

average agency costs, which would have the effect of raising the cost of capital for "good" managers and lowering it for "bad" ones.

5.   **The Corporation as a Contract.** Many economists view the corporation as a "set of contracts" or "series of bargains." Of course, the "bargaining" is usually, if not always, of the implicit kind. On this view, corporate law provides handy standard form contract terms, which the participants in an incorporated business may alter if they find it convenient to do so. Courts should interpret the terms, as modified by the parties, to effectuate the reasonable expectations of the participants. Advocates of additional legal constraints on top management accept only a modified version of this view. They argue that courts should interpret at least some of the terms of the "corporate contract" as mandatory, designed to protect shareholders from overreaching.

F. CORPORATE "SOCIAL RESPONSIBILITY"

1.   **To Whom Do Fiduciary Duties Run?** A number of academics have cheered the prospect that management of large businesses might have discretion to pursue goals other than profit maximization. These academics argue that management should use whatever discretion it might have to meet what they call the corporation's "social responsibility." Insofar as this argument seeks to justify expenditures that would otherwise not be made, it has elicited a number of objections: (i) diverting funds in this way is functionally equivalent to levying a tax and then deciding how the proceeds should be spent, a distinctly political process without the checks established by the political process; (ii) management lacks information about the real consequences of diverting funds; (iii) management cannot know how much diversion is justified; and (iv) management could readily use "social responsibility" as an excuse for inferior business results caused in fact by managerial shirking or pursuit of self-interest.

2.   **The Rise of Corporate Constituency Statutes.** Beginning in the early 1980s, 29 states have enacted statutes that authorize—and in some instances appear to command—directors to consider the interests of nonshareholder constituencies like employees, creditors, customers, and local communities. Many of these statutes apply only to corporate control transactions. (The threat of hostile takeovers prompted the lobbying that resulted in the enactment of these statutes.) Only a few of these statutes contain command language, and they may command precious little because they practically bar enforcement.

3.   **Objections to Constituency Statutes.** Requiring or permitting directors to serve both shareholders and nonshareholders may diminish the incentive to engage in economically efficient risk-taking. It may also expose directors to increased risk of litigation and liability—because the interests of these constituencies conflict—while rendering them effectively responsible to none. Constituency statutes put directors to the task of ascertaining the public interest, a task to which they may not be well-suited by virtue of personal characteristics or in-

centives. Moreover, nonshareholders can negotiate contractual protection much more readily than shareholders seeking protection for their contingent interest in the residual.

The ABA Committee on Corporate Laws urges that courts interpret these constituency statutes as permitting directors to "take into account the interests of other constituencies, but only as, and to the extent that, the directors are acting in the best interests, long- as well as short-term, of the shareholders and the corporation."

4. **The Judicial Development of Nonshareholder Fiduciary Duties.** In *Credit Lyonnais Bank Nederland, N.V. v. Pathe Communications Corp.*, 1991 W.L. 277613 (Del. Ch. 1991), the owner of 98% of the shares of nearly insolvent MGM alleged that the corporation's management and principal creditor had illegally blocked a high risk business strategy favored by the shareholder. The Chancellor held that the directors had acted properly, opining that, "[a]t least where a corporation is operating in the vicinity of insolvency, a board of directors is not merely the agent of the residual risk bearer, but owes a duty to the corporate enterprise." Shareholders with little to lose, he explained, may take economically inefficient risks. According to the casebook authors, the "clear implication" of this decision is that "investment decisions" appropriate for a solvent firm could constitute a breach of the directors' duties once the firm entered the vaguely defined "vicinity of insolvency."

Invoking the "trust fund" concept, the Chancellor held in *Geyer v. Ingersoll Publications Co.*, 621 A.2d 784 (Del. Ch. 1992), that the board owes fiduciary duties to creditors as of the moment of insolvency, not just when the corporation enters bankruptcy (thereby "prevent[ing] creditors from having to prophesy when directors are entering into transactions that would render the entity insolvent and improperly prejudice creditors' interests"). The duties imposed by this decision and *Credit Lyonnais* may prompt directors of nearly insolvent companies to file earlier for corporate bankruptcy and to reduce risk-taking.

G. THE GLOBAL PERSPECTIVE

In Germany and Japan, banks do a lot of the monitoring that the market does in the United States. Three "universal" banks control a majority of the shares of many large German corporations through stock ownership and by serving as custodians for individual shareholders. Shareholding is nearly as concentrated in Japan, and the concentration is supplemented by cross-ownership. Many large firms belong to a *keiretsu* whose members typically own about 50% of each other's stock collectively, but no more than 5% individually. Typically, one of the nation's large banks owns 5% of the stock of each major member of the *keiretsu* and supplies credit to its industrial members. Similar structures have not arisen in the United States, in part because of banking regulation.

The corporation laws of Germany and several other European countries provide for a nonemployee "supervisory board" that supervises a managers-only "management board." The supervisory board possesses limited powers with respect to management and business decisions, but it appoints and removes the members of the management board. Many of these laws require that employee representatives serve on the supervisory board.

II. BASIC NORMS AND DUTIES FOR MANAGEMENT OF CORPORATIONS

A. TRANSACTIONS OF CORPORATE BUSINESS

1. **The Allocation of Authority in the Standard Corporation.** Most corporation laws identify the board of directors as the group with the authority and responsibility for managing the regular business affairs of the corporation. The board may delegate most of its authority to one or more committees, including an "executive" committee. The directors choose the officers, and the officers conduct day-to-day business. The shareholders have limited powers. They elect the directors and, at least in some circumstances, may remove them. Under many corporation laws, the shareholders may adopt and amend the bylaws, but the shareholders typically delegate this power to the directors. The only other significant power held by the shareholders is the power to vote on fundamental corporate changes, such as dissolution, amendments to the articles of incorporation, mergers, and changes in the rights associated with each share. Shareholders may adopt all manner of resolutions dealing with other matters, but the directors have no obligation to heed them. Qualified shareholders may also initiate shareholder derivative suits against the officers and directors.

2. **Directors and the Formalities of Board Action.** Directors of large incorporated businesses typically exercise their power at formal meetings. At one time, corporation law may have required it, the idea being that the "shareholders . . . are entitled not only to the votes of the directors, . . . but also to their influence and argument in the discussion which leads to the passage of their resolutions." Almost all modern statutes permit directors to participate in meetings via conference call and, at least in some circumstances, to exercise their power without a formal meeting. Directors are entitled to notice of formal meetings, but this right is easily waived. Only a quorum of directors may take action, but some modern statutes permit a sub-majority quorum if the articles of incorporation so provide. If the statute does not expressly provide for the consequences of a failure to observe required formalities, controversy may well arise. One could argue that the consequences should depend on the function served by the relevant formalities, and this argument may explain the results in more recent cases.

3. **Officers.**

   a. **Authority.** While most corporation statutes still require corporations to have certain officers typically, a president, secretary and treasurer—these statutes rarely specify what these officers may or must do. By custom, and sometimes by statute, the secretary keeps the corporate records, including the minutes of board meetings, and the treasurer handles the firm's funds.

But who exercises the power to transact business on behalf of the corporation? Courts usually look to the law of agency for guidance in resolving this matter.

b. Inherent authority of corporation's president--

Menard, Inc. v. Dage-MTI, Inc., 726 N.E.2d 1206 (Ind. 2000).

Facts. Closely held Dage-MITI, Inc. (D), a manufacturer of electronic video products, owned 30 acres of land. Its board of directors authorized its president, Sterling, who was also a director and substantial shareholder, to negotiate for the sale of this acreage. Sterling had served as president from the time that D was organized, had managed its affairs for an extended period of time with little or no board oversight; and had purchased real estate for D without board approval. The board instructed Sterling to obtain its approval before contracting for the sale of this acreage. Sterling entered into negotiations with Menard, Inc. (P) in the course of which P became aware of the need for board approval. The board did not approve, but Sterling represented to P that he had authority from his board of directors to proceed with the transaction. He then purported to enter into a sales contract on D's behalf. P knew that D's corporate counsel had reviewed the contract. One of its terms provided that the persons signing this agreement on behalf of the seller are duly authorized to do so, and their signatures bind the seller in accordance with the terms of this agreement. Approximately three and one-half months after the board learned of Sterling's action, it notified P that Sterling had acted without its authority, and that the board did not wish to proceed with the transaction. P sued for specific performance and damages. The trial court entered judgment for D, and the court of appeals affirmed, concluding that this land transaction was "extraordinary" for a manufacturer of electronic video products, so Sterling was not performing an act that was appropriate in the ordinary course of the company's business.

Issue. Is D bound by the contract entered into purportedly on its behalf by its president?

Held. Yes. Judgment reversed.

♦ Indiana law has taken an expansive view of apparent authority which includes the concept of inherent agency power. Inherent authority derives solely from the agency relation and exists for the protection of persons harmed by dealing with the agent. It originates from the customary authority of a person in the particular type of agency relationship.

♦ Because Sterling had served as president of D since its inception, had managed its affairs for an extended period of time with little or no board oversight, and had purchased real estate for D in the past without board approval, Sterling's actions were acts that usually accompany, or are incidental to, transactions which he was authorized to conduct.

♦ Since P knew that the transaction required board approval, Sterling did not possess apparent authority to bind D, but Sterling nevertheless possessed the "inherent authority" to do so because he was D's president in a setting where he was the sole negotiator. It was reasonable for P not to question Sterling's representation that he had authority from his board of directors to proceed with the transaction, especially in light of the fact that: (i) Sterling was himself a director; (ii) the contract expressly stated that the persons signing this agreement on behalf of the seller are duly authorized to do so and their signatures bind the seller in accordance with the terms of this agreement; and (iii) P knew that D's corporate counsel had reviewed the terms of the agreement.

Dissent. The majority misapplied the principles of agency law.

------

c. **Chief executive officer.** The actions of a CEO bind the corporation if they are undertaken in the course of the corporation's "ordinary and usual business." Of course, what is "ordinary and usual business" will depend in part on the nature and size of the transaction, and the nature, size, condition, and organizational structure of the corporation. A CEO may possess powers beyond these implied or inherent ones by virtue of statute, the articles of incorporation, the bylaws, resolutions of the board of directors, or a course of conduct involving her exercise of "extraordinary powers" and board authorization or ratification.

d. **Corporate treasurer's guarantee.** The apparent authority of a corporate treasurer to bind the corporation on a guarantee depends in part on whether the corporation ordinarily makes guarantees and whether the particular guarantee appears, at least on the surface, to advance the corporation's interests. The treasurer's apparent authority also depends in part on the identity of the creditor and the creditor's relationship, if any, with the corporation.

e. **Special powers of the secretary.** Customarily, the secretary bears responsibility for preparing the minutes for all corporate proceedings. Accordingly, a secretary has the inherent power to certify resolutions of the board of directors, including those authorizing particular transactions. Certification usually involves affixing the corporate seal to a document. Even if the secretary provides an erroneous certification, the corporation is liable to the other parties to these transactions, unless the other parties knew, or should have known, of the secretary's error. If someone pretending to be the secretary certifies a purported resolution of the board, the corporation is still liable. The rationale for this liability is that corporate officers and directors are in a far better position than third parties to control access to the corporate seal.

f. **Officers of close corporations.** That a corporation is closely held may, and perhaps should, affect the power of the officers to bind it. In many closely held corporations, the principal officers think of themselves as partners and act accordingly. Courts frequently hold that the officers of such a corporation may bind it by acts apparently carried on to further its usual business, which is the power these officers would have had had they organized the business as a partnership.

4.   **"Ultra Vires."**

   a.   **The meaning of "ultra vires."** Literally, "ultra vires" transactions are those "beyond the powers" of the corporation. Even through mid-century, courts would decline to enforce such transactions unless wholly executed, although parties could sometimes recover in quasi-contract. This meshed well with the view that corporations were "mere creatures of the law," rather than the product of private contract. Of course, the risk of nonenforcement would make it more difficult, meaning more expensive, for corporations to do business (which may well have been the idea). So their lawyers responded by describing the purpose and powers of corporations in the broadest terms. For example, ABC Company would have the purpose to engage in "any lawful act or activity for which corporations may be organized." It would have the power to do whatever was necessary or convenient for carrying on ABC's business. This drafting reduced the threat posed by the ultra vires doctrine, especially once most corporation statutes expressly permitted such broad clauses or dispensed with the need for them. (Of course, those who wish to limit the purpose and powers of their corporation may still do so.) Reflecting the trend toward enabling and away from regulatory corporate law, every state except Hawaii has enacted legislation to eliminate most of the defenses that might otherwise be asserted by a claim of ultra vires.

   b.   **Benefit to majority shareholder but not to corporation--**

Real Estate Capital Corp. v. Thunder Corp., 31 Ohio Misc. 169, 287 N.E.2d 838 (1972).

Facts. Winthrop Homes, Inc. borrowed $105,000 from Real Estate Capital and Weissman (P). It secured its note with the personal guarantee of Winthrop's sole shareholder, Cohen, and a mortgage deed (and an assignment of rents and leases) on property belonging to Thunder Corp. (D), an unrelated company whose shares were held 80% by Cohen and 20% by Berman. Cohen signed the mortgage as a corporate officer without securing Berman's approval. Winthrop defaulted and P sues D to foreclose on the mortgage and to appoint a receiver.

Issue. May P enforce this mortgage?

Held. No.

- Since D received no benefit in return for its mortgage deed, it could further no corporate purpose. Thus, P may not enforce the mortgage over Berman's objection.

Comment. That giving the mortgage deed failed to benefit D may have figured less in the decision than the fact that giving it did benefit Cohen. By having D give the mortgage deed, Cohen probably breached his duty of loyalty, and P either knew or should have known of this breach. One could certainly argue that P was in a better position than Berman to prevent the breach. Thus, the judgment in this case may represent enforcement of fiduciary duties rather than an application of the ultra vires doctrine.

B. MANAGERS' RESPONSIBILITIES AND COMPENSATION

1. **Disinterested Conduct: Duty of Care and the Business Judgment Rule.** Officers and directors owe the shareholders collectively a duty to act with "reasonable care." (In this context, the shareholders collectively are often referred to as "the corporation." This is acceptable, but it can be confusing because, in other contexts, another grouping may be referred to in the same way.) Nevertheless, courts rarely require officers and directors to respond in damages simply for making an unsuccessful business decision. Doctrinally, this is known as "the business judgment rule." In *Joy v. North*, *infra*, the court offers an explanation for this "rule": "First, shareholders . . . voluntarily undertake the risk of bad business judgment. Investors need not buy stock, for investment markets offer an array of opportunities less vulnerable to mistakes in judgment by corporate officers. Nor need investors buy stock in particular corporations. In the exercise of what is genuinely a free choice, the quality of a firm's management is often decisive, and information is available from professional advisors. . . . Secondly . . . after-the-fact litigation is a most imperfect device to evaluate corporate business decisions. The circumstances surrounding a corporate decision are not easily reconstructed in a courtroom years later, since business imperatives often call for quick decisions, inevitably based on less than perfect information. The entrepreneur's function is to encounter risks and to confront uncertainty, and a reasoned decision at the time made may seem a wild hunch viewed years later against a background of perfect knowledge. . . . Third, because potential profit often corresponds to the potential risk, it is very much in the interest of shareholders that the law not create incentives for overly cautious corporate decisions. Some opportunities offer great profits at the risk of very substantial losses, while the alternatives offer less risk of loss but also less potential profit. Shareholders can reduce the volatility of risk by diversifying their holdings. In the case of the diversified shareholder, the seemingly more risky alternative may well be the best choice since great losses in some stocks will, over time, be offset by even greater gain in others."

a. Business judgment rule applied--

Shlensky v. Wrigley, 95 Ill. App. 2d 173, 237 N.E.2d 776 (1968).

Facts. The Chicago National League Ball Club, Inc., a Delaware corporation, owned and operated the Chicago Cubs and the team's home stadium, Wrigley Field. The Cubs played home games during the day since Wrigley Field lacked lights. Shlensky (P), a minority shareholder, sought to compel the installation of lights and the scheduling of night games as well as damages for past failure to do so. He brought a derivative suit against the corporation's directors, including Philip K. Wrigley (D), 80% owner and president. P alleged that the other major league teams played almost all nonweekend games at night in order to maximize attendance and, thus, revenues. In the years 1961-1965, the Cubs sustained losses from baseball operations. Except for 1963, attendance at Cubs' home games substantially trailed attendance at road games. Weekday home game attendance for the Cubs was substantially less than for the Chicago White Sox, who played at night. P further alleged that D had refused to install lights, not to advance any corporate interest, but because of his view that "baseball is a 'daytime sport'" and that light installation and night baseball would harm the neighborhood around Wrigley Field. Knowing all of this, the other directors acquiesced. According to P, the directors failed to use reasonable care in making these decisions. The trial court dismissed P's suit for failure to state a cause of action. P appeals.

Issue. Did P state a cause of action?

Held. No. Judgment affirmed.

♦ Corporate directors, not courts, should resolve questions of policy and business judgment. A court should presume that directors formed their judgment in good faith to promote the best interests of their corporation.

♦ P did not overcome this presumption because the motives assigned to D, and through him to the other directors, may not be contrary to the best interests of the corporation. For example, the directors could have legitimately considered the effect of lights and night games on the neighborhood because deterioration might affect both attendance and the sale value of Wrigley Field.

♦ Unless the directors' conduct borders on the fraudulent, illegal, or disloyal, the courts should not interfere.

♦ P failed to allege damage to the corporation. He did not allege that the other teams earned more profits as a result of playing night games. Nor did he allege that the Cubs would obtain a net benefit by doing so, for he ignored a variety of costs that the Cubs might well incur as a result.

♦ Failing to do what the other major league clubs did does not constitute negligence.

Comments.

♦ A court may be especially reluctant to second-guess a board's decision about a capital investment because the benefits and associated operating costs will necessarily accrue over the indefinite future.

♦ D's long-standing opposition to lights and night baseball at Wrigley Field could not have come as a surprise to Shlensky. Perhaps, then, the court was simply enforcing the parties' reasonable expectations. From the corporation-as-implied-contract perspective, this is quite proper. Indeed, the director's duty to act with "reasonable care" may simply reflect shareholders' reasonable expectations.

---

b.   **Illegal conduct--**

Miller v. American Telephone & Telegraph Co., 507 F.2d 759 (3d Cir. 1974).

Facts. The American Telephone & Telegraph Co. (D) was owed $1.5 million from the 1968 Democratic convention for telephone services supplied. When D failed to collect the bill, Miller and other stockholders (Ps) brought a derivative action on the grounds that: (i) it was against the corporate interest not to collect the bill and (ii) not collecting the bill amounted to an illegal corporate campaign contribution in violation of federal election laws. The trial court dismissed the complaint, and Ps appeal.

Issue. Is violation of a federal election law by noncollection from a debtor a sufficient ground for maintaining a stockholders' derivative action?

Held. Yes. Judgment reversed.

♦ Certain acts by directors of a corporation, even those acts advancing corporate interests, are a breach of the directors' fiduciary duty because they are illegal.

♦ Directors must be restrained from engaging in activities that are against public policy.

The federal prohibition against corporate political contributions has as its twofold purpose: (i) to destroy the influence of corporations over elections through financial contributions; and (ii) to stop the practice of using corporate funds to benefit political parties without the consent of the stockholders.

Ps are entitled to have their day in court to prove that D violated the election laws by making an illegal contribution in not collecting the phone bill.

♦ To prove their case at trial, Ps must prove that D made a contribution of money or anything of value to the Democratic National Committee in connection with a federal election for the purpose of influencing the outcome of the election. Proof of noncollection is insufficient unless Ps can also prove an impermissible motivation underlying the alleged inaction.

---

c. Informed judgment about merger proposals--

Smith v. Van Gorkom, 488 A.2d 858 (Del. 1985).

Facts. Trans Union was a profitable, multimillion-dollar leasing corporation that was not able to use all of the tax credits it was generating. Several solutions were explored. Van Gorkom (chairman of Trans Union) asked for a study by Romans (the corporation's financial officer) regarding a leveraged buy-out by management. Romans reported that the company would generate enough cash to pay $50/share for the company's stock, but not $60/share. Van Gorkom rejected the idea of this type of buy-out as a potential conflict of interest, but he indicated he would take $55/share for his own stock (he was 65 and about to retire). On his own, Van Gorkom approached Jay Pritzker, a corporate takeover specialist, and began negotiating a sale of Trans Union. He suggested $55/share and a five-year pay-out method without consulting the board or management. The price was above the $39/share market value, but no study was done by anyone to determine the intrinsic value of Trans Union's shares. In the final deal, Trans Union got three days to consider the offer, which included selling a million shares to Pritzker at market, so that even if Trans Union found someone else who would pay a better price, Pritzker would profit; for 90 days Trans Union could receive, but not solicit, competing offers.

Van Gorkom hired outside legal counsel to review the deal, ignoring his company lawyer and a lawyer on the board. He called a board meeting for two days later. At the meeting, Trans Union's investment banker was not invited, no copies of the proposed merger were given, senior management was against it, and Romans said the price was too low. Van Gorkom presented the deal in 20 minutes, saying that the price might not be the highest that could be received, but it was fair. The outside lawyer told the board that they might be sued if they did not accept the offer and that they did not need to get an outside "fairness" opinion as a matter of law. Romans said he had not done a fairness study but that he thought $55/share was on the low end. The discussion lasted two hours, and the merger offer was accepted.

Within 10 days, the management of Trans Union was in an uproar. Pritzker and Van Gorkom agreed to some amendments, which the board approved. Trans Union retained Salomon Brothers, an investment banker firm, to solicit other offers. Kohlberg, Kravis, Roberts & Co. made an offer at $60/share. Van Gorkom discouraged the offer and spoke with management people who were participating in it. Hours before a board meeting to consider the offer, it was canceled, and was never presented to the board. General Electric Credit Corp. made a proposal at $60/share, but wanted more time, which Pritzker refused to give, so it too was withdrawn.

On December 19, some shareholders (Ps) began this suit seeking rescission of the merger or, alternatively, damages against members of Trans Union's board (Ds). On February 10, 70% of the shareholders approved the deal. The trial court held that the board's actions from its first meeting on September 20 until January 26 were informed. Ps appeal.

Issue. Did the directors act in accordance with the requirements of the business judgment rule?

Held. No. Judgment reversed.

♦ The business judgment rule presumes that directors act on an informed basis, in good faith, and in an honest belief that their actions are for the good of the company. Ps must rebut this presumption. There is no fraud here, or bad faith. The issue is whether Ds informed themselves properly. All reasonably material information available must be looked at prior to a decision. This is a duty of care. Ds are liable if they were grossly negligent in failing to inform themselves.

♦ Ds were grossly negligent in the way they acted in the first board meeting that approved the merger: they did not know about Van Gorkom's role, and they did not gather information on the intrinsic value of the company. Receiving a premium price over market is not enough evidence of intrinsic value.

♦ An outside opinion is not always necessary, but here there was not even an opinion given by inside management. The Van Gorkom opinion of value could be relied on had it been based on sound factors; it was not and Ds did not check it. The post-September market test of value was insufficient to confirm the reasonableness of the board's decision.

♦ Although Ds knew the company well and had outstanding business experience, this was not enough on which to base a finding that they reached an informed decision. There is no real evidence of what the outside lawyer said, and, as he refused to testify, Ds cannot rely on the fact that they based their acts on his opinion.

♦ The actions taken by the board to review the proposal on October 9, 1980, and on January 26, 1981, did not cure the defects in the September 20 meeting. All directors take a unified position, so all are being treated the same way.

♦ The shareholder vote accepting the offer does not clear Ds because it was not based on full information.

Dissent. There were 10 directors; the five outside directors were chief executives of successful companies. The five inside directors had years of experience with Trans Union. All knew about the company in detail. No "fast shuffle" took place over these men. Based on this experience, the directors made an informed judgment.

Dissent. The record taken as a whole supports the conclusion that Ds' actions are protected by the business judgment rule.

d. **Rushed decisions do not always breach duty of care.** In *Citron v. Fairchild Camera & Instrumental Corp.*, 569 A.2d 53 (Del. 1989), the Delaware Supreme Court rejected a duty of care attack on the decision of the Fairchild board, operating under a three-hour deadline, to accept a "white knight's" tender offer in lieu of a hostile one. The court observed that the board "had been considering the possibility that the company would be sold for two years prior to receipt of [the] . . . unsolicited . . . proposal. The board . . . received investment advice from four leading investment banking firms, commissioned financial evacuations by three of them, shopped the company to roughly 75 potential buyers, and discussed the sale of the company at three separate board meetings over the course of three weeks. . . . [Whether the] time limits on the decisionmaking process . . . are self-imposed or attributable to bargaining tactics of an adversary seeking a final resolution to a belabored process must be considered. Boards that have failed to exercise due care are frequently boards that have been used." The court concluded that "the time constraints placed on the Fairchild board were not of the board's making and did not compromise its deliberative process."

e. **Duty to establish a corporate information-gathering and reporting system--**

In re **Caremark International, Inc. Derivative Litigation,** 698 A.2d 959 (Del. Ch. 1996).

Facts. Caremark International, Inc. ("Caremark"), a health care service provider, pled guilty to violating a federal law banning payments for the referral of Medicare or Medicaid patients during the period 1986-1993. Caremark agreed to pay criminal fines and civil reimbursement of approximately $250 million. The government did not charge Caremark's directors or senior officers with wrongdoing. Caremark shareholders (Ps) brought a derivative action against Caremark's directors (Ds), claiming that they had breached their fiduciary duty of care by failing to appropriately supervise and monitor the people who made the prohibited payments. The discovery record revealed that the board was informed that the company's reimbursement for patient care was frequently from government-funded sources and that such services were subject to federal regulation. But Ds appear to have been informed by experts that the company's practices, while contestable, were lawful. As early as 1989, Caremark's predecessor issued an internal "Guide to Contractual Relationships" ("Guide") to govern its employees in entering into contracts with physicians and hospitals. Most years, lawyers reviewed and updated the Guide. Each version of the Guide expressly prohibited payments to induce patient referrals. In 1993, the board adopted new policies requiring local branch managers to secure home office approval for all disbursements under agreements with health care providers and to certify compliance with the ethics program. In February of 1993, the Ethics Committee of the board received and reviewed an outside auditor's report by Price Waterhouse, which concluded that there were no material weaknesses in the corporation's control structure. Nevertheless, in April, the committee adopted a new internal audit charter requiring a comprehensive review of compliance policies and the compilation of an employee ethics handbook concerning such policies. In subsequent years, Ds caused employees to be given revised versions of the ethics handbook and required them to participate in training sessions concerning compliance with the law. After discovery, Ps and Ds entered into a settlement agreement, which did not require Ds to pay any money damages. The parties move for approval of the settlement.

Issue. In connection with a claim that directors had breached their duty of care by failing to detect illegal patient referral payments, is a settlement that does not require the directors to pay any money damages "fair" to the corporation if the directors had adopted a policy against such payments, communicated that policy to all concerned, and used internal and outside audits to ensure compliance?

Held. Yes. Settlement approved.

♦ Directors must establish a reasonable information gathering and reporting system even if they lack grounds for suspecting violations of the law—despite the Delaware Supreme Court's decision in *Graham v. Allis Chalmers,* 188 A.2d 125 (1963). In recent years the supreme court has articulated the seriousness with which corporation law views the role of the corporate board, especially in takeover cases. Moreover, to discharge its supervisory and monitoring role under section 141 of the Delaware General Corporation Law, the board must receive relevant information in a timely fashion. And creating a reasonable information gathering and reporting system renders a corporation eligible for reduced sanctions under the federal organizational sentencing guidelines.

♦ The level of detail that is appropriate for such an information system is a question of business judgment. No rationally designed information and reporting system will remove the possibility that the corporation will violate laws or regulations, or that senior officers or directors may nevertheless sometimes be misled or otherwise reasonably fail to detect acts material to the corporation's compliance with the law.

♦ Directors risk liability for unconsidered inaction if they fail to establish a corporate information gathering and reporting system designed to assure the board that appropriate information will come to its attention in a timely manner as a matter of ordinary operations, so that it may satisfy its responsibility.

♦ Ds were informed that the company's reimbursement for patient care was frequently from government funded sources and that such services were subject to federal regulation. But Ds appear to have been informed by experts that the company's practices, while contestable, were lawful. There is no evidence that reliance on such reports was not reasonable. It is not clear that Ds knew the detail found, for example, in the indictments arising from the company's payments. But, of course, the duty to act in good faith to be informed cannot be thought to require directors to possess detailed information about all aspects of the operation of the enterprise. Such a requirement would simply be inconsistent with the scale and scope of efficient organization size in this technological age.

- The corporation established an information and reporting system to remove the possibility that the corporation would violate laws or regulations, thereby representing a good faith effort to be informed of the relevant facts.

- To show that Ds breached their duty of care by failing adequately to control the corporation's employees, Ps would have to show either (i) that Ds knew or (ii) should have known that violations of law were occurring and, in either event, (iii) that Ds took no steps in a good faith effort to prevent or remedy that situation, and (iv) that such failure proximately resulted in the losses complained of (under *Cede & Co. v. Technicolor, Inc.*, 636 A.2d 956 (1994), this last element may constitute an affirmative defense).

- To establish directorial liability for ignorance of activities within the corporation that will render the corporation liable, a plaintiff would have to show sustained or systematic failure of the board to exercise oversight, such as an utter failure to attempt to assure a reasonable information and reporting system exits. Only such a showing would establish the lack of good faith that is a necessary condition to such liability. This demanding test of liability will promote the interests of shareholders generally by encouraging board service by qualified persons while prompting good faith performance of duty.

- No evidence in the record suggests that Ds failed on a sustained basis to exercise their oversight function. Caremark's information systems appear to be good faith efforts to keep Ds informed of relevant facts. If Ds did not know the specifics of the activities that led to the indictments, they cannot be faulted.

---

f. **Proximate cause.** Traditionally, a plaintiff claiming that one or more directors breached the duty of care could recover damages only if she could show that the breach caused a loss. The Revised Model Business Corporation Act section 8.31(b)(1) (1998) burdens such a plaintiff with the task of showing "harm to the corporation proximately caused by the director's challenged conduct." But in *Technicolor,* to which the chancellor referred in *Caremark,* the court asserted that such "tort principles . . . have no place in a business judgment rule standard of review analysis"; breach of "the duty of care rebuts the presumption that the directors have acted in the best interests of the shareholders, and requires the directors to prove that the transaction was entirely fair."

g. **Alternative approaches to the duty of care and the business judgment rule.**

    1) **Reformulate the standard.** Legislators and law professors have suggested a number of reformulations of the standard of care for officers

and directors. One of the better known appears in section 4.01(c) of the ALI's Principles of Corporate Governance (1994). It provides that a "director or officer who makes a business judgment in good faith fulfills his duty under this Section if he: (i) is not interested in the subject of his business judgment; (ii) is informed with respect to the subject of his business judgment to the extent he reasonably believes to be appropriate under the circumstances; and (iii) rationally believes that his business judgment is in the best interests of the corporation." According to the drafters, the "phrase 'rationally believes' is intended to permit a significantly wider range of discretion than the term 'reasonable,' and to give a director or officer a safe harbor from liability for business judgments that might arguably fall outside the term 'reasonable' but are not so removed from the realm of reason when made that liability should be incurred. . . . On the other hand, courts that have articulated only a 'good faith' test provide too much legal insulation for directors and officers. There is no reason to insulate an objectively irrational business decision—one so removed from the realm of reason that it should not be sustained—solely on the basis that it was made in subjective good faith." Serious questions remain, however, about whether this standard provides optimal room for risk-taking.

2) **Different standards for different directors.** The standard of care could vary depending on various characteristics of the director in question: inside vs. outside; expertise; reason for appointment to the board.

3) **Limit damages.** In principle, limiting damages could provide the same room for cost-effective risk-taking as relaxing the standard for liability. Conard suggests tying damage awards to a director's compensation while eliminating indemnification and insurance.

4) **Abolish liability.** Delaware General Corporation Law section 102(b)(7) authorizes a provision in corporate articles "eliminating or limiting the personal liability of a director to the corporation or its stockholders for monetary damages for breach of . . . [the duty of care,] provided that such provision shall not eliminate or limit the liability of a director . . . for acts or omissions not in good faith or which involve intentional misconduct or a knowing violation of a law. . . ." Other states have adopted mandatory provisions to the same effect, sometimes placing a heavier burden of persuasion on the person challenging the transaction as well. Note that eliminating liability for damages would not insulate officers and directors from internal corporate discipline or loss of reputation.

2. **Transactions in Which Directors, Officers, and Shareholders Have a Personal Interest: Duty of Loyalty.**

a. **Contracts with interested directors: the law's evolution.** Borrowing from the law of trusts, English judges developed the rule that a corporation could void any contract, no matter how fair, with one or more of its directors or with another business enterprise in which one or more of its directors played a significant role. Only ratification by informed shareholders could validate such a contract, and then only if the contract were "fair." American judges followed in this tradition, in some jurisdictions into the 20th century. As incorporated businesses became larger and entered more complicated fields, shareholders paid an increasingly steep price for the right to void interested transactions. Some people with experience in major businesses and financial institutions probably declined to serve as outside directors. Other directors probably declined to engage in transactions that could have benefited their corporations. Adapting to this changing economic environment, American judges began enforcing "interested transactions" where: (i) the interested directors disclosed pertinent information about the transaction to the disinterested ones, (ii) the disinterested ones constituted a quorum and a majority of them approved the transaction, and (iii) the transaction was "fair" to the corporation (with the burden of showing fairness allocated to those seeking enforcement). By the mid-20th century, few, if any, judges permitted corporations to void as of right any "interested transaction."

1) **Required disclosure and the meaning of "fairness"--**

Cookies Food Products, Inc. v. Lakes Warehouse Distributing, Inc., 430 N.W.2d 447 (Iowa 1988).

Facts. In 1975, L. D. Cook organized Cookies Food Products, Inc. ("Cookies") to produce and distribute his original barbecue sauce. Cookies never paid dividends; until a few months before Cookies' shareholders (Ps) filed this action, it could not have paid them without violating the terms of its Small Business Administration loan. To finance this closely held corporation, Cook sold stock at $5 per share to 35 people including Ps and Duane Herrig (D). When D purchased his 200 shares, he was the owner of an auto parts business, Speed's Automotive, and a business that distributed Speed's parts, Lakes Warehouse Distributors, Inc. ("Lakes").

Dismal first-year sales threatened Cookies with bankruptcy, so its board solicited D's interest in distributing its products. D agreed to market the sauce if Cookies would sell it to him at a 20% discount from its wholesale price. Using Lakes' trucks, he sold Cookies' sauce to his auto parts customers and to grocery stores located on the trucks' regular delivery routes. In May 1977, Cookies agreed that Lakes would serve as its exclusive distributor, with Lakes bearing the cost of warehousing, marketing, sales, delivery, promotion, and advertising in return for 30% of gross sales (raised to 32% in 1979). Gross sales revenues for 1976 ($20,000) grew five-fold by 1977, and 1978's doubled those for 1977. (When Ps filed suit in 1985, gross sales revenues amounted to $2.4 million.)

In 1981, majority shareholder Cook offered to sell his 8,100 shares to Cookies, but the board declined. D then offered Cook and all other holders $10 per share for their stock. Despite efforts to prevent D from becoming majority shareholder, he purchased 53% of Cookies' shares pursuant to his offer by January 1982. He then replaced four directors with people of his choosing. In April, the board purchased nearby short-term storage from Lakes at the "going rate." In July, the board extended the term of the exclusive distribution agreement just as it had in 1980 when four of the plaintiffs served on the board. Meanwhile, D had developed a recipe for taco sauce, and Cookies undertook to produce and distribute it. In August, the board agreed to pay D a royalty for the use of his recipe just as it had paid Cook for the use of his recipe for barbecue sauce. As a percentage of gross revenues, D's flat fee royalty slightly exceeded the percentage-of-gross-revenues royalty paid to Cook, but it left more for Cookies because producing the taco sauce was cheaper than producing the barbecue sauce. As sales increased, D devoted even more time to Cookies (averaging 80-hour weeks), and the board agreed in January 1983 to pay D a $1,000 per month "consultant fee" in lieu of salary. In August, the board agreed to pay him more and to pay Lakes an additional 2% of gross sales as a promotion allowance to expand the market for Cookies products outside of Iowa.

In a derivative action, Ps claimed that D breached his duty of loyalty in connection with all of the transactions that benefited him or Lakes. Ps' CPA expert opined that Cookies' income would have been much greater—double in 1985—had it hired an executive officer for $65,000 annually, paid a marketing supervisor and an advertising agency each a 5% sales commission, and built a new warehouse and hired a warehouseman. This expert did acknowledge that D had performed the work of at least five skilled people and conceded that D may have received less than his due for what he accomplished. Ps' food broker expert testified that for $110,856, his company would have provided all of the services that D performed for $730,637. The trial court found for D.

Issue. Did D breach his duty of loyalty in the challenged transactions?

Held. No. Judgment affirmed.

♦ That the trial court credited D and his evidence does not show it relieved him of the burden of persuasion that he bore.

♦ That Cookies might have obtained services of the kind provided by D at a lower price does not show that the challenged transactions were "unfair" because the evidence of record supports the finding that Cookies' profits would have been significantly smaller had it obtained these services from others.

♦ D had no duty to make any disclosures to minority shareholders in connection with the exclusive distributorship, royalty, warehousing, or consultant fee agreements because the board, not the shareholders, bears the responsibility for managing the company.

♦ All of the members of Cookies' board knew that D owned Lakes and Speed's. D had no duty to disclose the profits that he derived from the distribution and warehousing agreements, but the distribution agreement with Lakes gave the board the right to this information. Having found that the compensation he received from these agreements was fair and reasonable, we are convinced that D furnished sufficient pertinent information to Cookies' board to enable it to make prudent decisions concerning the contracts.

Dissent. Except for a little self-serving testimony, D did not produce evidence of the market price for the services (*e.g.,* distribution, freight, advertising, storage) that he provided or arranged. He did not rebut the testimony of Ps' expert that D was "grossly overcompensated for his services based on their fair market value." Therefore, he failed to discharge the burden of proving that the challenged transactions were fair to Cookies, and so Ps should prevail.

----

2) **Interested transaction issues.** The following are some commonly raised issues surrounding interested transactions.

   a) Which interests qualify as conflicting?

   b) What must the interested parties disclose? Is it enough that they identify themselves as interested? Must they explain precisely how they stand to gain and how much?

   c) In the absence of whatever disclosure is required, may a court uphold an interested transaction on the grounds that it is "fair"? The American Law Institute Principles of Corporate Governance section 5.02 provides that, in the absence of "appropriate disclosure," a court may set aside a "fair" transaction unless the transaction is ratified after the disclosure problem is remedied.

   d) Under what standard should a court evaluate the "fairness" of an interested transaction? The marketplace? The reasonable expectations of the parties? Some other standard?

   e) To what extent should a court defer to provisions of the articles or bylaws expressly authorizing interested transactions?

   f) Should a court review an interested transaction if it was approved by informed disinterested directors? What if the applicable statute does not provide for such review?

3) **Burden of persuasion.** With respect to some, perhaps many, "interested transactions," proving "fairness" or "unfairness" may pose quite a challenge. The party bearing the burden of persuasion may well lose. In the absence of an express statutory provision, courts must allocate this burden. Customarily, they allocate it to those who would

uphold the transaction. But they may consider making exceptions where a majority of the disinterested directors gave informed approval of the transaction or where the articles or bylaws specifically authorize the kind of interested transaction involved.

b. **Special problems of parent-subsidiary.**

1) **Introduction.** For a variety of reasons, an incorporated business might find it advantageous to organize some operations as a subsidiary corporation. Because of the parent's control, almost every transaction between the subsidiary and the parent, and others as well, will be an "interested" transaction. Therefore, if the subsidiary is not wholly owned, the other shareholders might challenge almost any one of these transactions on the grounds that the parent breached its duty of loyalty. If courts subjected these transactions to the same standard as other interested transactions, many an incorporated business might forgo the use of subsidiaries and the advantages that this form of organization offers.

2) **Exclusive benefit for majority shareholder--**

Case v. New York Central Railroad, 15 N.Y.2d 150, 204 N.E.2d 643, 256 N.Y.S.2d 607 (1965).

Facts. Minority shareholders of Mahoning Coal Railroad Co. (Ps) brought this shareholders' derivative suit against Central, Mahoning's parent (D), to rescind a tax liability consolidation agreement between the two corporations and to compel an accounting of all funds paid to D under the agreement. Mahoning leased railroad lines in Ohio to D, for which D paid all expenses of operating and maintaining plus 40% of the gross revenues realized. All of Mahoning's directors but one were D's employees. In 1956, D's directors proposed, and Mahoning's directors accepted, an agreement whereby Mahoning joined D's "affiliated group" for purposes of loss distribution (under the 1954 IRS Code) for tax purposes. The losses of unprofitable corporations (in this case, D) would thereby be spread among the profitable corporations to effect a tax savings for the benefit of all. During the three years in question, Mahoning saved $3,825,717.43 in taxes; but the terms of the agreement were such that, of that amount, $3,556,992.15 was given to D, the loss corporation, and only $268,725.28 was retained by Mahoning. Ps alleged that the agreement was unfair and that D, being in control of Mahoning's board of directors and 80% of its stock, violated its fiduciary duty to Mahoning and Ps not to take unfair advantage of its majority control position. The trial court found that, although the duty existed, the agreement, as a matter of fact, was not unfair. The appellate court disagreed and found that the agreement was unfair. As part of the decision a full accounting was ordered.

Issue. Did Ps fail to establish that D, as the majority shareholder, had taken such a degree of unfair advantage over the minority shareholders as to warrant judicial intervention for breach of fiduciary duty?

Held. Yes. Order reversed.

◆ Exercising, as it did, effective control over Mahoning's affairs by virtue of its majority stock ownership, D was required to follow a course of fair dealing toward the minority shareholders in managing the corporation's business. The basic ground for judicial intervention in minority complaint situations, however, is an advantage obtained by the dominant group to the disadvantage of the corporation or its minority owners. Loss to the corporation itself is the most prevalent criterion in the decided cases.

◆ Here, although D had a greater proportionate advantage, there was no actual loss or disadvantage to Mahoning. Ps complain that they should have gotten a larger share but they fail to spell out what amount would be right. Mahoning is still $268,725.28 better off than if the agreement had not been signed at all. Moreover, Mahoning had a vital interest in D's continued ability to pay the rent and operate the lines according to their lease agreement. Thus the appellate division is reversed and the trial court's decision is reinstated.

---

3) Subsidiary relationship--

Sinclair Oil Corp. v. Levien, 280 A.2d 717 (Del. 1971).

Facts. Sinclair Oil (D) owned 97% of the stock of Sinven, a subsidiary involved in the crude oil business in South America; D appointed all of the subsidiary's board members and officers. Then over six years D drained off dividends from the subsidiary to meet its own needs for cash. The dividends paid met the limitations of state law, but exceeded the current earnings of the same period. Levien (P), a shareholder of Sinven, brought a derivate suit charging that this limited the subsidiary's ability to grow. Further, P alleged that in a contract between D and the subsidiary for the purchase of crude oil, D had failed to pay on time and had not purchased the minimum amounts as required by the contract. The chancery court ordered D to account for damages. D appeals.

Issue. Is the intrinsic fairness test the appropriate standard to define the fiduciary duty of the parent corporation to its controlled subsidiary?

Held. Yes. Judgment for D on the dividend and expansion questions; judgment for P on the breach of contract issue.

◆ Where there is self-dealing, the intrinsic fairness test must be applied, which puts the burden on the majority shareholder to show that the transaction with the subsidiary was objectively fair. On the dividend issue there was no self-dealing (since the parent did not receive something from the subsidiary to the exclusion or detriment of the minority shareholders; they shared pro rata in the dividend distributions). On the expansion issue, D did not usurp any opportunities that would normally have gone to the subsidiary. Thus, the business judgment rule applies. The court will not disturb a transaction under this rule unless there is a showing of gross overreaching, which there was not.

♦　However, D did make its payments under a crude oil contract with the subsidiary on a late basis and failed to purchase the required minimum amounts of crude oil.

Comment. Although the court does not mention the parties' reasonable expectations, enforcing them may explain the different treatment of the different transactions. Investors in Sinven could not reasonably expect to earn revenues from Sinclair's worldwide operations. If they wished to do so, they had only to purchase Sinclair shares. On the other hand, they might reasonably expect to earn revenues from Sinven's sales to Sinclair under the contract.

---

c.　**Compensation of managers.** Like parent/subsidiary transactions, managerial compensation inevitably involves a conflict of interest. Most, if not all, corporation statutes address this conflict by authorizing the board to set the compensation of officers and directors. Some of these statutes explicitly permit the board to do this irrespective of any board member's personal interest.

1)　**Gifts to dependents of former employees--**

Adams v. Smith, 275 Ala. 142, 153 So. 2d 221 (1963).

Facts. This is a derivative action. The directors of Alabama Dry Dock and Shipbuilding Co. adopted a resolution to pay sums of money to the widows of its former president and comptroller. The gifts were ratified by a majority of the shareholders. Adams (P), a minority shareholder, objected to the payments as being unauthorized gifts without consideration to the corporation (and thus ultra vires acts). P filed a bill in equity against the corporation, the directors, and the widows (Ds) asking for an injunction and for a return of the money. Ds demurred; the demurrer was overruled, and Ds appeal.

Issue. May the directors, if their action is ratified by a majority of the shareholders, make corporate gifts to the dependents of former employees without return consideration?

Held. No. The trial court is reversed.

♦　Under the business judgment rule (which states that a board of directors has the power in good faith to manage the internal affairs of the corporation and may exercise its business judgment in matters during the course of ordinary business), the board of directors may make *bonus* or *retirement payments* to employees or dependents of former employees that are made for the benefit of the corporation.

- However, it is an ultra vires act to make such gifts for ***past services*** when there is no consideration to the corporation, even when such gifts are ratified by a majority of the shareholders. P alleged that this was done here. All employment contracts to the president and comptroller had already been paid, there was no obligation to make the payments, and no consideration was received for the payments. Thus, P's complaint states a cause of action.

---

2) "Reasonableness" of compensation--

Mlinarcik v. E.E. Wehrung Parking, Inc., 86 Ohio App. 3d 134, 620 N.E.2d 181 (1993).

Facts. In 1948, Edgar Wehrung organized E.E. Wehrung Parking, Inc., and until his death in 1967, owned the majority of its 150 shares and managed it. The corporation holds a lease on a parking garage; it derives its revenues from subleasing the garage. In the year in which this dispute arose, the corporation received $41,600. Edgar and his wife, Esther, who worked as the secretary for the corporation, received compensation for their services. After Edgar died, his wife owned one share; his son, Robert (D), owned 111 shares; Robert's wife, Marilyn (D), owned 9.5 shares; and Robert's sister, Shirley (P), owned 28.5 shares. Robert, Marilyn, and Shirley all became directors, but the board never met. Shirley did not know what she was supposed to do as a director and never asked. She did receive directors' fees. Robert became president of the company and managed it for $1,800 per year, which was less than his father received. He visited the garage monthly, prepared monthly payroll checks for himself and his wife, prepared and deposited a monthly payroll tax check and other checks, and went to the post office annually to mail shareholder reports. Marilyn worked as a secretary 30 to 35 hours yearly for $3,900 per year. In 1982, Robert raised his annual salary to $10,800 and his wife's to $7,200. P testified that she did not know of the salaries paid to Robert and Marilyn. P claimed that these post-1982 salaries were excessive. P's expert valued the yearly services performed by Robert and Marilyn at between $567— based on the nature of their work and the time required to perform it—and $2,000—"based on the cost of paying a management company to perform it." The trial court granted judgment for Ds. P appeals.

Issue. Does the evidence show that Robert and Marilyn received unreasonably high compensation?

Held. No. Judgment affirmed.

- P knew, or should have known, of the post-1982 compensation paid to Ds, but did not challenge it until 1989. In light of Ohio corporation law, which provides that "[t]he directors, by the affirmative vote of a majority of those in office, and irrespective of any financial or personal interest of any of them, shall have authority to establish reasonable compensation . . . for services to the corporation by directors and officers, or to delegate such authority to one or more officers or directors" [R.C. 1701.60(A)(3)], P bears the burden of showing that the compensation was unreasonable.

♦ P failed to carry her burden primarily because her expert used the wrong standard to measure the value of Ds' services. In almost every situation one can find that, compared to what a corporation pays its top executives, a management company can perform the same duties and more for a considerably lesser amount. A better standard is what other owners pay themselves in the local market for similar job performance.

♦ P's expert also failed to take into account the fact that Ds did not receive any fringe benefits.

Comment. The outcome may well be consistent with what the founder planned and, therefore, with the reasonable expectations of the parties.

———————————

3) **Stock options.** The holder of a stock option owns the right to purchase shares during a specified period at a set price. Corporate boards frequently grant stock options to officers and directors as part of a compensation package. Because certain stock options enjoy tax advantages, granting them may permit a corporation to get more compensation bang for its buck. Granting them may also give the holder a powerful incentive to take actions that will raise the price of the shares—if the exercise price is above the market price at the time that the stock option is granted.

4) **Stock option plans and the like--**

Eliasberg v. Standard Oil Co., 23 N.J. Super. 431, 92 A.2d 862 (1952), *aff'd*, 12 N.J. 467, 97 A.2d 437 (1953).

Facts. This case involves a shareholders' derivative action to challenge the propriety of a restricted stock option granted to certain key employees. Standard Oil (D) proposed a restricted stock option plan for key employees. The plan was put before the shareholders. They voted 78% to accept the plan, 2% to reject it, and 20% did not vote. Eliasberg (P), owner of 20 of the 60,571,000 shares, brought the present suit to challenge the propriety of the stock option agreement for key employees. P charged that the text describing the plan did not reveal the tax impact of the plan on the corporation and that the plan amounted to compensation without consideration since there was no increase in the duties or responsibilities of the key employees.

Issue. Is a stock option plan for key executives permissible, even if the executives need not perform increased duties and responsibilities?

Held. Yes.

♦ Since the plan has the shareholders' approval, the burden is on P to prove illegality.

♦ When stockholders have notice of the directors' interest and authorize the directors to enter into a contract, the agreement will be unassailable in the absence of actual fraud or want of power in the corporation.

♦ P contends the plan is illegal due to D's failure to specify the tax impact of the plan on the corporation. P errs. There is no duty to supply that information when the entire plan is given to the stockholders. The stockholder is chargeable with the knowledge he could have acquired.

♦ No stockholder testified that he was misled by the plan.

♦ Even if the plan gave executives additional compensation without additional responsibilities, it is not invalid. Stock options may be adopted as a form of compensation for continuance in employment. The stockholders overwhelmingly approved the plan and this court will not now substitute its opinion of the value of the executives' services for the shareholders' opinions.

---

5) Corporation must expect to receive benefit from stock option plan--

Beard v. Elster, 39 Del. Ch. 153, 160 A.2d 731 (S. Ct. 1960).

Facts. An independent board of directors approved a stock option plan for key management (Ds); the shareholders approved the plan. The options were exercisable over a five-year period as long as Ds were employed by the company. Two hundred eighty-nine employees received options under the plan. A shareholder (P) sued to cancel the plan on the basis that the corporation had received no consideration for issuance of the options. The vice-chancellor held that the options were invalidly granted.

Issue. Did the corporation receive valid consideration for issuance of the options?

Held. Yes. Judgment reversed.

♦ A valid stock option plan must contain conditions such that the corporation may reasonably expect to receive a benefit from the options. There must also be a reasonable relationship between the value of benefits to the corporation and the value of options granted.

◆ Here an independent board approved the plan; the salaries of Ds were lower than in comparable companies. Conditions are met here for validity.

Comment. The court cited a case where an interested board had approved and shareholders ratified. In that case the court would reverse if the value received by the corporation amounted to waste. But if the question was close, the court would let the option plan stand under the business judgment rule. Also, a plan allowing employees to exercise options six months after leaving the company would be invalid.

---

d. **Corporate opportunities and competition with the corporation.** At least in the absence of an agreement to the contrary, the duty of loyalty requires an officer or director to forgo: (i) some business opportunities in favor of the corporation and (ii) some activities that would compete with the corporation. But which opportunities and activities? Under what circumstances must the officer or director forgo them? The scope of the corporation's business may suggest answers to these questions.

1) **"Inability" of solvent corporation to take advantage of opportunity no excuse--**

Irving Trust Co. v. Deutsch, 73 F.2d 121 (2d Cir. 1934), *cert. denied*, 294 U.S. 708 (1935).

Facts. The trustee in bankruptcy (P) of what had been Acoustic (now Sonora Products) sued Bell and Biddle (Ds), who were an employee and a director of Acoustic, respectively. Acoustic needed the patents owned by DeForest Co., which was controlled by Reynolds & Co. (through an option Reynolds had to purchase the stock of DeForest). The Acoustic board of directors hired Bell to negotiate for the patents; he got a contract offer to Acoustic for one-third interest in the DeForest stock with a provision that Acoustic could name four of the nine directors and manage the affairs of the company, subject to its board's approval. The president of Acoustic (and a member of the board) then reported to the board that the corporation did not have, and could not get, the funds to fulfill the contract ($100,000 was needed), but that several of the board members were interested personally. The board resolved that Biddle would accept the contract on behalf of Acoustic, which was done, although the implied understanding was that Ds as individuals would really accept the contract and then license the patents to Acoustic. Ds made a large profit speculating in the DeForest stock. When Acoustic went bankrupt, P sued Ds for those profits.

Issue. If the corporation is not insolvent but cannot come up with the funds to fulfill a contract that it has signed, may the directors assume that opportunity for themselves?

Held. No. Judgment for P.

- Directors are fiduciaries; they may not take a position adverse to the interests of the corporation.

- Even if the corporation is financially unable to complete the contract, the fiduciaries may not take over the contract. To allow them to do so would encourage fiduciaries not to make their best efforts to see that the corporation exercises its opportunities. (It appears here that this is what happened; for example, the president owed the corporation $125,000, which it made no effort to collect.)

---

2) **Financial "inability" as an excuse for taking a corporate opportunity.** Because officers and directors wishing to take advantage of a corporate opportunity may also control the corporation's financial "ability," or its appearance, courts tend to treat this excuse with hostility. But courts do not always reject it, especially if the disinterested directors, having been fully informed, reject the opportunity.

3) **What constitutes a corporate opportunity--**

Rapistan Corp. v. Michaels, 203 Mich. App. 301, 511 N.W.2d 918 (1994).

Facts. In January 1987, Lear Siegler Holdings (P), a Delaware corporation, acquired Lear Siegler and its subsidiaries, one of which was Rapistan Corp. (P), another Delaware corporation. Rapistan was one of the largest United States manufacturers of materials handling conveyor equipment and systems, selling primarily to the warehouse-distribution market. At the time of the acquisition, Michaels (D) served as Rapistan's CEO, Tilton (D) as its vice president of finance, and O'Neill (D) as its vice president of marketing and sales. On September 6, 1988, Ds resigned. The next day, they signed employment contracts with Alvey Holdings, Inc., a corporation created by Raebarn, Inc., a merchant bank specializing in leveraged buyouts, for the purpose of acquiring Alvey, Inc. ("Alvey"). About two-thirds of Alvey's business was the manufacture of conveyors; about one-third was the manufacture of palletizers, a machine used by manufacturers to stack a uniform package into layers on a pallet for conveyance or distribution. Alvey Holdings, Inc. acquired Alvey on August 26, 1988, and Ds became Alvey's officers. Ps sued, claiming that Ds misappropriated Ps' corporate opportunity and illegally used proprietary or confidential information. Applying Delaware law, the trial court entered judgment for Ds on the basis of these findings: (i) Ds learned of Alvey's availability "in their capacities as individuals, not in their capacities as Rapistan managers," (ii) "the acquisition of Alvey was not essential to Rapistan," (iii) Ps had no "expectation in Alvey," and (iv) Ds had not used "sufficient Rapistan assets" to "estop" Ds from denying that Alvey was a Rapistan corporate opportunity. Ps appeal.

Issue. Did Ds misappropriate a Rapistan corporate opportunity?

Held. No. Judgment affirmed.

- Ps' assertion that they would have acquired Alvey had they known of its availability does not make it Ps' corporate opportunity.

- Whether Alvey was Ps' corporate opportunity may depend in part on the capacity in which Ds learned about it.

- It also depends on whether Alvey was "essential," *i.e.,* "so indispensably necessary to the conduct of [Rapistan's] business" that nonacquisition "threatened the viability of Rapistan." The evidence of record supports the trial court's findings even though Alvey's business was related to Rapistan's. The trial court was not obliged to consider that Ps would have benefited by acquiring Alvey.

- The evidence did not prove, as a matter of law, that Ps had an expectation or interest in the acquisition of Alvey, since the evidence did not show any urgent or practical need to acquire Alvey or that the acquisition fit into an established corporate policy or into the particular business focus of Rapistan.

- Because (i) the amount of Ps' assets used by Ds in connection with the acquisition, some of which was Ds' time, was minimal, especially in light of the $29.5 million cost of acquiring Alvey, and (ii) the evidence does not show a direct and substantial nexus between the use of Rapistan assets and the creation, development, and acquisition of the Alvey opportunity, Ds are not estopped from denying that Alvey was Ps' corporate opportunity.

- The evidence does not show that Ds used proprietary or confidential information.

---

4) The scope of a closely-held corporate business--

Burg v. Horn, 380 F.2d 897 (2d Cir. 1967).

Facts. Burg (P) filed a diversity stockholder's derivative action on behalf of Darand Realty Corporation ("Darand"), a New York corporation, which owned and operated three low-rent rooming and apartment buildings in Brooklyn. P held a one-third stock interest in Darand. The complaint alleged that George and Max Horn (Ds) had each breached a director's fiduciary duty not to appropriate for himself opportunities in which the corporation had an interest or a tangible expectancy. Ds were the managing officers and holders of a one-third stock interest each in Darand. P contended that, as a matter of law, Ds had a duty to acquire for Darand further properties like those it was operating even though there was no discussion or express agreement to that effect. P alleged that nine other buildings acquired by corporations wholly owned by Ds after the formation of Darand in September, 1953, were corporate opportunities, and P asked the court to impose a constructive trust covering the nine buildings for the benefit of Darand. Evidence showed that Ds, through wholly owned corporations, had acquired similar buildings prior to the formation of Darand and that three were still owned at the time of Darand's formation. Loans totaling $7,050 from Darand and P were used in the purchase of three of the nine contested buildings, but no express purpose or limitation was placed on the loans. To support his position, P cited commentators who stated that any opportunity within a corporation's "line of business" is a corporate opportunity, and hence Ds were in violation of their fiduciary duty if they appropriated them. However, on these facts, the trial court held that none of the nine properties were acquired by Ds in breach of their fiduciary duty to the corporation since none were corporate opportunities belonging to Darand. P appeals.

Issue. Did the trial court err in finding that Ds were not under a duty, as a matter of law, to acquire for Darand further properties similar to those it was operating where there was no agreement or understanding that Ds would do so, where none of the properties in question was offered to, sought by, or necessary to Darand, and where none of them came to Ds' attention while acting as directors for Darand?

Held. No. Judgment affirmed.

♦ Under the applicable New York law, property acquired by a director will be impressed with a constructive trust as a corporate opportunity only if the corporation had an "interest" or a "tangible expectancy" in the property. This doctrine is used to prevent a director's acquisition of property that the corporation needs or is seeking, or that a director is otherwise under a duty to acquire for it, such as when the offer or knowledge of the property came to him in his capacity as a director.

♦ Application of these general rules depends on the factual situation of each case, but there is no duty to take for a corporation any opportunity within the same line of business as the corporation's, absent some evidence of an agreement or understanding to that effect. Here, Ds were already in that same "line of business" when Darand was formed. Furthermore, the nine properties were not offered to Ds in their capacity as directors, nor were they necessary to Darand's continued success.

Dissent. A trustee is held to a standard characterized as the "punctilio of an honor the most sensitive," and certainly stricter than the morals of the marketplace. Application of that standard makes it clear that, as managing officers, Ds' primary function was to locate suitable properties for Darand and to offer them to the corporation before buying them themselves. An explicit agreement to that effect is not necessary.

III. AN INTRODUCTION TO CORPORATE FINANCE

A. WHY STUDY CORPORATE FINANCE

A working acquaintance with corporate finance permits a lawyer to better understand how to value corporate assets; and the better a lawyer understands valuation, the better she can: (i) evaluate and argue about claims that one or more people took actions that reduced the value of their corporation or of the claimants' interest in it; and (ii) explain how one interpretation of corporate law better facilitates maximizing the value of corporations than another.

B. VALUATION: HOW FINANCIAL ASSETS ARE VALUED

1. **Present Value (or Discounted Present Value).** Pretend that you were certain that you would receive a payment of a specified amount on a specified date. The "present value" of this payment equals the amount of money that, if invested today at the appropriate interest rate (the "discount rate"), would yield enough to make the payment on its due date. To figure the present value of a series of future payments—such as an annuity, a series of annual payments of a specified amount for a specified number of years—calculate the present value of each payment and add them together. The present value of a business project may be similarly computed. It is equal to the difference between the present value of the future revenues that the project will generate and the present value of the future outlays required to fund it. (Note that the higher the "discount rate," the smaller the weight given to the longer delayed outlays and revenues.) This net present value ("NPV") method of valuation lends itself to figuring the value of a business as well.

2. **Valuation Under Uncertainty: Risk and Diversification.**

    a. **Expected value.** The real world is full of uncertainty. This means that we must describe future cash flows probabilistically, *i.e.,* in terms of expected value—the average of all possible flows weighted in accordance with the odds of their occurring—and risk.

    b. **Risk.** In financial economics, "risk" refers to the odds that the value realized will differ from the expected value and the size of the difference. (Most people talk about risk in terms of what they consider bad outcomes, but in financial economics, risk refers to uncertainty, so a better than expected outcome represents the equivalent risk of a worse-than-expected outcome.) To measure this risk, financial economists customarily use a statistic called the "standard deviation." The larger the standard deviation, the higher the odds that the realized return will differ from the expected return. *Note:* To compute the standard deviation: (i) observe the difference between the expected value and each possible actual value, (ii) square each difference, (iii) add the differences together, and (iv) calculate the square root of this sum. This measure serves well ***provided that*** the distribution of actual returns corresponds to the familiar "normal" bell-shaped distribution. Most financial economists apparently believe that this holds true for publicly traded stocks.

c.   **Diversification.** Some events would affect the cash flow from all investments, and the probability of such events occurring is a component of the risk associated with every stock. On the other hand, some events would affect the cash flow only from an investment in a particular company or in one of a relatively small group of companies. The probability of such an event occurring is a component of the risk associated with the stock of that company (or those companies), but a shareholder need not bear this "firm-specific" or "nonsystematic" risk; he can avoid bearing this risk by holding a diversified portfolio of investments. A randomly chosen portfolio of 20 to 30 stocks will eliminate almost all nonsystematic risk. (Moreover, some events that would threaten to reduce the cash flow from one company would promise to increase the cash flow from another.)

Because a shareholder or other investor can use cheap self-help to shed nonsystematic risk, the capital market will not pay him to bear it. The market will pay him to bear only the "market" or "systematic" risk associated with his portfolio. He can construct his portfolio to suit his taste for risk-taking: an investor with a taste for more risk can indulge himself simply by using borrowed funds to expand the size of his portfolio; an investor with a taste for less risk can liquidate some of his portfolio and purchase practically riskless securities like short-term government bonds. As a measure of "market" or "systematic" risk, financial economists use the correlation between changes in the value of the market and changes in the price of a portfolio (or a stock). This correlation is called "beta."

d.   **The capital asset pricing model.** The ease with which investors can diversify away nonsystematic risk implies that neither this risk nor the risk-bearing tastes of individual investors will have any impact on how the capital market values a financial asset. *Note:* A company's top management cannot cause a rise in its market value by diversifying the company's real assets. But diversifying these assets could prove valuable to top management. A large portion of the portfolio of investments held by each senior manager might consist of the human capital he has devoted to the company. (If the company goes belly-up, the senior managers may find it difficult to earn comparable returns elsewhere.) The nonsystematic risk associated with the company would affect the value of this human capital, and the senior managers would find diversifying this risk away difficult. They would find it impractical to work two jobs or to sell financial assets representing claims on their future salary. Top management could reduce the impact of this risk on the value of their human capital by causing the company to diversify its real assets. An asset's expected return and its beta do have a dramatic impact on its value. In the widely used capital asset pricing model ("CAPM"), an asset's value is a function of only these two variables.

It is difficult to test the CAPM empirically because one must use a proxy for the market portfolio without knowing exactly how good the proxy is. According to the casebook authors, "the systematic risk of a security does not predict its return very well." Predictions improve if one takes into account firm size and the ratio of book equity to market equity, but this help may simply reflect the empirical techniques used. Some financial economists have developed multi-factor asset pricing models. In the arbitrage pricing theory ("APT"), the leading multi-factor model, an asset's value, is a function of liquidity, the rate of inflation, and several other risk factors, each with its own beta. According to the casebook authors, the proponents of these models have not yet explained why these other factors should matter.

3. **The Efficient Capital Market Hypothesis.** The efficient capital market hypothesis ("ECMH"), according to the casebook authors, "makes the bolder statement that the capital market in fact values financial assets as asset pricing theory says they should be. As such, it is necessarily a theory about what information is available to the capital market."

    The ECMH takes three forms: (i) weak, (ii) semi-strong, and (iii) strong. Weak form efficiency means that market prices reflect all information about past stock prices. (Past prices give no clues about future prices, even when studied by Wall Street "chartists.") Semi-strong form efficiency means that market prices reflect all publicly available information, such as earnings reports, so quickly that investors cannot make money by trading on this information. (Investors, at least ordinary investors, should hold a portfolio of securities that will earn the market return.) Strong form efficiency means that market prices reflect all information, nonpublic as well as public, that quickly.

    a. **Empirical tests of the ECMH.** Because one cannot compare the market price of an asset to the "correct" price, one cannot test the ECMH directly. Instead, financial economists test trading strategies that should prove profitable only if the ECMH is untrue in at least one of its forms. The reports of these tests, performed over 30 years, suggest that capital markets, particularly developed stock markets, are weak form and semi-strong form efficient. Prices on developed stock markets even reflect some nonpublic information, and so are strong form efficient to a limited extent.

    b. **Mechanisms of capital market efficiency and information costs.** The efficiency of these markets stems largely from securities trading informed not only by purposefully disseminated information, but also by information acquired by analysts or professional investors through research or by decoding "changes in trading volume and patterns." "Patterns" may include the trading of insiders, but not necessarily. It is true that analysts and others do make a point of trying to decode this trading, but to acknowledge the importance of trading by insiders for market efficiency would undermine beliefs that the casebook authors apparently hold dear. This professionally informed trading moves market prices quickly because of its volume.

Analysts and professional investors acquire information, analyze it, and act on it up to the point where they expect the cost of doing more would exceed the gain. A capital market possesses an "equilibrium level of inefficiency." A market's efficiency with respect to any particular kind of information will depend on the cost of acquiring, analyzing, and acting on it.

c. **Doubts about the ECMH and their significance.** The ECMH has evoked some opposition. Some opponents question whether "the market value of stocks . . . accurately reflects the present value of future cash flows" (whether "market prices actually reflect the value of a company's real assets, as opposed to the relative value of its financial assets"). Some ECMH opponents argue that "noise trading" impairs the efficiency of capital markets. Proponents of this view assert that a group of people persistently trade on the mistaken belief that some securities, even those traded on developed stock markets, are "underpriced" or "overpriced." These "noise traders," so the argument goes, provide a professional investor with a moneymaking opportunity that he might seize, using either an arbitrage or an "in-and-out" strategy. The arbitrage strategy would require that he trade in the opposite direction of the noise traders and cash in once the market realizes that the noise trading price is "wrong." In the interim, however, the professional investor would bear the risks and the transaction costs of purchasing and holding the securities in question, which would reduce the amount of arbitrage and, thus, market efficiency. The "in-and-out" strategy would require that a professional investor trade in the same direction as the noise traders and try to get out just before the market "corrected" the price of the relevant securities. Pursuit of this strategy would make markets less efficient.

The ECMH has important implications for the resolution of a number of issues arising under the law of corporations (and securities regulation), issues such as the materiality of undisclosed information and the measure of damages in shareholder suits. If capital market prices reflect some irrationality or "noise trading," the force of these implications would decline, but probably not enough to matter.

d. **Distribution of dividend--**

Kamin v. American Express Company, 383 N.Y.S.2d 807 (N.Y. App. Div. 1976).

Facts. In 1972, American Express Co. (D) acquired shares of publicly traded Donaldson, Lufken, and Jenrette, Inc. ("DLJ") stock for $29.9 million. Several years later, when the market value of these shares was about $4 million, D planned to distribute its DLJ shares to its stockholders as a special dividend. Two minority shareholders (Ps) requested that D sell these shares, use the $25 million capital loss to offset capital gains, and realize an $8 million reduction in taxes. The board rejected the request on the ground that such a sale could cause D to report less net income, which would depress the market value of D's stock. Ps filed a derivative action seeking a declaration that the special dividend constituted a waste of corporate assets. D moves for summary judgment and dismissal of Ps' complaint.

Issue. Does distributing D's DLJ shares as a special dividend rather than selling them and realizing an $8 million tax reduction constitute a waste of corporate assets?

Held. No. Ds' motion is granted.

♦ Whether a dividend should be declared is a matter of business judgment for the board of directors. Courts will not interfere with such a decision unless it appears that the directors acted in bad faith and for a dishonest purpose. Ps must show more than imprudence or mistaken judgment to prevail.

Comment. The court apparently ignored the implications of the ECMH. Perhaps the board did, too, although it would be interesting to know whether top management's compensation depended on D's net income.

C. CAPITAL STRUCTURE: OWNERSHIP STRUCTURE AND VALUE

The characteristics of financial interests in a corporation—such as common stock, preferred stock, and debt—vary in terms of control, return, and priority. Financial economists and lawyers call the mix of interests used by a corporation its "capital structure." A central issue in corporate finance is whether a corporation's capital structure affects its market value. The traditional answer was "yes"; each corporation has an optimal capital structure that would give it maximum value. Challenging the traditional answer, Nobel prizewinners Franco Modigliani and Merton Miller advanced the irrelevance proposition: in the absence of taxes and nontrivial information and transaction costs in the capital market, capital structure cannot affect a firm's value, as long as firms and investors can borrow and lend at the same rate;

arbitrage would see to it. Put simply, "the value of the corporation's real assets is unaffected by who owns them." Notice that the irrelevance proposition, which became the prevailing view, implies that departures from its assumption may cause capital structure to matter. The trick is to specify the departures and explain their significance.

1. **A Survey of Financial Assets.**

    a. **Common stock.** Common stock, which all corporations must issue, gives its holders the "residual" claim to corporate income and, upon sale or liquidation, to corporate assets: after owners of other interests receive their due, whatever remains, if anything, "belongs" to the holders of the common stock. Because of common stock's residual claim, its holders collectively possess the "right incentives to maximize the value of the corporation" (they must bear the consequences of their own decisions) and accordingly, corporation law vests control in them.

    b. **Debt.** Debt is a promise to pay back an investment with interest as provided in a contract. The claims of debtholders are almost always superior to the claims of holders of common stock, preferred stock, and other equity interests. A short-term debt instrument is called a *note*. A long-term debt is called a *bond* if it is secured by a mortgage on corporate property or a *debenture* if it is unsecured. In the context of a publicly-held corporation, the contract governing a debt instrument is called an *indenture*. The indenture limits the corporation's right to take specified actions that might put the debtholders at more risk. (It may also give the corporation the right to *call* a debt instrument, *i.e.,* repay the holders early.) In a sense, these provisions—and the common shareholders' incentive to maximize the value of the corporation—serves as a substitute for a vote, which debtholders almost always lack.

    c. **Preferred stock.** Preferred stock typically gives its holders a claim—superior to that of common stock—to a specified amount of corporate income (a dividend) and, upon sale or liquidation, to a specified amount of corporate assets. Typically, these specifications and related rights appear largely in the corporation's articles. (The relevant state corporation law will also define some of the rights of the preferred stockholders.) The articles usually provide that, if dividends on the preferred stock go undeclared for a specified period of time ("often between four to eight quarters"), the preferred shareholders become entitled to elect some directors. Otherwise, preferred stock typically gives its holders no vote, except in connection with mergers, amendments to the articles, and other unusual, major transactions that would affect these holders' rights. Preferred stock resembles debt, but it resembles common stock in that it typically gives its holders a contingent claim to income and assets that is subordinate to the claims of debtholders.

d. **Warrants.** Warrants give their holders the right to acquire stock at a specified price, the "exercise" price. Corporations frequently issue them in combination with other financial instruments.

e. **Hybrid financial assets.** Lawyers and others can custom-tailor financial instruments. They have found it especially useful to make some instruments convertible into others, to provide for the holders of nonequity instruments to share in residual income or assets, and to vary the voting rights associated with particular instruments or classes of instruments.

2. **Why Capital Structure Should Not Affect the Value of the Corporation: The Miller-Modigliani Irrelevance Proposition.** The irrelevance proposition is that, in the absence of taxes and nontrivial information and transaction costs in the capital market, capital structure cannot affect a firm's value, as long as firms and investors can borrow and lend at the same rate.

3. **Why Capital Structure May Affect Firm Value.** Now consider departures from these assumptions. Debt financing may increase a firm's value because (i) it receives favorable tax treatment; (ii) it signals management's informed belief that the firm will experience success; or (iii) it limits management's discretion to use the firm's assets to pursue its own interests at the expense of the passive investors. On the other hand, debt financing may reduce a firm's value because of bankruptcy costs.

a. **Taxes.** The tax laws treat interest and dividends differently. Both constitute taxable income for an investor, but a corporation may deduct only interest payments made to its debtholders, not dividends paid to its equity holders. This difference holds out the possibility of using debt financing to increase the value of a firm. Before 1986, however, some equity holders could more than offset equity's disadvantage by taking their return in the form of a capital gain, thereby deferring the tax due until sale and then paying at the then lower capital gains tax rate. The Tax Reform Act of 1986, however, caused personal tax rates to exceed corporate tax rates for the first time and largely eliminated the capital gains tax rate advantage.

b. **The information content of capital structure.** Increased debt financing may signal management's informed belief that the firm will experience success because (i) absent this belief, management would fear the increased odds of bankruptcy, which would cost management dearly due to its undiversified human capital invested in the corporation, or (ii) with this belief, management would conclude that the corporation would have to pay a higher return on equity than it should, given its prospects.

c. **Disciplinary effect of debt.** The obligation to pay interest will reduce management's discretion to use corporate cash flow to maximize management's satisfaction at the expense of the shareholders. The reduction of this discretion (or any "agency cost") should increase the firm's value.

    d.   **Bankruptcy costs.** Debt financing increases the risk of bankruptcy, and the bankruptcy process has proven costly. It has proven costly not only in terms of out-of-pocket expenses for professional services, but more importantly in terms of damage to intangible assets such as "reputation, expectation of future service, and the value of skilled employees." The higher the odds of bankruptcy and the greater the expected costs, the more debt financing will reduce a firm's value.

        This analysis suggests that a firm could approach its optimal capital structure by adding debt until the expected bankruptcy costs of an additional unit would at least equal the expected tax, signaling, and management discipline benefits.

D. OPPORTUNISM AMONG THE HOLDERS OF FINANCIAL CLAIMS

If a firm uses financial assets with different characteristics, the holders of each kind of asset will tend to pursue their own interests at the expense of the others. Holders collectively, however, would be better off if they rendered opportunistic transfers of value more difficult. This is because, the smaller the risk of opportunistic transfer, the lower the return demanded by a potential investor. Many business people find that the law does too little to prevent opportunistic transfers, so transactional lawyers and others must help. Of course, they cannot help unless they understand how holders of different kinds of financial assets might pursue their own interests. Option pricing theory sheds light on this subject, in part because many financial assets, including common stock, possess the characteristics of options.

    1.   **The Basic Structure of Put and Call Options.** An option holder is the person who buys it from the option "writer." The holder of a ***call option*** may purchase an asset from the writer at the "exercise" or "strike" price. The holder will exercise the option if it is "in the money," *i.e.,* if the value of the asset exceeds the exercise price. The holder will not exercise the option if it is "out of the money." The holder of a ***put option*** may sell an asset to the writer at the exercise price. The holder will only exercise it if the option is in the money, *i.e.,* if the exercise price exceeds the value of the underlying asset. If the option is out of the money, the holder will let it expire.

    2.   **Determinants of Option Value.** The value of an unexpired call option depends on:

        a.   **The current value of the underlying asset.** A decline in the value of the underlying asset will make the option worth less.

        b.   **The exercise price.** A decline in the real price (versus the face amount) will make the option worth more.

c. **The time value of money.** Because the holder of a call option defers payment until he exercises it, the present value of the exercise price is less than the face amount. The difference is greater the higher the interest rate and the longer the period until expiration. The greater the difference, the greater the value of the option.

d. **The variability in value of the underlying asset.** As the odds rise that the value of the underlying asset will differ from its expected value, so does the value of an option on the underlying asset. The reason is that if the option ends up out of the money, the holder will not exercise it anyway. So he can only gain on a rise in the odds that the value of the underlying asset will differ from its expected value by a lot. According to the casebook authors, variance has more impact on an option's value than any other factor.

e. **The length of the period until expiration.** A holder defers payment of the exercise price until he exercises his option. Therefore, the longer the period until expiration, the lower the present value of the exercise price and the higher the value of the option. Moreover, the longer this period, the greater the odds that the value of the underlying asset will move in the direction that favors the holder.

3. **Modes of Opportunistic Behavior Among Holders of Different Financial Assets.** The following are strategies by which holders of common stock can increase the value of their financial assets at the expense of the holders of more senior financial assets.

a. **Increasing the riskiness of the firm's investments.** In a sense, the holders of common stock sell their corporation's equity to the debtholders (retaining the right to manage the corporation) in return for the loan and a call option to repurchase the equity for the face value of the debt plus interest. When the debt comes due, the shareholders exercise their option by repaying the debt or let the option expire by defaulting. As the odds rise that the value of the corporation's investments (the "underlying asset") will differ from their expected value by a lot, the value of the "option," the common stock, also rises. Therefore, in corporations with debt (or preferred stock) outstanding, holders of common stock possess an incentive to push for more risky investments—even if the investments decrease the corporation's expected value. The incentive becomes stronger as the value of their stock declines.

b. **Withdrawing funds.** Viewed from another perspective, the holders of a corporation's debt grant the holders of its common stock a put option, *i.e.,* the stockholders may sell the corporation to the debtholders for the amount owed. The shareholders will exercise this option (default) when the debt exceeds the corporation's value. Paying a dividend, or otherwise distributing funds to shareholders, reduces the value of the corporation, the put option's "underlying asset," and so increases the option's value, the right to sell the corporation at a specified price.

  c. **Retaining control after default.** The term of the shareholders' "option" does not end upon default because the Bankruptcy Code gives a corporation's management the exclusive right, for four months, to propose a reorganization plan, the terms on which ownership will shift to the debtholders. Meanwhile, management stays in the saddle where it can pursue higher risk projects. And management can extend the term still more by securing an extension of the exclusivity period, requests for which bankruptcy courts grant routinely. Extending the term of an option increases its value to the holder at the expense of the writer. Shareholders of a bankrupt corporation frequently extract some value from the debtholders in return for foregoing additional extensions.

  d. **Likelihood of such opportunism.** The odds of such opportunism occurring depend in large measure on how well management's interests are aligned with the interests of the equity holders.

E. PROTECTION AGAINST INTRACORPORATE OPPORTUNISM

The "legal capital" regime imposed by most corporation statutes and the Uniform Fraudulent Conveyance Act (which, along with its revision, the Uniform Fraudulent Transfer Act, has been adopted by most states) provide some protection against the kind of opportunism analyzed in the preceding section. Debtholders can and do negotiate for additional protection in the form of *covenants* in the applicable indenture. After analyzing these sources of protection, we turn to the suggestion made by some commentators that courts should fill in the "gaps" of contractual protection by holding that, in limited circumstances, corporate boards owe a *fiduciary duty* to debtholders.

 1. **Weak Protection: The Statutory Legal Capital Structure.** Most corporation statutes bar a corporation from issuing common stock in return for certain kinds of intangible assets, such as unsecured notes or promises to render future services, and require that a corporation's accounts state the value ("par") of the (lawful) consideration that it did receive. These statutes bar the distribution of this "stated capital" as dividends or stock repurchases (as if creditors relied on "stated capital" in making their investment decisions, which no sensible creditor would do). This regulation provides very little protection to creditors because (i) it addresses only value transfers effected through dividends or stock repurchases, and (ii) shareholders and management easily and lawfully avoid the accounting limits.

Traditionally, these statutes limit dividends and stock repurchases to the amount by which a corporation's total assets exceed the sum of its liabilities and stated capital. Lawfully evading this limit is easy, however, because management can insure low stated capital by assigning a low par value to each share and allocating all remaining value to "capital surplus," which is available for distribution as dividends or stock repurchases. In the absence of capital surplus, management may be able to generate other forms of available surplus, such as a revaluation surplus, *i.e.*, the amount by which the market value of assets exceeds their book value.

Some corporation statutes limit dividend or stock repurchase distributions to a corporation's retained earnings ("earned surplus") as shown on its balance sheet. (They also bar distributions if the corporation is insolvent or if they would render it insolvent.) Lawfully evading this limit is also easy because accounting standards permit management to change the accounting principles used to prepare a corporation's balance sheet and to apply the new principles retroactively, even though doing so increases "earned surplus."

California's corporation statute provides that a corporation may make distributions up to the amount of its retained earnings (calculated in accordance with generally accepted accounting principles) and that it may distribute more if its accounts (maintained in accordance with generally accepted accounting principles) show certain financial ratios (ratios used in many indenture covenants governing distributions). The Revised Model Business Corporation Act provides that a corporation may make a distribution when it can pay its debts as they become due, and then only to the extent that its assets exceed its liabilities.

To the extent that sensible creditors care about all of this, they probably care less about the standard than that it be fixed.

2. **Fraudulent Conveyance Law.** The Uniform Fraudulent Conveyance Act provides a little more protection for creditors than the "legal capital" regime, in part because it addresses value transfers effected through loans and other nontraditional transactions. These statutes bar the transfer of assets or the incurring of debt (a) for the purpose of defrauding a creditor, or (b) in exchange for less than "reasonably equivalent value" (i) if the debtor was engaged or about to engage in a business or a transaction for which the remaining assets of the debtor were "unreasonably small in relation to the business or transaction," or (ii) if a reasonable person in the debtor's position would have expected to "incur debts beyond [its] ability to pay as they became due." [Uniform Fraudulent Conveyance Act §4; 7A U.L.A. (1985)] Creditors have sought to apply fraudulent conveyance law to leveraged buyouts, the impact of which on target company creditors resembles that of a dividend financed with borrowed funds. Courts have not rushed to embrace this application, perhaps because it requires that one calculate the probability of different cash flows from the proposed transaction.

3. **Contractual Protection: Bond Covenants.** Traditional covenants (i) restrict mergers, transfers of substantial assets, and other transactions most often used to change a corporation's risk profile; (ii) prohibit certain high-risk investments, or limit them to a specified amount; (iii) limit the incurring of debt (often defined to include debt substitutes such as sale and leaseback transactions) either

to a specified amount or to a percentage of the corporation's tangible assets; and (iv) limit dividends and stock repurchases. The advent of leveraged buyouts (in which an acquirer typically offers to buy a target's stock with the proceeds of a loan for which the target's assets will serve as collateral) and recapitalizations prompted many debtholders to insist on event risk covenants that, upon the occurrence of specified events, (i) give the debtholders the right to put the debt back to the corporation at face value, or (ii) cause the interest rate to increase to offset the increased risk (and thereby block the transfer of value to the shareholders). Debt covenants provide considerably more protection than the legal capital regime or the fraudulent conveyance law, but of course they still leave creditors at risk. Creditors can only anticipate so much and drafters bump up against language limits. Moreover, creditors find it advantageous to accept some risk because additional constraints may prompt management to forgo otherwise desirable investments (the creditors could waive the additional constraints, but the difficulties of acting collectively may render waiver impractical). (The Trust Indenture Act of 1939 requires, in connection with publicly held debt, a bondholder majority vote to approve amendments—except amendments relating to timely payment of principal and interest, which requires unanimous consent.)

4. **Fiduciary Duty and the Covenant of Good Faith and Fair Dealing.** According to the casebook authors, the legal capital regime, the Uniform Fraudulent Conveyance Act, and indenture covenants leave debtholders quite vulnerable to what the authors identify as the "most significant means" by which equityholders can appropriate value that would otherwise belong to debtholders—increasing the riskiness of the firm's business. Some commentators, and Chancellor Allen in *Credit Lyonnais Bank Nederland, N.V. v. Pathe Communications Corp.*, *supra*, have suggested that courts offer some protection against this by holding that, in limited circumstances, corporate boards owe a fiduciary duty to debtholders. This suggestion has generally met with judicial hostility. (Courts routinely hold that boards of insolvent corporations owe a fiduciary duty to debtholders.)

In *Credit Lyonnais*, Chancellor Allen analyzed the impact of threatened insolvency on the incentives of directors to put their corporation's creditors at greater risk than the creditors may have expected. In footnote 55, he considers a hypothetical solvent corporation that owes its sole creditors, its bondholders, $12 million. Its single asset is a judgment for $51 million against a solvent debtor, and the judgment is on appeal. Here is what may happen:

Outcome	Odds	Expected value
Affirm ($51mm)	25%	$12.75 million
Modify ($4mm)	70%	$2.8 million
Reversal ($0)	5%	$0

The expected value of the judgment is $15.55 million, and so the value of the corporation's equity is $15.55 million, less the $12 million owed to bondholders, or $3.55 million.

Now suppose that the appellant offers to pay $17.5 million to settle the matter. The creditors would favor accepting the offer because the $17.5 million would eliminate the 75% risk that the corporation would default, and would provide more than enough funds to satisfy the entire debt. In fact, the additional funds would raise the value of the corporation's equity to $5.55 million, but the stockholders might still favor taking their chances with the appeal. An affirmance would raise the value of their equity to $39 million, and so its expected value to them is 25% of $39 million, or $9.75 million.

Chancellor Allen suggests that because this hypothetical corporation is "in the vicinity of insolvency," its board cannot indulge the stockholders' preference without breaching a duty to its debtholders. The board cannot accept what the casebook authors call a "negative expected value investment." It is not clear whether such a "rule" would permit the board to accept a positive expected value investment if acceptance resulted in a substantial transfer from debtholders to shareholders. [*Note*: Perhaps it should, because only a negative expected value investment would have an impact on people other than the shareholders and debtholders.] In any event, the application of this rule and the ascertainment of the "vicinity of insolvency" involves considerable uncertainty. And this uncertain rule might deter managers from making risky investments that might have rescued their financially troubled firms.

IV. FORMING THE CORPORATION

A. SELECTION OF STATE OF INCORPORATION

People organizing a business as a corporation may incorporate it in any state, even one in which they do not plan to operate. (The desirability of this freedom was discussed in Chapter I.) The choice may have important implications, in part because the corporation laws of the various states differ in both language and interpretation. Because of these differences, the corporation laws of different states may best suit the needs and interests of different groups of people organizing different kinds of businesses. (The organizers may be able to draft around the important differences, but not always, and perhaps only at considerable expense.) Even where the relevant statutory language is substantially the same, its interpretation may be significantly more certain in a state with a well-developed body of case law, and certainty offers important advantages to those in business. The net benefits of one state's law, however, may not be worth the costs of incorporating under it. These costs include: payment of certain fees and taxes, some of which are assessed yearly, and submission to the jurisdiction of the courts of the state of incorporation. If the organizers plan anyway to operate in the state with the most attractive corporation law, the benefits of incorporating there are likely to exceed the costs. The reason is that the business will have to pay fees and taxes to that state and submit to the jurisdiction of its courts anyway. If the organizers do not plan to operate in that state, the relationship of benefits and costs may depend, in part, on the absolute size of the business.

B. COMPLIANCE WITH STATE REQUIREMENTS

1. **Preparation of Documents.** The process of incorporation may require the preparation of a number of documents, including shareholder agreements and subscription agreements (to buy shares when issued). It always requires the preparation of the articles of incorporation, sometimes called the "certificate of incorporation" or "charter." Under most statutes, the articles need only contain (i) the corporation's name, including some term indicating corporate status; (ii) the name and address of the corporation's agent for service of process within the state; (iii) a description of the rights (*e.g.,* voting, dividends, entitlement upon liquidation, purchase of newly issued shares) and restrictions (*e.g.,* transferability) associated with each kind of stock to be issued, and the number of each kind that may be issued; and (iv) the names and addresses of the incorporator(s) and of the directors, if any are named to serve before election. The articles may, and frequently do, contain other provisions. The more important ones will bear on control and perhaps duration.

2. **Meeting Statutory Formalities.** The incorporators must sign and usually verify or acknowledge the articles. They must then arrange to deliver the articles to bureaucrats working for a designated state officer, usually the secretary of state.

Certain fees and taxes must accompany the articles. If the bureaucrats detect no deficiencies, they send a certified copy of the articles to the incorporators. Some corporation laws require filing of the articles in one or more county offices, with some states placing this burden on the incorporators and others on the state bureaucrats. A few laws even require public notice of incorporation. Most state laws provide for a post-incorporation organizational meeting at which directors may be elected, officers selected, bylaws adopted, and "housekeeping" chores completed. About one-fifth of the states prohibit the transaction of any nonincidental business until a minimum capital, typically $1,000, has been paid in.

C. DEFECTIVE INCORPORATION

1. **The Problem.** People sometimes transact business purportedly as a corporation without having complied with the statutory requirements. When these transactions give rise to litigation, one of the issues becomes: to what extent, if any, should the court treat these people as if they had complied? The particular requirements involved, and their purpose, may bear on the answer. So, too, may the reason for noncompliance.

2. **Common Law Response: De Jure and De Facto Corporations and Corporations by Estoppel.** Some courts treated people as if they had observed the formalities if there had been "substantial compliance" with them. "Substantial compliance," they said, resulted in a de jure corporation. Some courts did not require this much. At least where the state was not involved, these courts treated people as if they had observed the formalities as long as they had made a good faith, "colorable or apparent" attempt to incorporate under an applicable law and exercised some corporate power. This, they said, resulted in a de facto corporation. Of course, just what constituted "substantial compliance" or "colorable or apparent" became the subject of litigation. So, too, did the consequences of a less than "colorable or apparent" attempt to incorporate. In some situations, courts held that one party or another was estopped from denying incorporation.

3. **Modern Statutes.** Some modern statutes appear to abolish or limit these common law doctrines. The interpretation of these statutes still gives rise to litigation.

4. **De Facto Incorporation and Incorporation by Estoppel Under Modern Statutes--**

Thompson & Green Machinery Co. v. Music City Lumber Co., 683 S.W.2d 340 (Tenn. App. 1984).

Facts. Purportedly as president of Music City Sawmill Co. ("Sawmill"), Walker (D) bought a wheel loader on credit from Thompson & Green Machinery Co. (P). In fact, unbeknownst to P and D, Sawmill did not become incorporated until the day after the sale. Sawmill defaulted and returned the equipment, which P resold at a substantial loss. About seven months later, P sued Sawmill and Music City Lumber Co., another business of which P was president, for the balance due. Three months later, when P discovered the date of Sawmill's incorporation, P amended its complaint to include D as a defendant. The amended complaint gave D his first notice of this fact. The trial court found for P, and D appeals.

Issue. If an individual contracts in good faith purportedly on behalf of a corporation, which does not in fact become incorporated until a later date, is the individual liable on the contract even if the other party believed that it was dealing with a corporation?

Held. Yes. Judgment affirmed.

♦   By statute (Tenn. Code Ann. section 48-1-1405), "all persons who assume to act as a corporation without authority so to do shall be jointly and severally liable for all debts and liabilities incurred or arising as a result thereof." This statute almost replicates section 56 of the Model Business Corporation Act, and its stated purpose is to eliminate the common law doctrines of de facto incorporation and incorporation by estoppel.

♦   The statute contains no exception for situations involving a plaintiff that believed it was dealing with a corporation.

Comment. Holdings like this one increase the incentive to verify compliance with the formalities of the incorporation statute, but it is not clear how much. On the other hand, they tend to frustrate the expectations of the parties to the contract. A court could honor the expectations of the parties without resorting to the doctrines of de facto incorporation or incorporation by estoppel by interpreting "inc." or "co." as shorthand for a nonrecourse debt.

---

5.   **Narrow Interpretation of Statutory Corporation by Estoppel--**

Don Swann Sales Corp. v. Echols, 160 Ga. App. 539, 287 S.E.2d 577 (1981).

Facts. Beginning in January 1980, Don Swann Sales Corp. (P) sold to Echols (D) on an open account in the name of Cupid's, Inc. Although neither P nor D realized it, Cupid's, Inc. did not become properly registered with the secretary of state until October 1980. P sued D individually, and not the corporation, for amounts due on pre-October transactions. The trial court entered judgment for D on the ground that P should have sued the corporation and was estopped from denying the existence of Cupid's, Inc. P appeals.

Issue. May one who sells on credit to an individual purporting to act for a corporation recover from the individual the amount due on sales made when, unbeknownst to either party, the corporation had not been registered with the secretary of state?

Held. Yes. Judgment reversed.

♦ By statute, "[a]ll persons who assume to act as a corporation before the Secretary of State has issued the certificate of incorporation . . . shall be . . . liable for all debts . . . incurred . . . as a result thereof." [Ga. Code Ann. §22-204]

♦ Such persons cannot shield themselves under the statutory doctrine of corporation by estoppel, section 22-5103, which provides that "[t]he existence of a corporation, claiming a charter under color of law cannot be collaterally attacked by persons who have dealt with it as a corporation." This doctrine estops a purported corporation from denying its own existence, and it estops an individual from denying the existence of a purported corporation when it sues to vindicate its own contractual rights.

♦ This is not a case where the corporation purportedly existed under "color of law."

♦ Any other ruling would permit an agent acting for a nonexistent principal to escape liability by claiming that he thought the corporation was in existence when, in fact, no such entity existed.

Comment. In *Cranson v. International Business Machines Corp.*, 234 Md. 477, 200 A.2d 33 (1964), the court invoked "estoppel" to shield from personal liability the president of a purported corporation when the attorney who drafted the articles had the president sign them, but inadvertently filed them late, and had advised the plaintiff seller that incorporation had occurred.

---

6. **Active vs. Inactive "Shareholders."** The liability of a purported shareholder in a defectively incorporated business may depend in part on how much the individual participates in the operation and control of the business.

7. **Failure to Pay In Minimum Capital Stated In Articles of Incorporation--**

Sulphur Export Corp. v. Caribbean Clipper Lines, Inc., 277 F. Supp. 632 (E.D. La. 1968).

Facts. Sulphur Export Corp. (P) sued to recover for damages resulting from a breach of contract for a charter party by Caribbean Clipper Lines, Inc. ("Clipper"). The officers and directors (Ds) of Caribbean entered into the transaction with P before the $1,000 stated in the articles of incorporation had been paid in to capitalize the corporation. Louisiana statute required that the capitalization provided for in the articles must be paid into the corporation before business is transacted. None of the individual defendants had objected to the transaction. P alleges that the individual defendants should be held personally liable for the full amount of the debt arising from the breach. Ds allege that their individual liability should be restricted to the $1,000 capitalization requirement.

Issue. Should corporate directors and officers who fail to object to a corporate transaction, which was entered into before the capitalization amount provided for in the articles of incorporation had been paid into the corporation, be held personally liable for the debts and liabilities of the corporation arising from the transaction?

Held. Yes.

♦   The measure of the joint and several liability of the non-dissenting directors and officers is the full corporate debt arising from the transaction that occurred before the required capitalization was paid into the corporation.

♦   The capitalization requirement of the statute was designed to promote a public policy of protecting corporate creditors of newly organized corporations.

♦   Limiting liability of nondissenting directors and participating directors would tend to frustrate the public policy embodied in the statute by emasculating the penalties provided for failure to properly capitalize.

Comment. Some states limit liability to the amount of the required capitalization.

D. DISREGARDING THE CORPORATE ENTITY

1.   **Limited Liability and Its Limits Generally.** Absent an agreement to the contrary, a shareholder generally bears no risk of corporate debt beyond her investment. A shareholder may not invoke this limited liability, however, if incorporation was part of a scheme to defraud a creditor. Courts "pierce the corporate veil," treating the debt as if it were incurred by the shareholder, not by a separate entity. Most courts also pierce the corporate veil in other situations as well, but it is usefully difficult to categorize these situations because the courts pin conclusory labels on them. Courts often refer to certain factors in piercing the corporate veil opinions: disregard of corporate formalities, commingling of corporate and personal funds, and the amount of "capitalization," meaning equity financing. A court's willingness to pierce the corporate veil may depend on: (i) how many people own shares and their involvement in the operation and control of the business; (ii) whether the shareholders are natural persons or other corporations; and (iii) whether the creditor has a tort or contract claim. When an incorporated business becomes bankrupt, judges sometimes engage in a process analogous to piercing the corporate veil whereby

they subordinate (or disallow entirely) the debts owed to shareholders to the debts owed to outside creditors.

2. Voluntary Creditor Accepting Risk--

Perpetual Real Estate Services, Inc. v. Michaelson Properties, Inc., 974 F.2d 545 (4th Cir. 1992).

Facts. Aaron Michaelson (D) organized Michaelson Properties, Inc. ("MPI") as an Illinois corporation with himself as president and sole shareholder, having invested $1,000. MPI entered into two joint ventures with Perpetual Real Estate Services, Inc. (P) to convert apartments to condominiums. In 1981, MPI and P organized the first one as a partnership, Bethesda Apartment Associates ("BAA"), in which they both invested $100,000. MPI also put up a $1 million letter of credit, and D and his wife agreed to indemnify P from their personal funds for any loss suffered on the letter of credit. BAA sold the last unit in 1983 and, in 1985, distributed about $600,000 in profits to each partner.

In 1983, MPI and P organized a second partnership, Arlington Apartment Associates ("AAA"), in which they both invested $50,000 and agreed to share pro rata in satisfying any AAA liabilities. AAA borrowed $24 million from P's parent, a bank, and $1.05 million from P. D and his wife personally guaranteed repayment of $750,000 of the first loan and all of the second. During 1985 and 1986, AAA distributed about $456,000 to each partner after they concluded, as required by their partnership agreement, that AAA held sufficient assets to meet its anticipated expenses. MPI distributed what it received to its sole shareholder, D.

More than a year after the last of AAA's distributions, some condominium purchasers sued AAA for breach of warranty. AAA settled by paying $950,000, all of which P paid. Seeking reimbursement for MPI's share of this settlement, P sued not only MPI but also D personally. The trial court instructed the jury that, under the applicable law (Virginia's), the jury could hold D personally liable if it found (i) D exercised "undue dominance and control" over MPI (as evidenced by D's failure to observe corporate formalities, keep corporate records, pay dividends, and elect other officers and directors), and (ii) D "used MPI to perpetrate 'an injustice or fundamental unfairness.'" The jury gave a verdict against D, and the trial court entered judgment on it. D appeals.

Issue. If D exercised "undue dominance and control" over MPI, does D become personally liable for MPI's contractual obligations to its partner if D used MPI to perpetrate "an injustice or fundamental unfairness"?

Held. No. Judgment reversed.

♦ That limited liability might yield results that seem "unfair" to jurors unfamiliar with the function of the corporate form cannot provide a basis for piercing the veil under Virginia law. Piercing requires a showing that the defendant used the corporation to "obscure fraud" or "conceal crime."

♦ A reasonable jury could not have so found. Knowing full well who controlled MPI and the nature and size of its capitalization, P entered into a long-standing contractual relationship with it. When they contemplated making distributions from AAA, P concluded that AAA would retain sufficient assets to meet its anticipated expenses and voted to make the distributions. P did not seek any limitation on what MPI could do with the funds that it received even though P knew or should have known that MPI would make a distribution to D (which it did long before any claims were filed against AAA). That P obtained personal guarantees from D in connection with other potential liabilities reinforces the conclusion that, with respect to these claims, P accepted the risk attendant to the limited liability provided by MPI. No evidence suggests that D misled P about MPI's financial condition or otherwise used MPI to disguise anything.

3. **Voluntary Creditor Ignorant of Unusually Small Equity Financing--**

Kinney Shoe Corp. v. Polan, 939 F.2d 209 (4th Cir. 1991).

Facts. Lincoln M. Polan (D) organized and became the sole owner of two corporations, Industrial Realty Co. ("Industrial") and Polan Industries, Inc. ("Polan"). He never held any meetings, kept any minutes, or elected any officers. Industrial issued no shares, and D made no capital contribution to it. Its sole asset and source of income was its sublease of a building leased by Kinney Shoe Corporation (P). Industrial subleased part of this building to Polan. D drew on his personal funds to make Industrial's first rental payment. P received no more rental payments, and Polan never paid any rent to Industrial. P sued D personally for the rent due on the sublease to Industrial. The trial court entered judgment in favor of D, holding that because P failed to undertake a reasonable investigation of D's credit record, P had assumed the risk that Industrial might be grossly undercapitalized.

Issue. May P recover from D personally for the rent due on Industrial's sublease?

Held. Yes. Judgment reversed.

♦ P met its burden of showing that D failed to (i) observe "the relatively simple formalities of creating and maintaining a corporate entity," and (ii) "adequately capitalize" Industrial. Indeed, P showed that D attempted to protect his assets by placing them in Polan and interposing Industrial between Polan and P.

♦ Because D made no investment in Industrial, P did not have to show that it undertook a reasonable investigation of D's credit record.

Comment. The appellate court's decision permits a party in P's position to assume that the other party's capitalization is not unusual, unless the other party discloses that it is.

This outcome may be efficient because the amount of credit extended by P may not have warranted much investigation.

---

4.   "Undercapitalization"--

Walkovsky v. Carlton, 18 N.Y.2d 414, 223 N.E.2d 6, 276 N.Y.S.2d 585 (1966).

Facts. Walkovsky (P) was injured in an accident with a cab. P sued the cab driver, the corporation owning the cab, and Carlton (D), owner of that corporation and of nine others, each of which owned two cabs with the minimum $10,000 liability insurance coverage required by state law. The complaint alleged that the corporations operated as a single entity and constituted a fraud on the public. D filed a motion for dismissal in that no cause of action was alleged. The motion was granted, but the appellate division reversed. D appeals.

Issue. Does P's complaint state a sufficient cause of action for piercing the corporate veil and holding D personally (or the other nine corporations he owns) liable?

Held. No. Order of the appellate division reversed and complaint dismissed with leave to amend.

♦   The courts will disregard the corporate form and pierce the corporate veil whenever necessary to prevent fraud or achieve equity. Whenever anyone uses control of the corporation to further his own rather than the corporation's business, he will be liable for the corporation's acts.

♦   There is nothing wrong with one corporation being part of a larger corporate enterprise. The issue is whether the business is really carried on in a personal capacity rather than for corporate purposes. It was not so alleged here.

♦   On the undercapitalization issue, the state has set the minimum insurance requirements for operating a cab, and thousands of individuals driving cabs have incorporated and taken out the minimum insurance. If the insurance protection provided by state law is inadequate, then the problem is the state legislature's to correct.

Dissent. An action lies against the shareholders if they incorporate a business without sufficient assets to meet prospective liabilities and possible business risks of the new business. Legislative setting of the minimum insurance does not prevent the court from requiring that incorporating shareholders provide further adequate capital for the intended business. This capital can be provided by additional insurance or other assets. But adequate capitalization was not provided here. So there is unfairness, and the veil should be pierced.

---

5. Parent Not Liable for Its Subsidiary Under Alter Ego Theory--

Fletcher v. Atex, Inc., 8 F.3d 1451 (2d Cir. 1995)

Facts. Fletcher and another computer user (Ps) sued Atex, Inc. ("Atex") and its parent, Eastman Kodak Co. ("Kodak") (Ds), for repetitive stress injuries that they suffered allegedly as a result of using computer keyboards manufactured by Atex. The district court granted Kodak summary judgment on Ps' alter ego theory of liability. Ps appeal.

Issue. Should the corporate veil of a subsidiary be pierced if (i) some of the members of its board also served on its parent's board; (ii) it could not lease real estate, make major capital expenditures, or negotiate for the sale of a minority interest in its own stock without its parent's approval; (iii) it participated in its parent's cash management system; and (iv) its parent played a significant role in the ultimate sale of its assets to a third party?

Held. No. Judgment affirmed.

- ♦ To prevail on the "alter ego" theory, a plaintiff must show that the parent and subsidiary "operated as a single economic entity."

- ♦ The overlap in the composition of the boards, which is common among parents and subsidiaries, was negligible. The board of Atex held its own meetings and hired its own management executives and employees. Atex filed its own tax returns.

- ♦ That Atex had to obtain Kodak's approval for a number of major transactions shows only that Atex was Kodak's subsidiary.

- ♦ Atex's participation in Kodak's cash management system does not show undue domination or control; nor did its participation result in a commingling of funds.

- ♦ A bare assertion that the parent "exploited" the subsidiary does not justify piercing the subsidiary's corporate veil.

Comment. Notice that the "alter ego" language must express the court's conclusion, not its reasoning. After all, the function of a wholly owned subsidiary is to serve as the "alter ego" of its parent.

---

6. **Tort vs. Contract Creditors.** On a contract claim, a defendant shareholder may plausibly argue that the creditor knew or should have known of the shareholder's limited liability and therefore assumed the risk that the corporation's assets would prove inadequate to satisfy its obligations. Should the creditor have known how thinly capitalized the corporation was? The an-

swer may, and perhaps ought to, depend on the additional cost of acquiring and evaluating the relevant information.

7.   **"Inadequate" Capitalization.** Considerable controversy surrounds the question of whether "inadequate" capitalization ("capitalization" here referring to equity rather than debt capital) should itself, or in combination with some other factor(s), prompt a court to pierce the corporate veil. If so, additional issues arise. How should a court measure the "adequacy" of the capitalization? When should it do so, at the time of incorporation or later? Are the shareholders of the "inadequately" capitalized corporation liable for the "inadequacy" or for the entire claim? The resolution of these issues may affect the propensity of entrepreneurs to undertake risky business ventures.

8.   **Parent's Liability for the Contractual Obligations of Its Thinly Capitalized Subsidiary--**

Bartle v. Home Owners Cooperative, 309 N.Y. 103, 127 N.E.2d 832 (1955).

Facts. Home Owners Cooperative (D) was a cooperative corporation composed mainly of veterans. It attempted to build low-cost housing for its members. To do so, it formed Westerlea Corporation ("Westerlea") to act as the builder of 26 homes. Costs turned out to be higher than anticipated, and Westerlea's contract creditors eventually took over and ran the corporation. Westerlea then went bankrupt. D had provided the original $50,000 capital for Westerlea; its officers and directors were the same as in Westerlea; but each corporation kept separate and correct corporate records. Bartle (P) was the trustee in bankruptcy for Westerlea; P tried to pierce the Westerlea veil to hold D liable. The trial court found for D, and P appeals.

Issue. In the absence of fraud, where a parent corporation and its subsidiary do not mingle their affairs together, will the parent be responsible for the contract debts of the subsidiary?

Held. No. Judgment affirmed.

♦   The law allows incorporation for the purpose of limited liability. The corporate veil will be pierced only if there is fraudulent use of the subsidiary by the parent or the parent has committed acts with the subsidiary for its benefit to the detriment of the creditors. There were no such acts in this instance.

♦   Here, the creditors had the opportunity to investigate the financial standing of Westerlea before extending it credit.

Dissent. D's business was done on the basis that Westerlea could not make a profit from the buildings it built. The homes were sold to D's members at cost. Westerlea was the mere agent of D in effectuating a fraud on creditors.

---

9. Subordination of Shareholder Claims Where Subsidiary Is Mere Instrumentality--

Stone v. Eacho, 127 F.2d 284 (4th Cir. 1942).

Facts. Tip Top Tailors, a Delaware corporation, operated nine retail clothing stores across the United States, one of which was incorporated in Virginia. The Virginia corporation was capitalized with $3. The officers of both the Delaware and the Virginia corporations were the same, and no separate corporate activity occurred within the Virginia store. The Delaware corporation paid all expenses for the operation of the Virginia store. In 1940, the Delaware corporation was adjudged bankrupt, and Stone (P) was appointed receiver on behalf of the creditors. An involuntary petition in bankruptcy was also filed against the Virginia corporation, which was similarly adjudged bankrupt. P then filed a claim for amounts owing to the Delaware corporation from the Virginia corporation. Eacho (D), the trustee in bankruptcy of the Virginia corporation, resisted the claim by P and asked that it be subordinated to the claims of other creditors of the Virginia corporation on the ground that the Virginia corporation was not a separate entity, but a mere instrumentality of the Delaware corporation. The claim was referred to a special master who found in favor of D. P appealed and asked in the alternative that the corporate entity of the Virginia store be disregarded and the bankruptcy proceedings of the two corporations be merged. The lower court affirmed the report of the special master, and P and three intervening creditors of the Delaware corporation appeal.

Issues.

(i)   Should the claims in bankruptcy of the parent corporation against its subsidiary be subordinated to the claims of the other creditors when it is shown that the subsidiary is undercapitalized and is a mere instrumentality of the parent corporation?

(ii)   In such a case, should the separate corporate entity of the subsidiary be disregarded and the bankruptcy proceedings of the two be consolidated?

Held. (i) Yes. (ii) Yes. Judgment reversed and remanded.

◆   It is well settled that the claims of a parent corporation against a subsidiary should be postponed where the subsidiary has, in reality, no separate existence.

◆   In a case such as this, where both a parent and a subsidiary are insolvent and where the subsidiary has no real existence, there is no reason why the courts should not ignore the subsidiary for all purposes, allowing the creditors of both corporations to share equally in the pooled assets.

◆   Courts will not be blinded by corporate form but will look through the form and behind the corporate entities involved to deal with the situation as justice may require.

Comment. When an incorporated business becomes bankrupt, the bankruptcy judge may treat the claims of shareholders as well as they would be treated if owned by outsiders. The judge may "subordinate" their claims, paying off others first, even though the claims of the others would ordinarily have the same or lower priority. Typically, the actions and circumstances that trigger subordination are the same as those that trigger piercing the corporate veil outside of bankruptcy. The bankruptcy judge may also subordinate the claims of a parent to the claims of minority shareholders in a subsidiary. This is what happened in *Taylor v. Standard Gas & Electric Co.*, 306 U.S. 307 (1939), involving Standard's Deep Rock Oil Corp. subsidiary, which is why this practice is known as the "Deep Rock doctrine."

E. PRE-FORMATION TRANSACTIONS

1. **Liability of the Corporation for Debts of Its Predecessor.** When an existing business becomes incorporated, questions may arise about the rights of the existing business's creditors. Of course, if the existing business had been organized as a proprietorship or partnership, the proprietor or partners remain personally liable. If it had been organized as a corporation, or part of one, that corporation remains liable. The questions relate to the liability of the new corporation. If the new corporation expressly accepts the existing business's obligations, say in the contract by which it acquires the existing business's assets, the creditors have the rights of third-party beneficiaries against the new corporation. But if the new corporation does not expressly accept these obligations, the creditors' rights may be subject to considerable controversy.

   a. **Avoidance of corporate liability due to predecessor sole proprietorship--**

Tift v. Forage King Industries, Inc., 108 Wis. 2d 72, 332 N.W.2d 14 (1982).

Facts. In 1975, Tift (P) suffered injury while operating a farm tractor allegedly as a result of the tractor's defective chopper box. Woodrow Wiberg's ("WW's") sole proprietorship, Forage King Industries, had manufactured the box in 1962. In 1968, Vernon Nedland became a partner in the business. Eventually, the partners formed a corporation, Forage King Industries, Inc. (D), and shortly thereafter, WW purchased all of Nedland's shares. Seven months before the accident, Tester Corporation bought all of WW's shares. At all relevant times, D continued to manufacture substantially the same products at the same location. P sued D, Nedland, and WW. The trial court granted Nedland summary judgment. It also granted D summary judgment, which the court of appeals affirmed. P appeals.

Issue. If a defective piece of machinery manufactured by a sole proprietorship causes injury, may the injured person seek recovery from the sole proprietorship's corporate successor, which manufactures substantially the same goods under the same trade name at the same location?

Held. Yes. Judgment reversed.

♦ That the allegedly defective product was manufactured by a business organized as a sole proprietorship rather than a corporation does not relieve the successor business of liability. Nor does the sole proprietor's amenability to suit.

♦ When a corporation purchases the assets of an existing business, the corporation bears liability for its predecessor's debts in two instances. First, liability exists where the transaction provides for such liability and where it constitutes a fraudulent conveyance. Second, corporate liability exists where the transaction amounts to a consolidation or merger and where the purchaser corporation is a continuation of the seller corporation. In the latter two circumstances, the original entity continues to exist, albeit in an altered form. This is the situation here. The corporation should therefore be treated as if it were in privity with the purchaser of the allegedly defective product.

♦ D and WW can better spread the cost and assume the liability than the helpless P.

Dissent. The reason for sometimes holding a successor corporation liable for the debts of a predecessor corporation is that the predecessor will not be amenable to suit. This reason does not apply where the predecessor business was organized as a sole proprietorship. Imposition of liability on D will give P a windfall. D, a creature of statute, should be held responsible only for its acts, not the totally independent acts of WW. P may not prevail here under the de facto merger or continuation exceptions to the rule of nonliability of successor corporations because P did not, and could not, show that the seller dissolved quickly and that the consideration for the sale of assets was the shares of the purchaser, which were distributed to the seller's shareholders.

---

b. Transfer for adequate consideration--

J.F. Anderson Lumber Co. v. Myers, 296 Minn. 33, 206 N.W.2d 365 (1973).

Facts. Anderson Lumber (P) obtained judgment against Richard T. Leekley Co. (D). After trial, but before entry of judgment, Richard Leekley and his wife, the sole stockholders of the corporation, formed a new corporation named Leekley's, Inc. The new corporation performed the same kind of home construction, had the same officers and stockholders, and purchased the assets of the preexisting corporation. The first corporation had been insolvent for some years before the second was incorporated. P sought to include the second corporation as an additional judgment debtor.

Issue. If an insolvent corporation transfers assets *for adequate consideration* to a successor corporation, can the successor corporation be held liable for the debts of its predecessor corporation (unless there is a consolidation or merger and a continuity of the business, or an agreement to assume the debts)?

Held. No.

♦ In the present case there is no evidence of any fraudulent transfer or other fraudulent act. There is clear evidence that the assets of the first corporation were transferred to the second corporation for full and adequate consideration.

♦ When one corporation sells or transfers all of its assets to another corporation, the latter is not liable for the debts and liabilities of the transferor, except when: (i) the purchaser expressly or impliedly agrees to assume the debts; (ii) the transaction amounts to a consolidation or merger; (iii) the purchasing corporation is merely a continuation of the selling corporation; and (iv) the transactions are entered into fraudulently in order to escape liability for debts by the first corporation.

♦ In the present case, there is no agreement by the transferee corporation to assume the debts of the transferor corporation. Before one corporation can be a mere continuation of another it is necessary that there be insufficient consideration running from the new company to the old one.

Comment. If Corporation A and Corporation B conduct an arm's length transaction, and there is no overlapping of ownership, then no matter what A receives from B, the creditors of A must look to the assets of A for repayment.

---

2. **Promoters' Contracts.**

   a. **Introduction.** "Promoters" help create incorporated businesses. It may be quite advantageous for promoters to engage in certain transactions prior to incorporation. Such transactions may give rise to a number of legal problems. This section focuses on the problems attending preincorporation contracts between promoters and those with no anticipated role in the yet-to-be-formed corporation: May the subsequently formed corporation enforce these contracts? Under what circumstances, if any, may the third party enforce the contract against the promoter? The corporation, once it is formed? To what extent is each liable?

   b. **Enforcement by corporation.** The courts almost always permit corporations to enforce preincorporation contracts entered into on their behalf by their promoters, but they experience some difficulty reconciling this sensible result with prevailing doctrine. "Ratification" customarily requires that the principal could have authorized the "agent's" act when it occurred, which a nonexistent corporation could not do. Courts sometimes treat the promoter's contract as an implied offer, and attempted enforcement by the corporation as an implied acceptance. This works fine unless the third party purports to "revoke" in the interim. When the promoter enters into an assignable contract, the court may permit the corporation to enforce it as the promoter's assignee. Alternatively, the court may permit the corporation to enforce it as a third-party beneficiary of the contract. Most often, courts say that the corporation has "adopted" the contract and so may enforce it.

c. **Enforcement by third parties.** The promoter's contract may explicitly address this problem. If it does not, litigation may well arise. The liability of the promoter may turn in part on whether the business ever becomes incorporated. If it does become incorporated, the liability of the corporation as well as the promoter may turn in part on whether the relevant corporate agents take any action with respect to the contract.

d. **Corporate liability through ratification--**

Kridelbaugh v. Aldrehn Theatres Co., 195 Iowa 147, 191 N.W. 803 (1923).

Facts. An attorney (P) sought to recover attorney's fees incidental to the incorporation of Aldrehn Theatres (D). P was hired to investigate the feasibility of the corporation. His plan was adopted by the three promoters, who then became the only directors of the new corporation. Subsequent to incorporation, P attended the first meeting of the board of directors. The three promoters requested that P obtain a permit to sell the corporation's stock in Iowa. On the basis of the sales, P was promised payment for both his preincorporation work and the present work. P alleged that his preincorporation contract with the promoters was adopted or ratified by the corporation after its creation through its board of directors. The trial court found in favor of P. D appeals.

Issue. Can a corporation be held liable for contracts entered into by promoters that were later adopted or ratified by the corporation?

Held. Yes. Judgment affirmed.

♦ Promoters are individually liable on their contracts, and this is true whether or not a corporation results from their efforts. The corporation, however, cannot be held liable as the principal (with the promoters as agents), since the corporation did not exist as a principal at the time the contract was entered into.

♦ On coming into existence, the new corporation does not adopt the preincorporation contracts merely by acquiescence.

♦ Here it was the express authorization by the board of directors (whose members had also been the preincorporation promoters) to have P provide legal services to the corporation, while at the same time recognizing that P should be paid for his past services, which provides a basis for holding the corporation liable on the promoter's contract.

Comment. The liability of the corporation may depend in part on whether it received any benefit from the promoter's contract and the promoter's subsequent role, if any, in the conduct of the corporation's business.

---

e.   **Promoter liability.** If the promoter contracts in the name of and solely on behalf of the corporation-to-be, then the promoter cannot be held liable if the corporation is never formed. Of course, if the promoter contracts in his own name, then the promoter may be held individually liable, even if the corporation is never formed (and may enforce the contract). The tough cases are the ones where both the promoter's name and the name of the corporation appear on the contract.

1)   **Corporate name only--**

Sherwood and Roberts-Oregon, Inc. v. Alexander, 269 Or. 389, 525 P.2d 135 (1974).

Facts. Alexander (D), a real estate developer, held title to land which he desired to develop. D sought financing through Sherwood and Roberts-Oregon, Inc. (P), which was in the finance business. P advised D to incorporate in order to obtain a more favorable interest rate. P required a deposit in the amount of 1% of the proposed loan that D was seeking. The deposit was refundable if no loan could be obtained, and was to be forfeited if a loan commitment was obtained by P but not accepted by D. D signed the deposit note in the name of the unformed corporation. P knew that there was not as yet any corporate entity. P obtained a loan which was rejected by D. D never formed the corporation. P brought this action to enforce the note against D.

Issue. Can a creditor of a still unformed corporation that indicates that it will rely only on the corporation for payment of the preincorporation contract debt hold a corporate promoter liable for a contract that he entered into only in the name of the corporation?

Held. No. D was entitled to summary judgment.

♦   P knew that there was no legal entity in any stage of incorporation. The contract entered into was, therefore, a preincorporation contract and D is in the position of a promoter. A promoter can be held personally liable on the contract unless the other party agreed to look to some other person or fund for payment.

♦   In the present case, P looked solely to the to-be-formed corporation for payment of the note. Unlike the creditor in the usual case, P is the party that insisted that the contract show a corporation as the obligor (and that it would not do business otherwise).

---

2)   Intent of parties as a factor--

How & Associates, Inc. v. Boss, 222 F. Supp. 936 (S.D. Iowa 1963).

Facts. Boss (D) signed a contract for architectural services as follows: "Edwin A. Boss, agent for a Minnesota corporation to be formed who will be the obligor." How & Associates (P), the other party to the contract, performed services worth $38,250 under the contract but was paid only $14,500. The corporation was never formed. P sued D individually to recover the balance due on the contract.

Issue. Is a person who signed for a nonexistent corporation liable under the contract if the corporation subsequently does not materialize?

Held. In this case, yes. Judgment for P.

♦   The Restatement (Second) of Agency states that when a promoter makes an agreement on behalf of a nonexistent corporation, the following alternatives may represent the actual intent of the parties:

> The other party is making a revocable offer to the corporation that will result in a contract if the corporation is formed and accepts the offer prior to its withdrawal.

> The other party is making an irrevocable offer to the corporation for a limited time. Consideration to support the promise to keep the offer open can be found in an express or implied promise by the promoter to organize the corporation and to use his best efforts to cause it to accept the offer.

> A present contract is formed by which the promoter is bound but with an agreement that his liability terminates if the corporation is formed and manifests its willingness to become a party to the contract.

♦   The general rule is that the person signing for the nonexistent corporation (the promoter) is to be held personally liable *unless* the intent is clearly expressed otherwise. Hence, D is liable here.

Comment. This case indicates that the test for whether the promoter is to be held liable is one of the intention of the parties. This intent may be either expressly stated in the contract or implied from all the circumstances. But the burden is on the promoter to prove that the intent was not to hold him personally liable.

---

3) Promoter's refusal to be named in contract--

Stewart Realty Co. v. Keller, 118 Ohio App. 49, 193 N.E.2d 179 (1962).

Facts. Keller (D), acting as a promoter, entered into a real estate contract for a prospective corporation. Stewart (P) knew that the corporation did not exist at the time of the contract. D expressly declined to execute any contract naming him as a party individually. The corporation was never formed. P sued, attempting to hold D personally liable on the contract. After hearing all the evidence, the trial court directed a verdict in favor of D. P appeals.

Issue. Can a promoter of a prospective corporation be held liable on a contract entered into only on behalf of the corporation if, at the time of the contracting, he expressly refused to have the contract name him personally?

Held. No. Judgment affirmed.

- ♦ Promoters are not personally liable on contracts made in the name of and solely on the credit of a future corporation when such intention is known to the other contracting party.

- ♦ It was clear from the evidence that P knew that only the corporation was to be bound and not D personally.

4) **Effect of knowing that the promoter is contracting for a corporation to-be-formed.** Generally, if a third party contracts with a promoter knowing that he is a promoter acting for a to-be-formed corporation, and the corporation subsequently ratifies the promoter's contract, when the third party goes to enforce the contract she can look only to the corporation.

V. CORPORATE DISCLOSURE AND SECURITIES FRAUD

A. OVERVIEW

The federal government and most, if not all, of the states regulate the dissemination of information by corporations, particularly publicly held ones. This regulatory regime mandates certain periodic and episodic disclosures and prohibits fraud and a variety of "misrepresentations." It also forbids "insiders" from trading shares in their corporations without disclosing "material, nonpublic" information in their possession. The Securities and Exchange Commission may enforce these regulations, and in some instances, private individuals may, too. The casebook authors justify this regulation on the grounds that: (i) the market for securities allocates scarce capital among competing users; (ii) proportionately more Americans than other nations' citizens invest their savings in this market; and (iii) individual investors cannot investigate or examine securities in the same manner that they can investigate tangible assets in which they might make investments. The casebook authors argue that federal securities law promotes allocative efficiency and distributive "fairness." They imply that it promotes allocative efficiency by helping to price shares "accurately," thereby directing capital to its most efficient uses. The casebook authors assert that the law promotes distributive "fairness" by, among other things, limiting trading by insiders in possession of material, nonpublic information. These goals may conflict. In particular, limiting the use of information in the name of "fairness" may reduce the incentive to search for information, thus impairing efficiency.

B. THE DISCLOSURE SYSTEM

1. **The Securities Act of 1933.** The 1933 Act primarily regulates the process of raising capital rather than trading in securities. The Act creates a scheme of mandatory disclosure for initial public distributions of securities by issuers, underwriters, and dealers (the "primary market"). Much of the scheme revolves around a disclosure document called a "registration statement," whose contents are prescribed by the S.E.C. The first part of a registration statement is called the "prospectus." The 1933 Act bars any effort to sell securities before the registration statement is filed with the S.E.C. From the time the registration statement is filed to the time the S.E.C. makes it "effective," the only written materials that an offeror may use are the registration statement and the prospectus. From the effective date to the completion of the distribution, usually a very short period, sellers may use other written materials but only in conjunction with the registration statement or prospectus. The 1933 Act renders issuing corporations strictly liable for material "misrepresentations" or omissions in their registration statements. It also subjects to liability other participants in the distribution unless they can show that they exercised "due diligence." This

costly and elaborate regulatory regime would apply to every sale of a security except that the 1933 Act exempts many securities and most securities transactions from its reach, including "transactions by any person other than an issuer, underwriter, or dealer."

2. **The Securities Exchange Act of 1934.** The 1934 Act primarily regulates securities trading among investors (the "secondary market"). It creates a scheme of mandatory continuous disclosure for corporations that: (i) list securities on a national exchange, (ii) own at least $5 million in assets and have at least 500 holders of any class of securities, or (iii) file a 1933 Act registration statement that becomes effective. These corporations must file with the S.E.C. annual, quarterly, and event-prompted reports. Investors do not receive these reports, although they may obtain them. Professional analysts use them, and through them, so do investors.

3. **Integrated Disclosure: Meshing the 1933 and 1934 Acts.** In 1977, the S.E.C. began prescribing disclosure documents responsive to both acts. Later, it promulgated regulations permitting some corporations to incorporate by reference material from their 1934 Act reports in their 1933 Act registration statements. Still later, the S.E.C. adopted Rule 415, permitting qualified corporations to register stock for future sale, "shelf registration." Once the corporation files a registration statement incorporating by reference subsequently filed 1934 Act reports, it may sell the registered securities at any time during the following two years. In promulgating these regulations, the S.E.C. relied on the "efficient capital market hypothesis" ("ECMH").

4. **"Blue Sky" Regulation.** The federal securities statutes explicitly provide for the simultaneous application of "blue sky" laws, state securities statutes. Many of these statutes subject brokers, dealers, and investment advisors to licensing regulations, most prohibit fraud, and most require securities registration with a state agency. Some of the state statutes authorize a state bureaucrat to bar sales of securities on "substantive" grounds, without regard to disclosure. The National Securities Markets Improvement Act of 1996 ("NSMIC") exempts all "covered securities" from state registration and other "blue sky" requirements. The Act defines "covered securities" as those traded on any S.E.C. approved exchange. The Securities Litigation Uniform Standards Act of 1998 preempted class actions and other consolidated or multiple party proceedings resembling class actions brought under state law for securities fraud in connection with "covered securities."

5. **Disclosure Requirements of Self-Regulatory Organizations.** The New York Stock Exchange, the American Stock Exchange, and the National Association of Securities Dealers Quotation System regulate the dissemination of information by listed corporations as part of their listing agreements. Generally, these self-regulatory organizations require the prompt disclosure of material information except where delay would serve a legitimate business purpose. The organizations enforce these obligations, not private investors.

6. When Does the Disclosure Obligation Arise?

a. Ripeness of information and due diligence in verification--

Financial Industrial Fund, Inc. v. McDonnell Douglas Corp., 474 F.2d 514 (10th Cir. 1973).

Facts. Financial Industry Fund, Inc. (P), a mutual fund, bought 80,000 shares of McDonnell Douglas (D) stock on the open market two days before D announced a share earning decline. Almost a month earlier, on May 27, D's president learned that its aircraft division was plagued by late delivery of components and worse-than expected performance by its work force. Corporate officials who investigated the extent of these problems reported that the delivery of 18 planes would be delayed until the next fiscal year. On June 4, D announced this delay to the press, stating that earnings for the current fiscal year would be adversely affected. On the same day, D's directors approved the issuance of new debentures. On June 7, the underwriter for these debentures issued a preliminary prospectus showing the December to April earnings as slightly below the same period for the prior fiscal year. On June 14, an officer in the comptroller's office received a regular report of aircraft division profit figures showing a May loss of several million dollars. This report prompted discussions with D's outside auditors about the advisability of revaluing inventory. On June 17, D's president sent a team to investigate the division. Three days later, the team formulated a 49¢ per share estimate of company earnings for the preceding six months. This estimate and consultations with the outside auditors led to a June 22 decision to substantially write down the company's inventory, which reduced the six-month earnings estimate to 12¢ per share. On this day P made its stock purchase. The next day, the president ordered the preparation of an earnings announcement, which was released to the press before the opening of the New York Stock Exchange on June 24. D's stock declined $2.75 per share to $76. On July 8, P sold its Douglas stock for $64.50 per share. P claimed that D violated rule 10b-5 by delaying disclosure of the earnings decline in order to facilitate the public offering of its debentures. The jury awarded P damages of $712,500. D appeals.

Issue. Did D violate rule 10b-5 by failing to announce the earnings decline earlier than it did?

Held. No. Verdict reversed.

◆ Since only the timing of the announcement is challenged, and timing requires the exercise of business judgment, the rationale of the business judgment rule applies: "to make the corporation function effectively, those having management responsibility must have the freedom to make in good faith the many necessary decisions quickly and finally without the impairment of having to be liable for an honest error in judgment."

◆ The information about which the issues revolve must be "available and ripe for publication" before there commences a duty to disclose. To be ripe, the contents must be verified sufficiently to permit the officers and directors to have full confidence in their accuracy. It also means that there is no valid corporate purpose dictating that the information not be disclosed. Nothing in the record suggests that D could have ascertained the extent of the May 1 loss and translated it into earnings figures at an earlier date to develop a statement ripe for publication. Thus the record shows that, as a matter of law, D exercised good faith and due diligence in the ascertainment, the verification, and the publication of the May loss.

♦ Upon a showing of the exercise of due care in the gathering and consideration of the facts, a presumption arose that the evaluation made was in the exercise of good business judgment although subsequent events might show the decision to have been in error.

Comment. The opinion does not address the question of whether management may, in the exercise of business judgment, delay disclosure of "ripe" information for legitimate business reasons. Nor does it address the question of whether management may invoke the rationale of the business judgment rule if some insiders have tipped or traded on the information.

---

b. Merger negotiations--

Basic, Inc. v. Levinson, 485 U.S. 224 (1988).

Facts. During the two years before Basic, Inc. (D) and Combustion Engineering merged, top management of both firms engaged in extensive merger negotiations. While these negotiations were pending, D issued three public statements denying either that any merger negotiations were taking place or that D knew of any corporate developments that would account for the heavy trading in its stock. Ex-shareholders who sold their stock between the first of these public statements and the announcement of the merger (Ps) sued D, claiming that by issuing these statements, D violated rule 10b-5. The district court entered summary judgment for D on the grounds that preliminary merger negotiations were immaterial as a matter of law because they were not "destined, with reasonable certainty, to result in a merger agreement in principle." The court of appeals reversed on the theory that merger negotiations not otherwise material became so when they were publicly denied. D sought and obtained certiorari.

Issue. For the purposes of rule 10b-5, were the merger negotiations material at the time that D denied them?

Held. It depends on the probability that the merger would occur and its anticipated magnitude in light of the totality of the company's activity. Judgment of the court of appeals reversed and case remanded.

- We adopt the *TSC Industries, Inc. v. Northway, Inc.* standard of materiality for the rule 10b-5 context: "there must be a substantial likelihood that the disclosure of the omitted fact would have been viewed by the reasonable investor as having significantly altered the 'total mix' of information made available."

- Because of the ever-present possibility that merger negotiations will not yield a merger, it is difficult to ascertain whether the reasonable investor would have considered the omitted information significant at the time.

- Lack of an agreement-in-principle about the price and structure of the proposed transaction does not necessarily render merger negotiations immaterial.

  Reasonable investors appreciate that proposed mergers may collapse any time before closing.

  That early disclosure might torpedo the merger bears on the issuer's duty to disclose the negotiations, not on their materiality.

  That a bright line rule would be easier to follow does not bear on the materiality of merger negotiations.

- A denial of merger negotiations cannot itself render them material because rule 10b-5 requires the plaintiff to show that "the statements were *misleading* as to a *material* fact," not just that they were false or incomplete.

- To assess the probability that a proposed merger will occur, a factfinder will need to look to indicia of interest in the transaction at the highest corporate levels (for example, board resolutions, instructions to investment bankers, and actual negotiations). To assess the magnitude of a proposed merger, a factfinder will need to consider such facts as the size of the two corporate entities and of the potential premiums over market value.

Comment. The decision may indicate that under rule 10b-5, a nontrading defendant may have no general duty to disclose.

---

c. **Duty to disclose in certain circumstances?** Prior to *Basic*, some lower courts or the S.E.C. had held that nontrading defendants have a duty to disclose: (i) when events make a prior statement misleading (leaving open the question of how long this duty lasts after each statement), (ii) or after "tipping" occurs (at least "tipping" in breach of a fiduciary duty). To what extent these duties survive *Basic* remains an open question. Even before *Basic*, courts refused to impose a duty on corporations to correct or verify rumors unless the rumors were attributable to the corporation.

d.   Duty to "update" previous statements--

Backman v. Polaroid Corp., 910 F.2d 10 (1st Cir. 1990).

Facts. In early 1978, Polaroid (D) introduced Polavision, an instant motion picture system, projecting sales that year of 200,000 units. In November 1978, D reported to its shareholders record earnings and sales but noted that its earnings "continued to reflect substantial expenses associated with Polavision" and that these expenses had increased D's total sales costs. D had then sold far fewer units than it had expected and had reduced Polavision production. In early February, D posted a $6.8 million reserve for Polavision-associated expenses and D's founder, Dr. Edwin Land, caused a foundation he controlled to sell 300,000 D shares. In late February, D issued a press release reporting that Polavision costs substantially exceeded sales revenues. D's stock dropped from $49.62 to $39.87. Purchasers of D stock or call options in the period from early January to late February (Ps) claimed that D violated rule 10b-5 by failing to disclose Polavision-related adverse developments. After a verdict for Ps, the trial court denied D's motion for judgment n.o.v. A panel of the First Circuit affirmed, noting sufficient evidence to support a finding that D's report of "Polavision's difficulties *became* misleading in light of the subsequent information acquired by [D] indicating the seriousness of Polavision's problems," including D's decision to stop Polavision production by its Austrian manufacturer, *"and its instruction to its Austrian supplier to keep this production cutback secret."* The First Circuit then heard the case en banc.

Issue. Did D have a duty to update its correct-when-disclosed report about Polavision expenses in light of subsequent Polavision-related developments even if these developments did not render the earlier disclosures incorrect or misleading?

Held. No. Judgment reversed.

♦   While under special circumstances, D may have had a duty to update a correct statement having a forward intent and connotation upon which shareholders may be expected to rely, it had no duty to update its statement about Polavision's expenses, which was precisely correct when made and remained precisely correct thereafter.

Comment. The opinion provides little certainty about when one has a duty to update.

e.   Duty to "correct" prior statements--

In re Time Warner Securities Litigation, 9 F.3d 259 (2d Cir. 1993).

Facts. With a more than $10 billion debt incurred thwarting Paramount Communications's hostile tender offer, Time Warner, Inc. (D) launched a highly publicized campaign to search abroad for "strategic partners" who would invest additional capital. D made hopeful statements about the ensuing negotiations; according to the reports of journalists and securities analysts, so did one or more of D's employees, but these reports did not identify the source(s). The search, however, proved largely unsuccessful. To generate more capital, D announced a stock offering structured so as to threaten shareholders with equity dilution unless they subscribed. In the week following the announcement, D's share price fell from $117 to $94, and later to less than $90.

Shareholders who purchased after the search for "strategic partners" began but before the announcement (Ps) filed a class action suit alleging that D violated rule 10b-5: (i) by misrepresenting the status of the negotiations (in its own statements and those of the unattributed source(s)); (ii) by failing to disclose problems in the negotiations with potential strategic partners; and (iii) by D's active consideration of a "coercive" stock offering as an alternative means of generating capital.

The district court dismissed Ps' suit on the grounds that: (i) D bore no liability for unattributed statements reported by journalists or securities analysts; (ii) D's statements were accurate when made; (iii) problems in the strategic alliance negotiations did not give rise to a duty to correct D's prior statements about them; and (iv) D did not have to disclose its active consideration of a "coercive" stock offering as an alternative means of generating capital because it and a strategic alliance were not mutually exclusive alternatives. P appeals.

Issues.

(i)   Can unattributed statements quoted or paraphrased by reporters or securities analysts be material for the purpose of rule 10b-5?

(ii)   Did D affirmatively misrepresent its strategic alliance negotiations in its hopeful statements about them?

(iii)   Having made hopeful statements about its strategic alliance negotiations, may D have become obligated to "correct" the statements when problems arose in connection with the negotiations?

(iv)   Having made hopeful statements about its strategic alliance negotiations, may D have become obligated to disclose its active consideration of a "coercive" stock offering as an alternative means of generating capital?

Held. (i) No. (ii) No. (iii) No. (iv) Yes. Judgment of trial court reversed because D may have become obligated to disclose its active consideration of a "coercive" stock offering.

♦   Unattributed statements reported by journalists or securities analysts are not material for the purpose of rule 10b-5 because investors tend to discount information in newspaper articles when the author is unable to cite specific, attributable information from the company.

♦   With regard to the expressions of opinion and projections in D's statements, P's complaint made no allegations from which one could infer that D did not subscribe to the opinions and projections or that they lacked any basis in fact. The assertions of fact in D's statements were true when made.

♦ While "a duty to update opinions and projections may arise if [they] have become misleading as the result of intervening events," D's statements about the negotiations lack "the sort of definite positive projections" that require correction. The statements expressed hope for success, but they do not assess its likelihood.

♦ A duty to disclose arises whenever secret information renders prior public statements materially misleading, not merely when that information completely negates the public statements. D's statements could have been understood by reasonable investors to mean that the company hoped to solve the entire debt problem through strategic alliances. Secret information may have rendered these statements materially misleading. When a corporation pursues a specific business goal, makes that goal publicly known, and announces a strategy for reaching the goal, the company may owe a duty to disclose alternative methods of achieving the goal once they are under active and serious consideration. Cases of this sort require a court to balance two interests: (i) deterring fraud that is "served by recognizing that the victims often are unable to detail their allegations until they have had some opportunity to conduct discovery" and (ii) "deterring the use of litigation process as a device for extracting undeserved settlements as the price of avoiding the extensive discovery costs that frequently ensue once a complaint survives dismissal, even though no recovery would occur if the suit were litigated to completion."

---

7. **The Sarbanes-Oxley Act of 2002.** Accounting irregularities took center stage in the high profile bankruptcies of Enron, Tyco, Adelphia, and WorldCom. A Government Accounting Office study found that between 1997 and 2002, 10% of the listed corporations in the United States restated their financial statements at least once (meaning that financial information once certified by their independent auditors as correct and in compliance with GAAP was revealed to be false). According to the casebook authors, "[t]he plain import of this wave of accounting irregularities was that the United States' system for the disclosure of financial information had less transparency than it had formerly prided itself on. Corporate managements could seemingly game me system to inflate earnings, while hiding expenses and liabilities, exploiting highly technical accounting rules that few investors understood." These irregularities set the stage for quick passage of the Sarbanes-Oxley Act (the "Public Company Accounting Reform and Investor Protection Act of 2002"). According to the casebook authors, this act sought to upgrade the quality of financial disclosure by establishing a new regulatory body with jurisdiction over auditing standards (the Public Company Accounting Oversight Board), by upgrading the requirements for membership on the audit committee, by requiring new certificates from corporate executives, and by toughening the criminal laws pertaining to securities fraud.

a. **Registration of public accounting firms required.** All accounting firms that prepare audit reports for public companies must register, and only registered firms may participate in the preparation or issuance of any audit report with respect to an issuer.

b. **The Public Company Accounting Oversight Board.** The Act directs the Public Company Accounting Oversight Board, a private not-for-profit organization subject to S.E.C. oversight, to:

    1) Establish or adopt . . . auditing, quality control, ethics, independence and other standards relating to the preparation of audit reports for issuer";

    2) Conduct inspections of registered public accounting firms;

    3) Conduct investigations and disciplinary proceedings concerning, and pose appropriate sanctions where justified upon, registered public accounting firms and associated persons of such firms; and

    4) Enforce compliance with the Act, the rules of the Board, professional standards, and the federal securities laws relating to the preparation and issuer of audit reports and the obligations and liabilities of accountants.

c. **Auditor independence.** Section 201 of the Act prohibits accounting firms from providing an audit client with a wide variety of non-audit services— (i) bookkeeping or other services related to accounting records or financial statements of the audit client; (ii) financial information systems design and implementation; (iii) appraisal or valuation: services, fairness opinions, or contribution-in-kind reports; (iv) actuarial services; (v) internal audit outsourcing services; (vi) management functions or human resources; (vii) broker or, dealer, investment, adviser, or investment banking services; (viii) legal services and expert services that are unrelated to the audit—but it permits these firms to provide tax services. Section 202 requires that all appreciable audit and non-audit services provided to a "reporting" company by a registered public accounting firm requires advance approval by the corporation's audit committee and that such approval be disclosed on Form 10-Q or Form 10-K. Section 204 requires auditors to rotate the lead audit partner, the partner with primary responsibility for conducting the audit, at least every five years. Section 206 prohibits an accounting firm from auditing any public company whose chief executive officer, controller, chief financial officer, chief accounting officer, or "any person serving in an equivalent position" was, at any time in the past year, an employee of the accounting firm.

d. **Corporate governance.** The Act provides that national securities exchanges require, as a condition of listing, that a corporation's audit committee consist entirely of independent board members which the Act defines as those "unaffiliated" with the company or any subsidiary who receive no "consulting, advisory, or other compensatory fee from the issuer" (directors fees only). [See §10A(m)(3)(B) of the Securities Exchange Act of 1934] The exchanges must also require that at least one member of the audit committee qualify as a "financial expert" by virtue of education and experience. Section 301 of the Act provides that the audit committee "be directly responsible for the appointment, compensation, and oversight of the work" of the independent auditor and that the audit firm "shall report directly to the audit committee." This provision seems to trump state law and thereby limits the authority of corporate officers, fellow board members, and shareholders. The Act also appears to trump state law when it provides (i) that an audit committee may engage independent counsel and other advisers, whose fees are to be paid by the company; and (ii) that the audit committee establish procedures for the receipt and evaluation of anonymous communications from employees about "questionable accounting or auditing matters."

e. **Executive certifications.** Section 302 mandates that the S.E.C. adopt rules requiring that, in connection with each filing of a company's periodic reports, its CEO and CFO certify that:

(i) He has reviewed the report, that to his knowledge it contains no material misstatement or omission, and that "the financial statements, and other financial - information included in the report, fairly present in all material respects the financial condition and results of operations of the issuer as of, and for, the periods presented in the report"; and

(ii) He has designed internal controls as necessary to ensure that material information relating to the issuer was made known to him during the reporting period and that he disclosed to the company's auditors and to its audit committee all significant deficiencies in the design or operation of these controls—in addition to any fraud, whether or not material, that involves management or other employees who have a significant role in the issuer's internal controls.

The Act also requires—subject to criminal penalties—that the CEO and CFO certify that any periodic report containing financial statements filed with the S.E.C., pursuant to Securities Exchange Act section 13(a) or §15(d), "fully complies with the requirements" of these Exchange Act sections, and that "information contained in the periodic report fairly presents, in all material respects, the financial condition and results of operations of the issuer." This requirement makes no reference to generally accepted accounting principles ("GAAP") which leaves open the possibility that a signing officer could face liability even though the financial statements complied with GAAP—as did Enron's.

f.   **Restatements of financial results.** If a company must restate its financial results because of material noncompliance resulting from "misconduct," the CEO and CFO must reimburse the company for any incentive-based or equity-based compensation that they received during the 12 months following the issuance or filing of the financial report and for any profits they made on their sale of company stock during this period. [§304(a)]

g.   **Executive loans.** An issuer may not make, renew, or arrange for a "personal loan" to any director or executive officer or otherwise directly or indirectly extend credit to such an individual. [§402(a)—even though state corporation codes expressly permit a company to do so]

h.   **Financial reports.** Section 409 requires companies to disclose material changes in their financial condition or operations on a "rapid and current basis "and in plain English." Section 401 mandates that the S.E.C. require disclosure of all material off-balance-sheet transactions, arrangements, obligations (including contingent obligations) and other relationships that might have a "material current or future effect" on the financial health of the company. The Act requires that this information be "presented in a manner that . . . reconciles it with the financial condition and results of operations of the issuer under generally accepted accounting principles"— which restricts the use of pro forma financial information.

i.   **S.E.C. authority over attorneys.** Section 307 directs the S.E.C. to prescribe "minimum standards of professional conduct for attorneys" who practice before the Commission. These standards must require attorneys to report evidence of a material violation of securities law or breach of fiduciary duty or similar violation by the company or any agent thereof to the company's chief legal counsel or CEO, and if these officers do not take appropriate action, to the company's audit committee, its independent directors, or to the entire board.

C. CIVIL LIABILITY

1.   **Introduction.** Common law, "blue sky" laws, and the 1933 and 1934 Acts all provide private remedies for material misstatements or omissions in connection with a securities transaction. Because of the procedural advantages of suing in federal court and the relatively accommodating liability standards of federal law, attorneys representing aggrieved investors tend to prefer 1933 Act and 1934 Act causes of action, especially the implied cause of action under rule 10b-5.

2.   **Common Law Remedies.** An aggrieved investor might obtain rescission if she can show that she reasonably relied on a misrepresentation of a material fact by a person with whom she was in privity. She might obtain damages for deceit if she can also show scienter ("the intent to deceive, to mislead, to con-

vey a false impression") and causation (damages attributable to misrepresentation). In fact, damages for deceit are available even in the absence of privity as long as the misrepresentation was made to the investor. Note that common law limited liability to misrepresentations of "facts," as distinguished from expressions of "opinion" or "value."

3. **Blue Sky Statutes.** Most state securities laws expressly provide for private damage suits by those defrauded in connection with securities transactions. Thirty-six states have adopted section 410(a) of the Uniform Securities Act, which is closely modeled after section 12 of the 1933 Act, except that it lists a broader range of secondary participants who are presumptively liable. As the federal courts have narrowed their interpretation of rule 10b-5, plaintiffs have made increased use of these blue sky laws.

4. **Fiduciary Duty of Disclosure--**

Malone v. Brincat, 722 A.2d 5 (Del. 1998).

Facts. The shareholders (Ps) of Mercury Finance Company ("Mercury"), purportedly a class, alleged that since 1994, Mercury's S.E.C. filings and direct communications to shareholders materially overstated earnings, financial performance, and shareholders' equity. Ps claimed that these alleged overstatements reflected a knowing and intentional breach by Mercury's directors (Ds) of a fiduciary duty of disclosure and that as a direct result of the false disclosures the company had lost virtually all of its value (about $2 billion). Ps also alleged that KPMG, Mercury's public accountant, knowingly participated in the claimed breach. The court of chancery dismissed the complaint for failure to state a claim on the ground that directors have no fiduciary duty of disclosure under Delaware law in the absence of a request for shareholder action. The chancellor opined that "[w]hen a shareholder is damaged merely as a result of the release of inaccurate information into the marketplace, unconnected with any Delaware corporate governance issue, that shareholder must seek a remedy under federal [securities] laws," which "ensure the timely release of accurate information into the marketplace." Ps appeal.

Issue. In the absence of a request for shareholder action, may corporate directors breach a fiduciary duty by knowingly disseminating to the stockholders false information about the financial condition of the company?

Held. Yes. Judgment affirmed in part, reversed in part, and remanded.

♦   Directors may breach their duty of loyalty and good faith by knowingly disseminating false information to the stockholders.

♦   Since Ps did not sell their shares, recognizing their claim would not implicate federal securities laws that relate to the purchase or sale of securities.

♦   The beneficial owners of the corporation, the shareholders, are entitled to rely on those charged with managing the corporation for their benefit, the directors, to tell the truth when they disseminate information. Knowing dissemination of materially false information to the stockholders may provide the basis for a direct or a derivative claim for which the remedy may be damages or equitable relief.

♦ Since Ps apparently complained about an injury to the corporation, but failed to expressly assert a derivative claim or compliance with Chancery Rule 23.1, which requires pre-suit demand or cognizable and particularized allegations that demand is excused, the chancellor properly dismissed the complaint. But the chancellor should have permitted Ps to replead.

––––––––––––

5.   **Federal Law: Express Causes of Action.**

a.   **Section 11 of the 1933 Act.**

1)   **Liability.** Section 11 renders all participants in the distribution process liable for material misrepresentations or omissions in the registration statement. The aggrieved investor need not show scienter, reliance, or causation although his knowledge of the untruth or omission can defeat his claim.

2)   **"Standing."** To invoke section 11, an investor must trace his shares back to those registered under the defective statement. This "linear privity" requirement practically limits section 11 to investors who purchased from the underwriters or dealers who participated in the distribution.

3)   **Damages.** An investor may recover the difference between the price he paid, up to the price at which the security was offered to the public, and either: (i) the value of the security at the time the suit was filed, or if he no longer owns it, then (ii) the price at which he sold it.

4)   **The "due diligence" defense.** Defendants other than the issuer may invoke the "due diligence" defense. They can avoid liability if they show that, "after reasonable investigation," they had "reasonable ground to believe and did believe" that the registration statement accurately disclosed all material information. With respect to portions of the registration statement "purporting to be made on the authority of an expert," they need only show that they "had no reasonable ground to believe and did not believe . . . that the statements therein were untrue or that there was an omission to state a material fact. . . ." In the landmark case of *Escott v. BarChris Construction Corp.*, 283 F. Supp. 643 (S.D.N.Y. 1968), the court rejected the argument of the issuer's directors that they had to meet only the due diligence standard for "expertised" portions of the registration statement because

the entire registration statement had been on the authority of experts: lawyers and accountants. Nevertheless, the court held lawyers to a standard of diligence incorporating the profession's own standards. It held other defendants to varying standards depending in part on the individual's training and role in the corporation and the securities offering. S.E.C. Rule 176 may permit more reliance than did the court. The Rule provides in pertinent part: "In determining whether or not the conduct of a person constitutes a reasonable investigation or a reasonable ground for belief [within the meaning of section 11], relevant circumstances include . . . [r]easonable reliance on officers, employees and others whose duties should have given them knowledge of the particular facts (in light of the functions and responsibilities of the particular person with respect to the issuer and the filing). . . ."

b. **Section 12(1) of the 1933 Act.** Section 12 renders all "sellers" strictly liable for noncompliance with the registration requirements of section 5, which contains the basic operating rules of the Act. But who is a "seller" for section 12 purposes? In *Pinter v. Dahl*, 486 U.S. 622 (1988), the Supreme Court limited section 12 "sellers" to those in privity with the buyer and solicitors who are "motivated at least in part by a desire to serve [their] own financial interests or those of the securities owner." By implication, this decision may limit liability for aiding and abetting a securities offense.

c. **Section 12(2) of the 1933 Act.** Like section 11, section 12(2) prohibits material misrepresentations and omissions made in connection with the sale of securities. Unlike section 11, section 12(2) applies to oral as well as written communications. Moreover, it directs that statements be analyzed from the perspective of the time of sale, not the effective date of the registration statement, and it provides for a rescission measure of damages. In *Gustafson v. Alloyd Co.*, 513 U.S. 561 (1995), however, the Supreme Court held that section 12(2) applies only to initial public offerings. Moreover, section 12(2) only reaches those in privity with the purchaser or those who solicited the purchase (and presumably qualify under *Pinter v. Dahl, supra*) Defendants may avoid liability by establishing a "reasonable care" defense. In defining "reasonable care," section 12(2) makes no reference to "reasonable investigation," so courts split on the issue of whether this standard is easier to meet than "due diligence."

6. **Federal Law: Implied Civil Liabilities.**

a. **The controversy over implied causes of action.** Since the federal securities laws expressly provide for private causes of action, one might argue that courts ought not "imply" additional ones. That the express causes of action are subject to a number of important constraints supports this argument. The courts did not accept this argument, and now implied causes of action dominate securities litigation. The most frequently invoked is the rule 10b-5 cause of action alleging material "misrepresentations" and omissions in securities transactions. Two other commonly invoked ones arise under rule 14a-9 and section 14(e), which prohibit material "misrepresentations" and omissions in proxy solicitations and tender offers, respectively.

    b.   **Rationale and scope.**

        1)   **Implied cause of action to further the remedial purposes of the securities laws--**

J.I. Case Co. v. Borak, 377 U.S. 426 (1964).

Facts. J.I. Case Company (D) entered into a merger agreement with American Tractor Corporation. When the agreement was submitted to the shareholders for approval, D solicited proxies with a statement that allegedly contained false information. The shareholders approved by a narrow margin. Borak (P), a shareholder in D, sought an injunction against the merger, damages, and other relief for violation of section 14a. The trial court held that it could not redress the alleged violations of section 14a except to grant declaratory relief under section 27 of the Act. The court of appeals reversed, and the Supreme Court granted certiorari.

Issue. Does section 27 of the Act authorize a federal cause of action for a shareholder seeking rescission or damages for a consummated merger authorized pursuant to a proxy solicitation allegedly containing false and misleading statements in contravention of section 14a?

Held. Yes. Judgment of court of appeals affirmed.

◆   Section 14a specifically grants district courts jurisdiction over all suits at equity or law. The stated purpose of the section is to protect investors. A section intended to protect investors would not deny them the right to adequate redress.

◆   The S.E.C. is not in a position to review every proxy statement for factual errors. Shareholders can assist the S.E.C. by policing this type of conduct. A private right of action provides additional deterrence.

◆   The courts may grant more than declaratory relief. They may fashion whatever remedy that they deem appropriate. To limit them would foreclose many shareholders from adequate reparations.

Comment. The opinion does not really come to grips with the controversy about implied causes of action. Moreover, the opinion relies on a strained interpretation of section 27, which probably just authorized federal courts to hear S.E.C. claims and private actions expressly provided for by the Act.

---

2) **Post-*Borak* limits on implied causes of action.** In *Piper v. Chris-Craft Industries, Inc.*, 430 U.S. 1 (1977), the Court rejected the argument that those allegedly aggrieved by violations of the securities laws could always bring a private cause of action. It also rejected the argument that the S.E.C.'s "institutional limitation" inevitably requires the implication of a private cause of action. The Court invoked the four factors identified in *Cort v. Ash*, 422 U.S. 66 (1975), as relevant to the question of whether an implied cause of action was available: (i) the plaintiff's membership in the "class for whose ***especial*** benefit the statute was enacted"; (ii) "indication of legislative intent, explicit or implicit, either to create such a remedy or to deny one"; (iii) the "[consistency of a private cause of action] with the underlying purposes of the legislative scheme"; (iv) whether "the cause of action is one traditionally relegated to state law. . . ." In post-*Piper* decisions, the Court has emphasized the fourth factor.

3) **Congressional intent determinative--**

Touche Ross & Co. v. Redington, 422 U.S. 560 (1979).

Facts. Touche Ross (D), an accounting firm, had audited the books of Weis Securities ("Weis"), a broker dealer, which became insolvent. The Securities Investor Protection Corp. ("SIPC") and Redington (P), Weis's trustee, sought damages allegedly suffered as a result of D's improper audit and certification of Weis's section 17a reports. P claimed that, had D not erred, Weis's financial condition would have become known in sufficient time for remedial action that would have reduced the customers' losses. The district court dismissed the suit on the ground that section 17a created no private cause of action. The second circuit reversed, and the Supreme Court granted certiorari.

Issue. Do customers of brokerage firms required by section 17a to file financial reports with regulatory authorities have an implied cause of action under this section against accountants who audit such reports for damages allegedly attributable to misstatements contained in them?

Held. No. Judgment of court of appeals reversed.

♦   SIPC's argument in favor of implication of a private right of action based on tort principles is entirely misplaced. Our task is limited solely to determine whether Congress intended to create the private right of action. Thus whether an implied private remedy is necessary to "effectuate the purposes of this section" and whether the cause of action is one traditionally relegated to state law have little relevance to the decision in this case.

♦ Only when the statute in question at least prohibited certain conduct or created federal rights in favor of private parties have courts implied a private cause of action. Section 17a does neither.

♦ The intent of section 17a is simply to require certain regulated businesses to keep records and file periodic reports to enable the relevant governmental authorities to perform their regulatory functions.

♦ In the 1934 Act, section 17a is flanked by provisions that explicitly grant private causes of action. Obviously, when Congress wished to provide a private damages remedy, it knew how to do so and did so expressly.

♦ Section 18a permits people who trade in reliance on a materially misleading statement appearing in a document filed with the S.E.C. to sue accountants who "make or cause to be made" such a statement. Evidence suggests that Congress intended this as the exclusive remedy for misstatements appearing in such documents. In any event, where the principal express civil remedy for misstatements in reports created by Congress contemporaneously with the passage of section 17a is by its terms limited to purchasers and sellers of securities, we are extremely reluctant to imply a cause of action in section 17a that is significantly broader than the remedy that Congress chose to provide.

♦ Section 27 creates no implied cause of action for it is strictly jurisdictional and procedural.

♦ The invocation of the "remedial purposes" of the 1934 Act is unavailing.

Comment. This decision appears to reject *Borak* and adopt the argument that Congress's silence about a private cause of action probably indicates that it did not intend to authorize one.

---

4) **Do express causes of action exclude implied ones?** In *Herman & MacLean v. Huddleston*, 459 U.S. 375 (1983), the Court held that purchasers of registered securities could sue under rule 10b-5 even though they could have sued under section 11 of the 1933 Act. According to the Court, "Section 11 places a relatively minimal burden on a plaintiff. In contrast, Section 10b is a 'catch-all' antifraud provision, but it requires a plaintiff to carry a heavier burden to establish a cause of action."

c. **Section 10b and rule 10b-5.** Rule 10b-5 makes it unlawful in connection with the purchase or sale of any security for any person, directly or indirectly by the use of any means or instrumentality of interstate commerce, or of the mails, or of any facility of any national securities exchange to:

(i) Employ any device, scheme, or artifice to defraud;

(ii) Make any untrue statement of a material fact or to omit to state a material fact necessary to make the statements made, in light of the circumstances under which they were made, not misleading; or

(iii) To engage in any act, practice, or course of business conduct that operates or would operate as a fraud or deceit upon any person.

1) Standing under rule 10b-5: limiting the plaintiff class.

a) Only purchasers and sellers may recover under rule 10b-5--

Blue Chip Stamps v. Manor Drug Stores, 421 U.S. 723 (1975).

Facts. Blue Chip Stamps (D) was subject to an antitrust consent decree to offer a substantial number of its shares to retailers who had used its stamp service. It registered the offering under the 1933 Act, and about 50% of the stores purchased shares. Two years later, Manor Drug Store (P), one of the nonpurchasing offerees, sued under rule 10b-5 on the basis that the prospectus was overly negative, so that P did not purchase, allowing D then to offer the shares to the public at a higher price. The district court dismissed P's complaint, but the court of appeals reversed. The Supreme Court granted certiorari.

Issue. Does a plaintiff who is neither a purchaser nor seller have standing to sue under rule 10b-5?

Held. No. Judgment reversed.

♦ The legislative history and the language of rule 10b-5 indicate that only purchasers or sellers are covered. All lower courts considering the question have so held, and Congress has not amended the section to broaden the language, although urged by the S.E.C. to do so. Where Congress wanted to cover more, it has done so (for example, section 17 of the 1933 Act applies to offerees).

♦ The 1934 Act has a provision limiting damages to "actual" damages.

♦ Most of the sections of the securities acts passed the same time as section 10b relate to actual purchasers or sellers.

♦ Rule 10b-5 lawsuits are particularly vexatious. The rule should therefore be limited. Such lawsuits frustrate normal business activity; they have a high settlement value; there are liberal discovery rules by which valuable business information can be obtained. It is too easy to establish claims based merely on oral evidence put in by a plaintiff, with no verification (*i.e.,* "I would have purchased"). Securities transactions take place across exchanges with no privity between the seller and would-be buyer and no verification of a plaintiff's intention unless the plaintiff is an actual buyer or seller.

♦ P argues that the consent decree amounts to a "contract to purchase." It does not. Standing will not be given to exceptional situations where plaintiffs argue the rationale of the "purchaser-seller" requirement does not apply. In the interest of commercial certainty, the rule as it is will stand.

Dissent (Blackmun, Douglas, Brennan, JJ.). This is an unusual case. The alleged fraud was designed to prevent Ps from becoming "purchasers."

---

b) **Exceptions to the purchaser/seller rule?** In *Blue Chip Stamps*, the Court embraced the second circuit's *Birnbaum* rule. [*See* Birnbaum v. Newport Steel Corp., 193 F.2d 461 (2d Cir. 1952), *cert. denied*, 343 U.S. 956 (1952)] Whether the Court will also embrace the second circuit's exceptions to its rule remains an open question. The exceptions permit a non-purchasing, nonselling shareholder to sue: (i) when the shareholder seeks an injunction rather than damages; (ii) when the shareholder has become a "forced seller," one obliged to sell as a result of some pending transaction like a merger or liquidation (the lower courts have divided on the question of whether a shareholder who cannot sell because her stock has become worthless qualifies for this exception); and (iii) when the shareholder is a "frustrated seller," one claiming that she deferred sale in reliance on a misrepresentation by a broker-dealer, thereby incurring a greater loss. *Blue Chip* appears to sound the death knell of at least the frustrated seller exception.

2) **"In connection with."** Rule 10b-5 addresses only those statements made in connection with the purchase or sale of securities. One could argue that a statement made by a nontrader must fall outside the rule. The courts have rejected this argument, eventually concluding that rule 10b-5 reached any statement if it was "reasonably foreseeable."

3) **Materiality.**

a) **Materiality of an event depends on probability of occurrence and magnitude--**

S.E.C. v. Texas Gulf Sulphur Co., 401 F.2d 833 (2d Cir. 1968).

Facts. Texas Gulf Sulphur Co. ("TGS") (D) detected a large promising anomaly near Timmins, Ontario. It drilled a test hole, a sample of which contained an extraordinary level of mineral content. A few in-the-know corporate officers purchased TGS stock on the open market before public disclosure of the discovery. The S.E.C. (P) claimed that D and these officers violated rule 10b-5. The district court ruled that the test results were not material at this point because extensive drilling would be required to establish the commercial value of the strike. P appeals.

Issue. Were the test results immaterial as a matter of law?

Held. No. Judgment reversed.

♦ The test for materiality need not, as the trial court suggested, be a conservative one in the sense of assessing facts solely by measuring the effect that knowledge of them would have upon prudent and conservative investors.

♦ The basic test of materiality is whether a reasonable person would attach importance to the information in making choices about the transaction. This test encompasses any fact that in reasonable and objective contemplation might affect the value of the securities. The speculators and chartists of Wall and Bay Streets are also "reasonable" investors entitled to the same legal protection afforded conservative traders.

♦ Whether facts are material when they relate to a particular event will depend at any given time upon a balancing of both the indicated probability that the event will occur and the anticipated magnitude of the event in light of the totality of the company's activity. Here the undisclosed facts might well have affected the price of TGS stock, and would certainly have been important to a reasonable, if speculative, investor in deciding whether to buy, sell, or hold the stock of D. It certainly would have affected the stock price and as such, it was material.

Comment. The court's balancing test for materiality requires that the magnitude of an event be discounted by the probability of its occurrence and that the resulting expected value be compared to the company's financial posture.

---

b) **The relevant audience.** The court's deference to the chartists of Wall and Bay Streets raises the question of whether information might be considered material because it is of particular interest to other investors with special interests. The S.E.C. defines materiality in terms of economics.

c) **"Integrity disclosures."** The S.E.C. has also taken the position, however, that corporations must disclose information relevant to the integrity of senior management, even though unimportant financially. But where the allegedly questionable conduct by senior management does not involve self-dealing, the S.E.C. seems to weigh heavily the financial significance of the conduct in deciding whether information about it must be disclosed.

d) **"Might" vs. "would."** In *TSC Industries, Inc. v. Northway, Inc.*, 426 U.S. 438 (1976), a case involving an allegedly misleading proxy solicitation, the Court reformulated the *Texas Gulf Sulphur* materiality test: "An omitted fact is material if there is a substantial likelihood that a reasonable shareholder would consider it important in deciding how to vote." In *Basic, Inc. v. Levinson, supra*, the Court expressly adopted this test for rule 10b-5 purposes.

e) **Projections and soft information.** Investors find projections and forecasts much more useful than the historical information that the S.E.C. traditionally requires corporations to disclose. Yet, for many years, the S.E.C. banned them from its prescribed documents. Even when the ban was lifted, securities lawyers advised their clients that including predictions and forecasts would put them at considerable risk because, by their nature, such statements usually prove wrong and often appear unreasonable in hindsight.

(1) **S.E.C. "safe harbor" rules.** Rules 175 and 3b-6 now provide that a "forward looking statement" only runs afoul of rule 10b-5 and similar prohibitions if the corporation lacked a "reasonable basis" for the statement or made it "other than in good faith." But the rules define "forward looking statement" to exclude predictions of asset or market values.

(2) **Directors' beliefs or opinions--**

Virginia Bankshares, Inc. v. Sandberg, 501 U.S. 1083 (1991).

Facts. First American Bankshares, Inc. ("FABI") planned an acquisition of First American Bank of Virginia ("Bank") through a freeze-out merger with FABI's wholly owned subsidiary, Virginia Bankshares, Inc. ("VBI"). VBI owned 85% of Bank's shares. FABI hired an investment banking firm to give an opinion about the appropriate price to pay for shares owned by Bank's minority holders. On the basis of market quotations and unverified information from FABI, the investment banking firm opined that a fair price would be $42 per share.

Virginia law required that shareholders approve the planned merger at a meeting after management circulated a statement of information to them. The law did not require that management solicit proxies, but it did anyway, even though VBI owned enough shares to guarantee approval. The solicitation stated that the "Plan of Merger has been approved by the Board of Directors because it provides an opportunity for the Bank's public share-holders to achieve a high value for their shares." It also described the terms of the merger as "fair." Most of the minority shareholders gave their proxies to management, except for Sandberg (P). Following approval of the merger at the shareholders meeting, P sued FABI, VBI, and Bank's directors for damages, claiming (i) they had solicited proxies in violation of section 14(a) and rule 14a-9, and (ii) they had breached their state law fiduciary duties. P alleged that the directors had not believed that $42 per share was high or that the terms of the merger were fair, but had recommended the merger because failure to do so would have resulted in their removal from the board. The trial court instructed the jury that it could find for P even if she failed to show that she relied on the alleged misstatements, as long as she showed that they were material and that the proxy solicitation was an "essential link in the merger process." The jury found for P on both claims, awarding her $18 per share, the difference between the $42 per share she received and the $60 that the jury found she would have received had Bank's stock been valued appropriately. The trial court entered judgment accordingly, and the court of appeals affirmed.

Issue. Can a statement in a proxy solicitation that the board recommends approval of a merger by minority shareholders because the merger would permit them to obtain a "high" price for their stock, or that the merger's terms were "fair," qualify as "materially misleading" within the meaning of section 14(a)?

Held. Yes. Judgment reversed. Such a statement may qualify as "materially misleading" within the meaning of section 14(a), but a member of a class of minority shareholders whose votes are not required to approve a transaction cannot prove damages compensable under section 14(a).

♦ A reasonable shareholder would probably consider directors' reasons for recommending a course of action important in deciding whether to approve the action, thus making these reasons "material" under *TSC Industries, Inc. v. Northway, Inc.* (*supra*).

♦ A statement of reasons or beliefs makes factual assertions about their subject matter and conveys that the "directors do act for the reasons given or hold the belief stated." Holding such statements actionable under rule 14a-9 need not implicate the *Blue Chip Stamps* (*supra*) concern about vexatious litigation over "many rather hazy issues of historical fact the proof of which depended almost entirely on oral testimony. . . . " The root of those concerns was a plaintiff's capacity to manufacture claims of hypothetical action, unconstrained by independent evidence. Reasons for directors' recommendations or statements of belief are, in contrast, characteristically matters of corporate record subject to documentation, to be supported or attacked by evidence of historical fact outside a plaintiff's control. Such evidence would include circumstantial evidence bearing on the facts that would reasonably underlie the reasons claimed and the honesty of any statement that those reasons are the basis for a recommendation or other action, a point that becomes especially clear when the responses or beliefs go to valuations in dollars and cents.

- In a commercial context, conclusory terms such as "high value" or "fair value" are reasonably understood to rest on a factual basis that justifies them as accurate, the absence of which renders them misleading. Whether $42 was "high" and the proposal "fair" to the minority shareholders depended on whether provable facts about the Bank's assets, and about the actual and potential levels of operation, substantiated a value that was above, below, or more or less at the $42 figure, when assessed in accordance with recognized methods of valuation.

- The evidence showed that the price of Bank's stock had little significance for the calculation of Bank's value because the market for it was "closed, thin, and dominated by FABI," points not disclosed in the solicitation. The evidence "indicated" that $42 per share represented no premium over Bank's book value if calculated on the basis of the appreciated value of Bank's real estate holdings. Some evidence not disclosed in the solicitation did suggest that Bank's "going concern" value exceeded $60 per share.

- Mere disbelief, or undisclosed belief or motivation, however, should not alone suffice for liability under section 14(a), absent proof by the sort of objective evidence described above that the statement also expressly or impliedly asserted something false or misleading about its subject matter. If it did, some section 14(a) litigation would revolve around the "impurities" of a director's "unclean heart," threatening just the sort of strike suits and attrition by discovery that *Blue Chip Stamps* sought to discourage. This requirement does not substantially narrow the cause of action because it would be rare to find a case with evidence solely of disbelief or undisclosed motivation without further proof that the statement was defective as to its subject matter.

---

(3) Duty to include "soft information"--

Flynn v. Bass Brothers Enterprises, Inc., 744 F.2d 978 (3d Cir. 1984).

Facts. Bass Brothers (D) made a successful tender offer for National Alfalfa Dehydrating and Milling Co. ("National Alfalfa") at $6.45 per share. In connection with this tender offer, D obtained asset appraisals of National Alfalfa that estimated that an orderly liquidation could yield $12.40 per share, while operating National Alfalfa as a going concern could yield $16.40 per share. Various National Alfalfa officials partially corroborated these appraisals. D did not disclose them. Minority shareholders in National Alfalfa (P) claimed that D thereby violated rule 10b-5 and section 14(e) of the 1934 Act.

Issue. Did D have a duty to disclose the asset appraisals?

Held. No, because they were prepared by nonexperts for special purposes and were insufficiently reliable.

- In failing to require disclosure of such soft information in the past, courts relied in part on S.E.C. policy against inclusion in S.E.C. prescribed documents, but that policy has begun to change.

- Shareholders value soft information highly. The considerable time lag between the circulation of a document containing soft information and the final adjudication of a challenge to that document "retard[s] the evolution of the law concerning disclosure."

- Therefore, corporations may have a duty to disclose soft information depending on the balance between "the potential aid such information will give a shareholder . . . [and] the potential for harm such as undue reliance, if the information is released with a proper cautionary note." The relevant "factors" are: (i) "the facts upon which the information is based; (ii) the qualifications of those who prepared or compiled it; (iii) the purpose for which the information was originally intended; (iv) its relevance to the stockholders' impending decision; (v) the degree of subjectivity or bias reflected in its preparation; (vi) the degree to which the information is unique; (vii) and the availability to the investor of other more reliable sources of information."

Comment. This decision does inform securities lawyers that omitting soft information from corporate disclosures will not immunize their clients from liability, but other than that it provides almost no guidance whatsoever. It should generate more work for such lawyers and raise their malpractice insurance premiums.

---

(4) "Bespeaks caution" doctrine--

In re **Donald Trump Casino Securities Litigation,** 7 F.3d 357 (3d Cir. 1993).

Facts. Ps purchased bonds issued to finance the construction of Atlantic City's largest and most lavish casino resort. The prospectus for the bonds said that management believed that "funds generated from the operation of the casino will be sufficient to cover all its debt service (interest and principal)." The prospectus also contained extensive and detailed cautionary statements about the risks of lending to a start-up of "unprecedented size and scale. . . ." For example, it stated "the ability of the [Ds] to serve its debt . . . is completely dependent upon the success of that operation and such success will depend upon financial, business, competitive regulatory and other factors affecting the Taj Mahal and the casino industry in general as well as prevailing economic conditions. . . ." After Ds disclosed their plan to file a Chapter 11 bankruptcy petition, Ps filed suit under rule 10b-5 and section 12(2) of the 1933 Act. They alleged that the statement of management's belief about generating funds to repay the bondholders was a material misrepresentation "because [Ds] lacked a reasonable belief in its truth and because [Ds] failed to disclose additional facts, such as that the Taj Mahal would require an average daily 'casino win' of approximately $1.3 million simply to break even." Invoking the "bespeaks caution" doctrine, the district court dismissed Ps' complaint.

Issue. Can a statement of management's belief about generating funds to repay bondholders be material if the prospectus containing the statement also contains warnings and cautionary language addressed to the uncertainty about repayment?

Held. No. Judgment affirmed.

♦ The "bespeaks caution" doctrine is essentially shorthand for the well-established principle that a statement or omission must be considered in context, so that accompanying statements may render it immaterial as a matter of law. The prospectus here took considerable care to convey to potential investors the extreme risks inherent in the venture while simultaneously carefully alerting the investors to a variety of obstacles the Taj Mahal would face. The prospectus warnings and cautionary language precisely address the uncertainty concerning Ds' prospective ability to repay the bondholders. Because of these warnings and cautionary language, any reasonable shareholder would believe that the bonds constituted a high risk speculative investment that might well result in a loss. Therefore, the statement of management's belief about generating funds to repay the bondholders was immaterial as a matter of law.

---

    4) Causation.

        a) Causation and the failure to disclose--

Affiliated Ute Citizens v. United States, 406 U.S. 128 (1972).

Facts. The Ute Indian tribe formed the Ute Development Corporation ("UDC") to receive lands from the United States government. Shares were issued to members of the tribe. A Utah bank was the transfer agent, and two of its employees encouraged the tribe members to sell their stock (the employees buying the stock and then reselling to prearranged buyers, usually for a price much in excess of what the tribe members got for the stock). The employees also bought and sold some stock for their own account. The bank employees did not disclose the nature of their resale arrangements or the prices that they received on resale, and that they received commissions, etc. Tribe members who formerly owned UDC stock and sold it through the bank (Ps) sued the employees and the bank (Ds).

Issue. Have Ps established reliance and causation in a case of nondisclosure of material facts?

Held. Yes. Judgment for Ps.

♦ Rule 10b-5 applies since Ds were purchasers and market makers in UDC stock.

♦ The fact that Ds were making a market in UDC stock and buying and then reselling Ps' stock at a great price are material facts, which Ds were under an obligation to disclose.

♦ All that Ps needed to show to prove reliance was the existence of an undisclosed material fact. The same thing proves causation-in-fact.

Comment. The opinion appears to equate materiality with "transaction causation" (reliance) so that a plaintiff need not prove the latter as part of her prima facie case. But the decision may reflect the fact that a long-standing course of conduct induced reliance. The opinion seems to leave open the possibility that proof of lack of reliance might defeat a plaintiff's claim.

---

b) **Proof of reliance after** *Affiliated Ute***.** On the question of whether plaintiff must prove reliance in a misrepresentation case, the courts have split. Some have found the nondisclosure/misrepresentation distinction elusive, allocating the burden of proof to the party best able to bear it. According to the casebook authors, courts generally require plaintiffs to prove reliance in cases involving misrepresentations in face-to-face transactions. They dispense with the requirement "where the plaintiff can allege more than a simple misrepresentation and seeks to show collateral conduct by the defendant amounting to a scheme to defraud."

c) **Fraud-on-the-market--**

Basic, Inc. v. Levinson, 485 U.S. 224 (1988).

Facts. *See supra.*

Issue. May defendants satisfy the rule 10b-5 reliance requirement by showing that they sold in reliance on the market price that presumably reflected the alleged misrepresentation (the "fraud-on-the-market" theory)?

Held. Yes.

♦ The market performs a substantial part of the valuation process performed by the investor in a face-to-face transaction. The market acts as the unpaid agent of the investor, informing him that given all the information available to it, the value of the stock is worth the market price.

♦ Requiring a plaintiff to show a speculative state of facts, *i.e.*, how he would have acted if the misrepresentation had not been made, would place an unnecessarily unrealistic evidentiary burden on the rule 10b-5 plaintiff who has traded on an impersonal market.

♦ Presuming reliance on the market price supports the policy embodied in the 1934 Act, whose premise is that securities markets are affected by information. The presumption is "supported by common sense and probability" as well as empirical data.

Comment. The Court embraces the Efficient Capital Market Hypothesis, apparently the "semi-strong" version. Recall that the data supporting this version relates almost exclusively to organized stock exchanges. It is not clear that other markets, for example, the "new issue" market, impound all publicly available information in prices with comparable speed. In cases involving such markets, perhaps evidence to this effect might rebut the presumption.

---

     d)   **Rebutting the fraud-on-the-market presumption.** In its *Basic* opinion, the Court suggests that the presumption might be rebutted by "any showing that severs the link between the alleged misrepresentation and either the price received (or paid) by the plaintiff, or his decision to trade at a fair market price. . . ." For example, if the misrepresentations had not been believed or the truth had become known, the defendant would prevail.

     e)   **Loss causation.** Even though a misrepresentation may have induced a purchase or sale, it may have had nothing to do with the subsequent loss. If that is the case, the plaintiff cannot recover.

     f)   **No presumption of loss causation--**

Litton Industries, Inc. v. Lehman Brothers Kuhn Loeb, Inc., 967 F.2d 742 (2d Cir. 1992).

Facts. Seeking a friendly acquisition, Litton Industries, Inc. (P) planned a tender offer for Itek Corp. Dennis Levine, an employee of P's investment banker, Lehman Brothers (D), illegally tipped the planned offer to an arbitrageur whose purchases of Itek stock spurred a price rise from $26 to $33 per share. P deemed the risk of its tender offer failing unacceptably high unless its offer price exceeded the preannouncement price by 50%. Accordingly, P raised its planned tender offer price from $42.50 to $48. The Itek board accepted the higher offer. When P found out about the tip, it filed suit to recover its increased acquisition costs, the profits of those involved in the insider trading, and the fees received by D. The district court dismissed P's suit on the ground that P did not even raise a genuine issue of material fact about one element of "loss causation": whether the Itek board would have accepted a lower offer from P had the price of Itek stock not reflected the illegal tip.

Issues.

(i)   Does P bear the burden of production and persuasion with respect to "loss causation" in general, and in particular, with respect to whether the Itek board would have accepted a lower offer from P had the price of Itek stock not reflected the illegal tip?

(ii)   If so, did P raise a genuine issue of material fact about whether the Itek board would have done so?

Held. (i) Yes. (ii) No. Judgment reversed and remanded because P raised a genuine issue of material fact about whether the Itek board would have accepted a lower offer from P had the price of Itek stock not reflected the illegal tip.

◆   The rationale for presuming "transaction causation" (here, that P relied) does not apply to "loss causation." Proof whether the Itek board relied on the market involves few of the evidentiary uncertainties exhibited in either the omission or fraud-on-the-market context. Unlike the omission situation—Itek knew of the crucial information, that the market price of Itek stock had risen and that P had plans to acquire Itek. And—unlike the fraud-on-the-market context—the face-to-face negotiations in a friendly tender offer situation make the question of the target board's reliance an issue of determinable fact. Nor does this proof require P to bear the "burden of establishing the inclinations of a large number of shareholders." P bears the burden of production and persuasion with respect to whether the Itek board would have accepted a lower offer from P had the price of Itek stock not reflected the illegal tip.

◆   "The most favorable interpretation" of the district court's dismissal is that the market price of Itek stock was not a "substantial factor" in the Itek board's assessment of P's offers because the board believed that the "inherent value" of Itek stock exceeded any untainted market price plus premium that P might have offered. Many board members claimed to have held this belief, but they did not discuss Itek's "inherent value" at the relevant meetings nor commission a study of it. Some claimed that they believed its "inherent value" exceeded $50 per share, yet they did not reject P's $46 per share offer and they all voted to recommend P's $48 per share offer. A finder of fact could reasonably interpret this behavior as reflecting a search for the best offer the market would bear, a search in which market price would play a critical role. It is difficult to imagine any pricing decision by a responsible target board in which market price considerations played no role.

5)   **Scienter.**

    a)   **Negligence insufficient; scienter required--**

Ernst & Ernst v. Hochfelder, 425 U.S. 185 (1976).

Facts. Ernst & Ernst (D), an accounting firm, audited books of a small securities firm and prepared its statements to the S.E.C. and the Midwest Stock Exchange. Customers of the firm (Ps) gave the firm's president money by personal check to be invested in "escrow accounts." In fact, the president embezzled the money. The president had a firm rule that no mail addressed to him or to the firm in his care should be opened by any other person. Ps charged that if D had not been negligent in its audit, it would have discovered this rule and an investigation of this rule would have led to discovery of the fraud. No reports of the escrow accounts ever showed up in the statements that D prepared. The district court granted D's motion for summary judgment, but the court of appeals reversed. The Supreme Court granted certiorari.

Issue. Does rule 10b-5 apply when the defendant has been negligently nonfeasant in performing its duties, thus aiding and abetting the perpetration of a fraud?

Held. No. Judgment reversed.

- ♦   The language and history of rule 10b-5 show that Congress did not intend for it to apply to negligent conduct. Thus, P must show intentional conduct.

Dissent (Blackmun, Brennan, JJ.). An investor can be victimized just as much by negligent conduct as by positive deception.

---

b)   **Recklessness as the required scienter.** The Supreme Court has yet to rule on the question of whether recklessness suffices for rule 10b-5 liability. All of the appeals courts that have addressed the question have answered "yes," but this apparent consistency is deceptive, for the opinions use "recklessness" to mean different things. Some use it to mean awareness of a substantial risk that a reasonable person would not have disregarded. Others use it to mean something close to actual knowledge. Still others use it as an epithet.

c)   **Scienter and the S.E.C.** In *Aaron v. S.E.C.*, 446 U.S. 680 (1980), the Court held that the S.E.C. must establish scienter to prevail on a rule 10b-5 claim, even if the S.E.C. seeks only an injunction. The Court also held, however, that the S.E.C. did not have to "establish scienter as an element of an action to enjoin violations of sections 17(a)2 and 17(a)3 of the 1933 Act" (which contain language identical to paragraphs (2) and (3) of rule 10b-5).

6)   **Damages.**

a) Which measure?--

Mitchell v. Texas Gulf Sulphur Co., 446 F.2d 90 (10th Cir. 1971), *cert. denied*, 404 U.S. 1004 (1971).

Facts. Reynolds, Stout, and Mitchell (Ps) owned shares in Texas Gulf Sulphur Co. ("Texas Gulf") prior to the April 12, 1964, press release concerning its major ore discovery (found to be misleading in the *Texas Gulf Sulphur* case). On April 16, Texas Gulf announced that there really was a large discovery after all. Reynolds was informed by his broker about the April 12 release, and again on the 16th that there were rumors of a strike "but that it was mere propaganda," whereupon he sold his shares. Mitchell was told of the April 12 release on the 16th, whereupon he ordered his broker to sell his shares, delivering an additional 20 shares for sale on the 17th; he testified that he had no knowledge of the April 16 release when he gave the sell orders. After hearing about the April 12 release, Stout sold on April 21. Ps sued Texas Gulf and its executive vice president (Ds). The trial court gave damages to Ps based on the average price of the highest daily selling price for the 20-day period following April 16, less the price at which Ps actually sold their stock. Both Ps and Ds appeal.

Issue. When a defendant has published a materially misleading press release, which is shown to be a substantial factor in a plaintiff's sale of stock, may the plaintiff recover damages?

Held. Yes. Trial court judgment is altered in some respects.

♦ To recover, the misleading press release must have been a substantial factor in causing Ps' sale. There is sufficient evidence in the trial court record to find that it was.

♦ Ps must also show that they exercised due diligence and good faith in their trading. Stout did not sell until April 21, and Mitchell did not actually sell the additional 20 shares until April 23. The April 16 press release was given very large circulation, and so neither Stout nor Mitchell can show their good faith and due diligence with regard to these sales.

♦ Ps should be restored to the position they would have enjoyed had they not been fraudulently induced to sell their stock.

> Ps should have damages based on the highest value of Texas Gulf stock between Monday, April 20 (when a reasonable shareholder would have had notice of the April 16 release) and a reasonable time thereafter, which would give the investor the time to reinvest in Texas Gulf stock after evaluating the press release (thus limiting his damages from future gains in the stock price).

> Restitution is inappropriate in this case since Ps did not deal personally with Ds in selling their securities, and such a measure would be unfair to Ds,

Because of the uniqueness of this type of litigation, no uniform rule on damages should be set.

Comment. Some cases are more lenient than this one, giving plaintiffs damages based on the difference between the value of the securities at the time of the trial and the consideration paid by or to plaintiffs. This case is important because it allowed damages to be assessed within a reasonable time after discovery of the fraud rather than at the instant of the sale (it reasoned that the market may not immediately reflect the true value of the stock). Likewise, it allowed the correction of misstatements published in newspapers by holding, in effect, that a published retraction is deemed to have come to the attention of the plaintiffs.

---

b) **Alternative measures of damages for rule 10b-5 violations.** Since rule 10b-5 does not expressly create a private cause of action, it does not provide a formula for measuring damages. Courts have used all of the following:

(1) **"Out of pocket."** "Out of pocket" means the difference between the price paid and the value received in the transaction. (This is not the "expectation" measure of damages; courts have rejected the "benefit of the bargain" measure, citing section 28 of the 1934 Act, which prohibits any person from recovering "a total amount in excess of his actual damages on account of the act complained of.")

(2) **Rescission.** In *Randall v. Loftsgaarden*, 478 U.S. 647 (1986), the Court declared that when a plaintiff's loss fell short of the defendant's profit, the law's deterrent function would be served by permitting the plaintiff to recover the defendant's profit, ***provided*** that the plaintiff did not hold onto the stock hoping that it would rise, only to seek rescission when the price declined. The Court expressly declined to decide whether plaintiffs could choose between rescissionary and out-of-pocket damages. Of course, in the absence of a secondary market, calculating out-of-pocket damages is very difficult, so rescission would be the norm. In support of the rescissionary measure of damages, courts have also invoked section 29 of the 1934 Act, which purports to void any contract made in violation of the Act or any rule adopted thereunder.

(3) **"Cover."** In *Mitchell, supra*, the court gave the plaintiffs a reasonable period after disclosure of the fraud to reinvest or "cover" (in the U.C.C. sense), arguing that disclosure

presented the plaintiffs with a second investment decision. To put it in terms of "causation," the fraud would not cause the plaintiffs to suffer any loss after it was disclosed.

(4) Consequential damages. Courts have occasionally allowed recovery for consequential damages when the plaintiff can prove that losses were proximately caused by the defendant's misrepresentations.

c) **Statute of limitations applicable to rule 10b-5.** In *Lampf, Pleva, Lipkind, Prupis & Petigrow v. Gilbertson,* 501 U.S. 350 (1991), the Court held that the statute of limitations applicable to section 10(b) is the one that appears in sections 9(e) and 18(e) of the 1934 Act: the earlier of (i) one year after discovery of the facts constituting the violation, or (ii) three years after such violation, which may not be equitably tolled. The one-year period begins on discovery of the facts constituting the violation, but courts have held that when a prospectus discloses the risks associated with an investment, a plaintiff claiming fraud in that prospectus has one year from the date of sale to bring her claim.

7) **The policy dilemma surrounding securities class actions: do the benefits exceed the costs?**

a) **Common criticisms of securities class actions.**

(1) Such suits are often triggered simply by a significant drop (often estimated as any one-day decline of 10% or more) in a stock's trading price, which penalized companies whose share price was highly volatile. (In one study, of the 33,206 one-day stock drops of 10% or greater surveyed, 1,584, or 4.4%, triggered class actions.)

(2) In the standard "stock drop" case, members of the class typically recovered at the expense of the other shareholders in the same corporation. (Diversified shareholders will likely be in the plaintiff class as often as not, but they will suffer a loss because of the high transaction costs—primarily attorneys' fees—incident to this compensation system.)

(3) Such suits frequently settle based on their "nuisance value" not the merits.

b) **The Private Securities Litigation Reform Act of 1995**. The 1995 Act sought to:

(1) Reduce the ability of the plaintiff to obtain a favorable settlement in a non-meritorious case based on the action's

nuisance value by (i) toughening the pleading standards for securities fraud—allege conduct giving rise to a "strong inference of fraud" (§21D(b)(2) of the Securities Exchange Act of 1934); (ii) mandating a stay of discovery while a motion to dismiss was pending; and (iii) substituting a regime of proportionate liability for joint and several liability except where a defendant was found to have acted with "actual knowledge" of the misstatement or omission;

(2) Make it easier for members of the class rather than members of the plaintiffs' bar to control securities class actions by creating a presumption that the investor with the largest economic stake in the action would be named the "lead plaintiff " and would be entitled to choose the counsel for the class;" and

(3) Protect predictive and other "forward-looking statements" by creating a safe harbor for them.

c) **The impact of the 1995 Act.** Several studies reported that the number of securities class action filings declined in 1996 but in subsequent years rose to their pre-Act levels or higher. Some class actions migrated to state court which Congress stopped in 1998 with a law that preempts securities class actions in state court. Some evidence also suggests that a significantly larger "stock drop" is now necessary to trigger the filing of a securities class action. Accountants were sued far less often in these actions—at least they were before Enron collapsed—and projections and other "forward-looking statements" figured in far fewer of them. Most of the complaints in these actions now allege insider trading violations as the conduct giving rise to a "strong inference of fraud."

d. **Transactions not covered by rule 10b-5.**

1) **Corporate mismanagement.**

a) **Breach of a fiduciary's duty as a "fraud" or "deceit" cognizable under rule 10b-5--**

Superintendent of Insurance v. Bankers Life & Casualty Co., 404 U.S. 6 (1971).

Facts. The stock of Manhattan Insurance Co. was sold by Bankers Life & Casualty Co. ("Bankers") to Begole for $5 million, who, in conspiracy with others, then sold the bond portfolio of Manhattan for the $5 million and through a complicated series of transactions used the $5 million to pay off the bank loan used to initially pay D. Thus, Manhattan sold its bonds but never received any of the proceeds, and it ended up bankrupt. The Insurance Department of the State of New York (P) sued Bankers and the bank that gave Begole the loan, Irving Trust, (Ds), under rule 10b-5. The district court dismissed the complaint, and the court of appeals affirmed. The Supreme Court granted certiorari.

Issue. Has there been a "fraud" "in connection with" the sale of securities?

Held. Yes. Case remanded for trial on the defenses.

◆ There has been a deception "in connection with" the sale of Manhattan's securities.

◆ Manhattan is a "seller" of securities (its bond portfolio).

◆ The seller of corporate control—here Bankers—can be held liable for the subsequent violation of rule 10b-5 that occurred (as an aider and abettor) if the subsequent fraudulent conduct was "sufficiently foreseeable" by the seller (Bankers).

---

b)   Limiting *Bankers Life*--

Santa Fe Industries v. Green, 430 U.S. 462 (1977).

Facts. Santa Fe Industries (D) owned more than 90% of the outstanding stock of a subsidiary corporation and, desiring to eliminate the minority shareholders (Ps), used a Delaware short-form merger statute that allowed a corporation holding more than 90% of the stock of a subsidiary to merge the subsidiary corporation, paying cash to the subsidiary's minority shareholders, giving notice to them within 10 days of the merger, and restricting the minority shareholders to an appraisal action in the state courts if they were dissatisfied with the price they received. D adopted the merger plan, disclosed all material information relative to the value of the subsidiary's stock, offered Ps $150 per share (when it had been appraised by a brokerage firm at $125 per share), and notified Ps of their option to seek an appraisal in the state courts. Ps sued in federal court to enjoin the merger or for damages based on a violation of rule 10b-5. They alleged that rule 10b-5 was breached in that: (i) there was no business purpose for the merger except to freeze out the minority and (ii) a grossly inadequate price was offered. The district court dismissed and, on appeal, the dismissal was reversed. D appeals.

Issue. Does rule 10b-5 provide a remedy for breach of a fiduciary duty by officers and directors and majority shareholders (*i.e.,* is there a fraud) in connection with a sale of the corporation's securities by its majority shareholders even if there is full disclosure of all the facts, no misrepresentations are made, and the transaction is permitted by state law?

Held. No. Judgment for Ps reversed.

♦ The states should be free to regulate the conduct of corporate officials except for the specific areas regulated by federal statute. Expansion of rule 10b-5 to cover this form of activity would be an unnecessary intrusion on the powers of the states.

♦ Section 10(b) was designed to protect investors by requiring full and truthful disclosure so that investors could make informed choices as to their course of action.

♦ Here the investors were fully informed of their rights and options *and had an adequate state remedy (appraisal) for the wrong alleged* in the complaint.

---

c) *Santa Fe* **distinguished--**

Goldberg v. Meridor, 567 F.2d 209 (2d Cir. 1977).

Facts. UGO issued shares to its controlling shareholder, Maritimecor (D), at below market prices. Several press reports released by UGO represented that the transaction would benefit the company. Minority stockholders (Ps) brought a derivative action alleging that UGO's board of directors had violated rule 10b-5 by accepting inadequate consideration for UGO stock while misrepresenting the corporate benefits of the transaction. The district court dismissed the complaint on the ground that, since Ps could not have prevented the stock sale, they could not have relied on the alleged misstatements. Ps appeal.

Issue. Does misrepresenting the corporate benefits of a below-market-price sale of stock to a majority shareholder violate rule 10b-5?

Held. Yes. Complaint reinstated and remanded to the district court.

♦ While a mere breach of fiduciary duty does not give rise to a cause of action under rule 10b-5, here Ps alleged deceit upon the minority shareholders.

♦ In a derivative action, when the corporation has allegedly been deceived, the alleged misrepresentations are material if the facts "would have assumed actual significance in the deliberations of reasonable and disinterested directors or created a substantial likelihood that such directors would have considered the 'total mix' significantly altered"—even if all directors were parties to the alleged misrepresentations.

♦ Under state law, Ps would have been able to enjoin the proposed sale had full and honest disclosure been made. Thus Ps relied on the misleading statements in not suing for an injunction.

Concurrence and dissent. If the directors breached their fiduciary duty, Ps may obtain relief in state court. The majority has unnecessarily added a federal cause of action to police the same conduct. Rarely, if ever, will one planning to breach a fiduciary duty announce these plans in advance, and therefore, plaintiffs will have an additional remedy under rule 10b-5.

Comment. The "sue facts" doctrine may render material any information that would provide the basis for a state lawsuit. Some courts, however, have required plaintiffs invoking the doctrine to show that they would have won or had a "reasonable probability of success." Of course, this requirement implicates the "fairness" of the underlying transaction, which the Supreme Court held irrelevant to rule 10b-5 litigation in *Santa Fe Industries*.

---

2) Aiding and abetting.

a) No rule 10b-5 liability for aiding and abetting--

Central Bank of Denver v. First Interstate Bank of Denver, 511 U.S. 164 (1994).

Facts. To finance a land development project, a public housing authority issued bonds in 1986 and 1988, which were secured by land owner assessment liens. The bond covenants promised that the value of the land subject to the liens always equals or exceeds 160% of the bond's outstanding principal plus interest. The covenants required that the project developer furnish the bond indenture trustee, Central Bank of Denver (D), with an annual report containing evidence of compliance with the 160% provision. In January 1988, the developer's report contained an updated appraisal showing land values almost unchanged from the 1986 appraisal despite declining property values in the relevant real estate market. This updated appraisal prompted a letter from the senior bond underwriter to D about possible noncompliance with the 160% provision. In response, D's in-house appraiser recommended a review by an outside appraiser. Following an exchange of correspondence between D and the developer, however, D agreed to delay this review until year end, six months after the expected closing on the 1988 bond issue. The authority defaulted before the outside appraiser completed the review. The bond purchasers sued under section 10(b), naming D as an aider and abettor. The district court granted summary judgment for D. The court of appeals reversed, holding that a reasonable factfinder could conclude (i) D's delay of the review had substantially assisted the principal offenders, and (ii) D was reckless with respect to the primary violation.

Issue. Does one who aids and abets a violation of section 10(b) bear liability to a private claimant?

Held. No. Summary judgment for D is affirmed.

♦   Section 10(b) does not expressly provide for aiding and abetting liability.

- Since Congress did not provide for aiding and abetting liability in connection with any express private right of action under the securities law, it likely would not have done so in connection with section 10(b).

- Interpreting section 10(b) as rendering aiders and abettors liable would exact "costs that may disserve the goals of fair dealing and efficiency in the securities markets." Since the rules of aiding and abetting liability offer little predictive value, those who provide services to people trying to raise capital or trade securities would probably find themselves incurring significant expenses to fend off even flimsy claims or settling these claims. In anticipation of such outcomes, many of these service providers might raise their fees or decline to serve riskier businesses that would prove costly to investors, the very people that the statute is supposed to help.

Dissent (Stevens, Blackmun, Souter, Ginsburg, JJ.). The majority should follow the long history of aider and abettor liability under section 10(b), which has been recognized by all 11 courts of appeals.

Comment. Gauging the impact of this case is difficult because subsequent section 10(b) decisions have held professionals, such as attorneys and accountants, liable as principals for preparing or certifying documents containing misleading financial statements.

---

b) **Aiding and abetting liability under the Private Securities Litigation Reform Act of 1995.** The Private Securities Litigation Reform Act of 1995 added section 20(e) to the Securities Exchange Act of 1934, empowering the S.E.C. to bring an injunctive action or to seek administrative penalties against "any person that knowingly provides substantial assistance to another person in violation of a provision of this title, or of any rule or regulation issued under this title."

D. INSIDER TRADING

1. **Under Rule 10b-5.**

   a. **Seminal case--**

In the Matter of Cady, Roberts & Co., 40 S.E.C. 907 (1961).

Facts. Cowdin, a director of Curtis-Wright Corp. and a Cady, Roberts partner, participated in a Curtis-Wright board meeting during which the board voted to cut the dividend. Cowdin left the meeting and called one of his partners, Gintel, to inform him about the decision before it was publicly announced. Gintel then sold the Curtis-Wright stock in the accounts of the firm's customers. He also had the firm sell "short," which is selling stock that one does not own with the hope that the price will decline so that the seller may make good on his sale with cheaper stock. The enforcement staff of the S.E.C. (P) charged Gintel and his firm (Ds) with violating rule 10b-5 and section 17(a) of the 1933 Act.

Issue. Did Gintel's sales of Curtis-Wright stock without disclosure of the dividend cut information obtained from Cowdin violate rule 10b-5 and section 17(a)?

Held. Yes.

♦ To prevent fraud, manipulation, or deception in connection with securities transactions, rule 10b-5 and section 17(a) aim at reaching misleading or deceptive activities, whether or not they are sufficient to sustain a common law action for fraud or deceit.

♦ An affirmative duty to disclose material information has been traditionally imposed on corporate "insiders," particularly officers, directors, or controlling shareholders. If disclosure prior to trading would be improper or unrealistic under the circumstances, we believe the alternative is to forgo the transaction. Simply refraining from making any express representations does not suffice.

♦ Analytically, the obligation rests on two principal elements; first, the existence of a relationship giving access, directly or indirectly, to information intended to be available only for a corporate purpose and not for the personal benefit of anyone, and second, the inherent unfairness involved where a party takes advantage of such information knowing it is unavailable to those with whom he is dealing.

♦ The disclose or abstain duty runs to nonshareholder purchasers as well as shareholders.

♦ Gintel has this duty because he received the information from a director knowing that the information had not been publicly disclosed. It affects all of his selling, not just that on his own account. He violated at least paragraph (3) of section 17(a) and rule 10b-5.

---

b. **The harms from "insider trading."**

1) **Corporate harm.**

a) A corporation that has developed valuable confidential information may see that value dissipated by "insider" trading if the trading itself reveals the information.

b) Some, including the casebook authors, argue that the allure of "insider trading" gains may divert the attention of corporate employees to searching for material undisclosed information.

c)   Perhaps the market discounts the price of a stock heavily traded by insiders.

2)   Allocational efficiency and the injury of delayed disclosure. The prospect of "insider trading" gains could create an incentive to delay disclosure, thus impairing the efficient allocation of capital accomplished by the market. Whether any such delay would be significant is open to serious doubt. And "insider trading" may, as noted above, increase the flow of information to the market.

3)   Investor injury. It is a challenge to figure out how "insider trading" could hurt investors engaging in open market transactions because they would have traded whether the "insider" was trading or not. Most of those who favor limits on "insider trading," including the casebook authors, assert that such trading is "unfair." They also assert that, without limits, investors will "lose confidence in the market."

c.   **The "benefits" of "insider trading."**

1)   "Insider trading" may promote market efficiency by causing prices to more rapidly reflect confidential information.

2)   The potential gains from such trading may serve as the most cost-effective incentive that some businesses can employ to encourage managerial risktaking.

d.   **The enforceability of the prohibition.** Even if it were clear that the harms exceeded the benefits, limiting "insider trading" might itself do more harm than good if enforcing the limits were very costly, both out-of-pocket and in terms of deterring useful activities, especially the activities of market professionals.

e.   **Tippee analyst's duty to disclose or refrain from trading--**

Dirks v. S.E.C., 463 U.S. 646 (1983).

Facts. Dirks (D) was an officer of a broker-dealer firm that specialized in providing investment analyses of insurance company securities to institutional investors. He received information from a former officer of Equity Funding ("EF") that, due to fraudulent practices, EF's assets were grossly overstated. D investigated these charges, upon which several regulatory agencies had failed to act. The allegations were corroborated by other EF employees. D urged the *Wall Street Journal* to publish the story, but the *Journal* declined. Neither D nor his firm owned or traded any EF stock. However, D discussed his findings with a number of clients and investors, some of whom subsequently sold their EF stock. The price of EF stock dramatically declined. Trading on the stock was halted and other parties began looking into the situation. EF's fraudulent practices came to light and it went into receivership. The S.E.C. (P) investigated D's role in exposing the fraud, and ruled that D had aided and abetted violations of securities laws, including rule 10b-5. The appellate court upheld the ruling. D appeals.

Issue. Is a tippee always under an obligation to disclose inside information before trading or to refrain from trading?

Held. No. Judgment reversed; judgment for D.

- Tippees inherit the insider's duty to shareholders to disclose material, nonpublic information before trading or to refrain from trading only when the information has been *improperly* disclosed to them by the insider.

- Imposing this duty solely because a person knowingly receives material, nonpublic information from an insider and trades on it could have an inhibiting influence on the role of market analysts, which the S.E.C. itself recognizes is necessary to the preservation of a healthy market. The purpose of the tip will usually determine whether its disclosure constitutes a breach of the insider's fiduciary duty. The test is whether the insider will receive a direct or indirect personal benefit from the disclosure. If the insider does not stand to personally gain, he has not breached his duty to the shareholders, and there can be no derivative breach by the tippee.

- Here, those who provided D with the information about EF's conduct did not receive any personal benefit from the disclosures. The facts showed that they were motivated by a desire to expose the fraud. The insiders did not breach their duty, so D was not under any derivative obligation to EF's shareholders when he passed the nonpublic information to his clients.

Dissent (Blackmun, Brennan, Marshall, JJ.). The Court's ruling is another limitation placed on provisions intended to protect investors. The requirement of showing improper purpose has no basis in law, and results in excusing knowing and intentional violations of the insider's duty to shareholders. The Court justifies D's action because the benefits to society in general outweigh the harm caused shareholders when D's clients sold their EF stock before the fraud became public. This does not change the fact that D's clients profited from inside information, and that innocent parties paid for those gains. The insider gave D the information knowing that D would cause his clients to trade on it. Therefore, D was obligated to publicly disclose the information or to refrain from actions that he knew would lead to trading.

Comment. Under section 10(b), mere possession of material, nonpublic information does not give rise to a duty to disclose or abstain. A fiduciary relationship between the insider and the shareholders must already be in place before the tippee's role will be examined.

---

    f.   **Post-*Dirks* issues.**

1) What knowledge must the plaintiff show the tippee to have had in order to recover?

2) What "indirect benefit" will render the tipper's disclosure "improper," thus putting the tippee at risk?

3) Must a plaintiff show a "breach of fiduciary duty" if she invokes rule 14c-3, which prohibits trading in securities affected by a tender offer by everyone except the bidder who possesses material, nonpublic information about it?

g. **The background to *Dirks*.** *Chiarella v. United States*, 445 U.S. 222 (1980), arose in connection with the criminal conviction of a financial printer who had purchased shares of a company that was the target of a planned tender offer after he decoded the company's name from the documents on which he was working. The Supreme Court reversed the conviction emphasizing that those with a fiduciary duty to a company or its shareholders bore the duty to disclose or abstain.

h. **S.E.C. rule 14e-3(a).** In the wake of *Chiarella*, the S.E.C. announced, in connection with a proposed rulemaking under section 14(e) of the Exchange Act, that it "continue[d] to have serious concerns about trading by persons in possession of material, nonpublic information relating to a tender offer. This practice results in unfair disparities in market information and market disruption. Security holders who purchase from or sell to such persons are effectively denied the benefits of disclosure and the substantive protections of the Williams Act. If furnished with the information, these security holders would be able to make an informed investment decision, which could involve deferring the purchase or sale of the securities until the material information had been disseminated or until the tender offer has been commenced or terminated."

1) The Commission adopted rule 14e-3(a), which provides in relevant part:

(a) If any person has taken a substantial step or steps to commence, or has commenced, a tender offer (the "offering person"), it shall constitute a fraudulent, deceptive or manipulative act or practice within the meaning of §14(e) of the [Exchange] Act for any other person who is in possession of material information relating to such tender offer which information he knows or has reason to know is nonpublic and which he knows or has reason to know has been acquired directly or indirectly from:

(1) The offering person,

(2) The issuer of the securities sought or to be sought by such tender offer, or

(3) Any officer, director, partner or employee or any other person acting on behalf of the offering person or such issuer, to purchase or sell or cause to be purchased or sold any of such securities or any securities convertible into or exchangeable for any such securities or any option or right to obtain or to dispose of any of the foregoing securities, unless within a reasonable time prior to any purchase or sale such information and its source are publicly disclosed by press release or otherwise.

2) Section 14(e) of the Exchange Act provides in relevant part: "It shall be unlawful for any person . . . to engage in any fraudulent, deceptive, or manipulative acts or practices, in connection with any tender offer . . . . The [S.E.C.] shall, for the purposes of this subsection, by rules and regulations define, and prescribe means reasonably designed to prevent, such acts and practices as are fraudulent, deceptive, or manipulative." The validity of rule 14e-3(a) was challenged in *United States v. O'Hagan, infra.* So, too, was the validity of the "misappropriation theory" of 10b-5 liability.

i. Selective disclosure and Regulation FD.

1) **Why disclose selectively.** Selectively tipping information about material corporate developments to selected institutional investors and security analysts prior to its general release could (i) "guide" the expectations of securities analysts, thereby reducing the volatility of the corporation's share price; (ii) curry favor with large institutions who hold or could hold a sizeable number of the corporation's shares; and (iii) reward securities analysts for positive reports or recommendations or punish analysts for negative ones. Ordinarily, such tipping would not qualify as a personal benefit under *Dirks* and is much less likely than a public announcement or S.E.C. filing to result in rule 10b-5 liability. During the 1990s, selective tipping frequently occurred in invitation-only conference calls hosted by the CEO and CFO. According to the casebook authors, selective disclosure hurt small investors (although it is not obvious that it hurt those who invested through institutional investors).

2) **Regulation FD.** In 2000, the S.E.C. adopted Regulation FD ("Fair Disclosure") to regulate selective disclosure. Regulation FD's requirements come into play when material nonpublic information is disclosed by an issuer, or any person acting on its behalf (which the

S.E.C. defined as senior officials of the issuer and public relations employees and agents.), to any of the following people: a broker, dealer, investment adviser, institutional investment manager, investment company, person associated with any of the foregoing, or "a holder of the issuer's securities, under circumstances in which it is reasonably foreseeable that the person will purchase or sell the issuer's securities on the basis of the information."

When this happens, Regulation FD provides that the issuer must make public disclosure of this information simultaneously, in the case of an intentional disclosure (which, according to the S.E.C., is one made by a person when he "knows or is reckless in not knowing that the information so communicated is both material and nonpublic"), and promptly, in the case of a non-intentional disclosure. According to the S.E.C., "prompt" means "as soon as reasonably practicable (but in no event after the later of 24 hours or the commencement of the next day's trading on the New York Stock Exchange) after a senior official of the issuer learns that there has been a non-intentional disclosure or is reckless in not knowing.

Disclosing the material nonpublic information by filing a Form 8-K complies with Regulation FD as does disseminating the information through another method or combination of methods of disclosure that is reasonably designed to provide broad, non-exclusionary distribution of the information to the public.

Regulation FD does not apply to a disclosure made to a person who owes a duty of trust or confidence to the issuer (such as an attorney, investment banker, or accountant) or to an entity whose primary business is the issuance of credit ratings, provided the information is disclosed solely for the purpose of developing a credit rating and the entity's ratings are publicly available. Nor does the Regulation FD apply to the public offering process ("road shows" open to analysts and institutions are OK).

Only the S.E.C. may enforce Regulation FD (no private cause of action).

j.   **Trading on the basis of misappropriated information about a planned tender offer--**

United States v. O'Hagan, 521 U.S. 642 (1997).

Facts. In connection with a planned tender offer for Pillsbury Company, Grand Metropolitan PLC ("Grand Met") retained the law firm of Dorsey & Whitney, where O'Hagan (D) was a partner. Both Grand Met and Dorsey & Whitney took precautions to protect the confidentiality of Grand Met's plans; O'Hagan did no work for Grand Met. In September and October of 1988, O'Hagan purchased common shares of Pillsbury and options to purchase such shares. When Grand Met announced its tender offer in October, the price of Pillsbury stock rose to nearly $60 per share, and O'Hagan sold his Pillsbury call options and stock for a profit exceeding $4.3 million. A grand jury indicted O'Hagan under S.E.C. Rules 10b-5 and 14e-3(a) (and under statutes prohibiting mail fraud and money laundering) for defrauding his law firm and its client, Grand Met, by using for his own trading purposes material, nonpublic information regarding Grand Met's planned tender offer. A jury convicted D on all counts. A divided panel of the Eighth Circuit Court of Appeals reversed, holding that rule 10b-5 liability could not be grounded on the "misappropriation theory" and that rule 14e-3(a) exceeded the rulemaking authority granted to the S.E.C. by section 14(e) of the 1934 Act because the rule does not require a showing that a defendant breached a fiduciary duty. (The eighth circuit reversed the mail fraud and money laundering convictions because they rested on the securities law violations.) The United States (P) appeals.

Issues.

(i)   Does a person violate section 10(b) and rule 10b-5 by trading in securities for personal profit using nonpublic information obtained or used in breach of a fiduciary duty to the source of the information?

(ii)   Does section 14(e) of the Securities Exchange Act of 1934 give the Commission the power to adopt rule 14e-3(a), which prohibits trading on material, nonpublic information relating to a tender offer even if the trader had no duty to disclose?

Held. (i) Yes. (ii) Yes. Judgment reversed and remanded.

♦   When a fiduciary uses a principal's undisclosed information for self-serving securities transactions in breach of a duty of loyalty and confidentiality, he deceives the principal into believing that the fiduciary is loyal and defrauds the principal of the exclusive use of the information. Thus, such "misappropriation" qualifies as a "deceptive device" within the meaning of section 10(b) and rule 10b-5. Section 10(b) and rule 10b-5 do not expressly require deception of an identifiable purchaser or seller.

♦   The deception occurs "in connection with the purchase or sale of a security," as required by rule 10b-5, because the fraud is consummated when, without disclosure to the principal, the fiduciary uses the information to transact in securities, thereby gaining an unfair market position to the detriment of the investing public.

The misappropriation theory targets information of a sort that misappropriators ordinarily capitalize on to gain no-risk profits through the purchase or sale of securities.

The theory would not reach the misappropriation of money to purchase securities because the misappropriation would be sufficiently detached from a subsequent securities transaction that section 10(b)'s "in connection with" requirement would not be met. If a misappropriator put confidential, nonpublic information to some unauthorized use other than trading securities, he would not violate rule 10b-5.

♦ Imposing liability for such misappropriation helps insure honest securities markets and thereby promotes investor confidence. Although informational disparity is inevitable in the securities markets, investors likely would hesitate to venture their capital in a market where trading based on misappropriated nonpublic information is unchecked by law. An investor's informational disadvantage vis-a-vis a misappropriator with material, nonpublic information stems from contrivance, not luck; it is a disadvantage that cannot be overcome with research or skill. Rejecting the misappropriate theory would mean that a lawyer like O'Hagan violates section 10(b) and rule 10b-5 if he works for a law firm representing the target of a tender offer, but not if he works for a law firm representing the bidder, a result that would inhibit participation in the market, undermining the congressional purposes underlying section 10(b).

♦ The three Supreme Court decisions on which the eighth circuit relied, *Chiarella, Dirks,* and *Central Bank of Denver,* do not preclude liability predicated on a duty owed to the source of nonpublic information. *Chiarella* expressly left open the validity of the misappropriation theory. *Dirks* involved a tipper who breached no duty to the source of his information, his former corporate employer, when he tipped a financial analyst about massive fraud within the corporation, since the tipper acted not for personal profit, but to expose the fraud, and absent such a breach, the analyst could not be liable because his liability would have been derivative. Moreover, the tipper neither wanted nor expected the analyst to keep the tip confidential. *Central Bank* held that accomplices to rule 10b-5 offenses could not be held liable under the rule. The opinion observed that "[a]ny person or entity, including a lawyer, accountant, or bank, who employs a manipulative device or makes a material misstatement (or omission) ***on which a purchaser or seller of securities relies***" [emphasis added], which was the Court's effort to clarify that some accomplices might qualify as principal offenders, not to reject the misappropriation theory.

♦ Criminal prosecutions do not present the dangers the Court addressed in *Blue Chip Stamps,* so that decision is "inapplicable" to indictments for violations of section 10(b) and rule 10b-5. To establish a criminal violation of rule 10b-5, the government must prove that a person "willfully" violated the provision. Furthermore, a defendant may not be imprisoned for violating rule 10b-5 if he proves that he had no knowledge of the Rule. O'Hagan's charge that the misappropriation theory is too indefinite to permit the imposition of criminal liability thus fails not only because the theory is limited to those who breach a recognized duty.

♦ Rule 14e-3(a), as applied to cases of this genre, qualifies as a means reasonably designed to prevent fraudulent trading on material, nonpublic information in the tender offer context within the meaning of section 14(e). Trading on such information is likely because so many people acquire confidential information during a tender offer, few of them have any long-term loyalty to the issuer, and those in the know stand to reap very large short-term profits. But a prosecutor would find it difficult to prove that a trader obtained confidential information about a planned tender offer in breach of a fiduciary duty owed either by the trader or by the ultimate insider source of the information, much less that the trader knew or should have known of that breach, because, in most cases, the only parties to the information transfer will be the insider and the alleged tippee. Moreover, because Congress authorized the Commission to prescribe legislative rules, the Commission's judgment is entitled to controlling weight unless it is arbitrary, capricious, or manifestly contrary to the statute.

Comments.

◆ **Congressional action**: Congress may have endorsed the "misappropriation theory" of rule 10b-5 liability in the Insider Trading and Securities Fraud Enforcement Act of 1988 (*see infra*).

◆ **Use vs. possess**: Citing the majority's assertion that the fraud is consummated when, without disclosure to his principal, the defendant uses the information to purchase or sell securities, courts have held that the plaintiff in a rule 10b-5 suit must show that the undisclosed information was at least a substantial factor in the defendant's investment decision. The S.E.C. has weighed in on the use/possession distinction by adopting rule 10b5-1 discussed *infra*.

◆ **"Warehousing"**: In proposing rule 14e-3(a), the S.E.C. was trying to stamp out, among other things, "warehousing"—leaking a planned tender offer to allies of the bidder so that they might purchase the target's stock before announcement of the bid. Such purchases would breach no duty to the bidder. In *O'Hagan*, the majority left "for another day" whether the Commission's proscription of warehousing falls within its section 14(e) authority to define or prevent fraud.

◆ **Pre-offer conduct**: Rule 14e-3(a) prohibits trading when a substantial step to commence a tender offer has been taken. Focusing on this provision, O'Hagan urged the Supreme Court to strike down the rule on the grounds that (i) this provision exceeded the reach of section 14(e), which prohibits fraudulent acts "in connection with any tender offer"; and (ii) that this provision fails to comport with due process in that it does not give fair notice as to when, in advance of a tender offer, a violation of section 14(e) occurs, and that it eliminates the need to show scienter. The Supreme Court declined to address these arguments because O'Hagan did not raise them in his briefs before the court of appeals and the court had not addressed them; the Supreme Court did acknowledge that the court of appeals could consider them on remand if O'Hagan had preserved them.

----

k. **Rule 10b5-1 and the use/possession distinction.** In 2000, the S.E.C. adopted rule 10b5-1 which addresses trading on the basis of material nonpublic information in insider trading cases. The rule (i) prohibits the purchase and sale of a security of any issuer *on the basis of* material nonpublic information about that security or issuer, in breach of a duty of trust or confidence that is owed directly or indirectly to the issuer of that security or the shareholders of that issuer, or to any other person who is the source of the material nonpublic information and, (ii) provides that a purchase or sale of a security of an issuer is on the basis of material nonpublic information about that security or issuer if the person making the purchase or sale was aware of the material, nonpublic information when the person made the purchase or sale unless the person can show that before becoming aware of the information, the person had entered into a binding contract to purchase or sell the security, instructed another person to purchase or sell the security for the instructing person's account, or adopted a written plan for trading securities. The rule also provides that, in connection with institutional investors such as investment banks, traders do not trade on the basis of material nonpublic information known to members of the institutional investor's non-trading divisions if the investor uses a qualifying information partition system.

l.   Remote tippee--

United States v. Chestman, 947 F.2d 551 (2d Cir. 1991).

Facts. Ira Waldbaum, the president and controlling shareholder of Waldbaum, Inc. ("Waldbaum") agreed to sell Waldbaum to A&P. The agreement required Ira to tender a controlling block of Waldbaum shares for $50 per share. Ira invited his sister to tender her shares as part of the controlling block, warning her not to discuss the pending sale. (He also disclosed the pending offer to three of his children who worked for Waldbaum, giving them a similar warning.) Ira's sister told her daughter, warning her to disclose the sale only to her husband, Keith Loeb. When the daughter disclosed it to him, she warned him not to discuss it. Nevertheless, according to Loeb, he disclosed it to his stockbroker, Robert Chestman (D), in a telephone conversation the next morning, November 26, between 9 a.m. and 10:30 a.m. D denied talking with Loeb on November 26.

According to Loeb, he told D that Waldbaum was about to be sold at a substantial premium over its market value. D had learned of Loeb's relationship with the Waldbaum family in the course of executing several trades in Waldbaum stock on behalf of Loeb and his wife over the preceding four years. According to Loeb, he asked D whether he should buy Waldbaum stock, but D declined to advise him "in a situation like this." At 9:49 a.m., D bought 3,000 Waldbaum shares for his own account at $24.65 per share. Between 11:31 a.m. and 12:35 p.m., he purchased 8,000 shares for his clients' discretionary accounts (1,000 for the Loebs) at $25.75 to $26.00 per share. D explained these purchases as the product of his research, his reading of trade reports, and his observation of high volume trading in Waldbaum stock on November 25. According to Loeb, late that afternoon he again asked D by phone whether he should buy Waldbaum stock, and D again declined to advise him "in a situation like this," but said that D's research put Waldbaum stock on his buy list. Subsequently, Loeb ordered 1,000 shares.

At trial, a jury found D guilty of perjury and mail fraud and of rule 10b-5 and rule 14e-3(a) violations. [*Note:* rule 14e-3(a) defines "fraudulent, deceptive or manipulative act" for the purpose of section 14(e) of the Securities Exchange Act of 1934, which regulates tender offers (added by the Williams Act) to promulgate rule 14e-3(a). According to the Rule, one such act is the purchase or sale of a security by one "who is in possession of material information related to a tender offer which information he knows or has reason to know is nonpublic and which he knows or has reason to know has been acquired directly or indirectly" from the offeror, the issuer of the securities sought, or someone acting on either's behalf.] A panel of the Second Circuit Court of Appeals reversed these convictions, but the court granted rehearing en banc except with respect to the panel's reversal of the perjury conviction.

Issues.

(i)   Did the S.E.C. possess the authority to define "fraudulent, deceptive or manipulative act" for the purpose of section 14(e) as it did in rule 14(e)-3(a) so as to dispense with common law elements of fraud, including breach of a fiduciary duty?

(ii)   Did Loeb owe a fiduciary or functionally equivalent duty to his wife or the Waldbaum family?

Held. (i) Yes. (ii) No. Rule 14(e)-3(a) convictions affirmed; rule 10b-5 conviction reversed.

♦   Section 14(e) (i) makes it "unlawful . . . to make any untrue statement of a material fact or omit to state any material fact necessary in order to make the statements made, in the light of the circumstances under which they are made, not misleading, or to engage in any fraudulent, deceptive, or manipulative acts or practices, in connection with any tender offer, . . ." and (ii) provides that the S.E.C. "shall, for the purposes of this subsection, by rules and regulations, define and prescribe means reasonably designed to prevent such acts and practices. . . ." The plain language represents a broad delegation of rulemaking authority, reflecting Congress's recognition of the highly sensitive nature of tender offer information, its susceptibility to misuse and the often difficult task of ferreting out and proving fraud. The Act's minimal legislative history reinforces this interpretation, as does its subsequent enactment of the Insider Trading Sanctions Act of 1984 when it "acknowledged and left untouched the force of rule 14(e)-3(a)."

♦   Since section 14(e) itself prohibits common law fraud, forbidding the S.E.C. from defining other conduct as fraud would render its rulemaking power superfluous.

♦   In any event, section 14(e)'s grant of the power to "prescribe means reasonably designed to prevent such acts and practices" authorizes the S.E.C. to define other conduct as fraud in the tender offer context.

♦   The Supreme Court's rejection of the parity of information rule in *Chiarella v. United States,* 445 U.S. 222 (1980), does not require that the S.E.C. define fraud for the purpose of section 14(e) so as to include all common law elements. *Chiarella* interpreted section 10(b), the "general antifraud statute," not section 14(e), an "antifraud provision specifically tailored to . . . tender offers, an area . . . that the Williams Act makes clear deserves special regulation," and in any event, Rule 14(e)-3(a) "creates a narrower duty." Moreover, 14(e) provides that the S.E.C. "shall" make rules while section 10(b) provides that the S.E.C. "may" do so.

♦ The Supreme Court held in *Schreiber v. Burlington Northern, Inc.*, 472 U.S. 1 (1985) that misrepresentation or nondisclosure is an indispensable element of a section 14(e) violation and does not require that the S.E.C. define fraud for the purpose of section 14(e) so as to include all common law elements. *Schreiber* speaks to the meaning of "manipulative," and in any event, rule 14(e)-3(a) "remains a disclosure provision."

♦ Because D was convicted under rule 10b-5 as an accomplice in Loeb's misappropriation of nonpublic information in breach of a fiduciary duty and as a tippee of this information, these convictions can survive on appeal only if Loeb owed a fiduciary or functionally equivalent duty to his wife or to the Waldbaum family. Since rule 10b-5 can result in criminal prosecution, a broad interpretation of this duty would offend not only the rule of lenity but due process as well.

♦ That Loeb received confidential information does not itself give rise to any such duty. Nor does the fact that he received it from his wife, who asked him not to disclose it. That Loeb was Ira Waldbaum's nephew-in-law does not give rise to any such duty absent evidence of "repeated disclosure of business secrets" (as in *United States v. Reed*) to Loeb by members of the Waldbaum family.

Concurrence and dissent. D's rule 10b-5 convictions should be affirmed. Misappropriation of confidential information enables those who have not paid for corporate information to reap a benefit from it. Disclosure of such information to a few buyers of securities may send a message to others that the stock is worth more than the market price. If the law fails to punish those who misappropriate confidential information, corporations will have less incentive to invest in its costly acquisition. This analysis, when applied to family-controlled corporations, dictates that family members who have benefited from the family's control of the corporation owe a duty not to disclose confidential corporate information that comes to them in the ordinary course of family affairs. The family relationship enables its members to learn of confidential information to maintain the relationship. If information were kept secret between family members, it would foster distrust and misunderstanding.

----

m. **Causation and damages.**

1) **Insider Trading and Securities Fraud Enforcement Act of 1988.** Section 20A(a) creates an express cause of action for "insider trading," but leaves the concept undefined. It provides: "[a]ny person

who violates any provision of this title or the rules or regulations thereunder by purchasing or selling a security while in possession of material, nonpublic information shall be liable in an action in any court of competent jurisdiction to any person who, contemporaneously with the purchase or sale of securities that is the subject of such violation, has [traded in the opposite direction] securities of the same class." Subsection (b) limits liability. In particular it caps damages at the profit gained or loss avoided by the defendant.

2) Profit gained or loss avoided as cap on damages--

Elkind v. Liggett & Myers, Inc., 635 F.2d 156 (2d Cir. 1980).

Facts. Shareholders (Ps) brought a class action suit against Liggett & Myers, Inc. (D) for wrongful tipping of inside information about an earnings decline to selected shareholders who then sold Liggett's shares on the open market. When the decline was made public, the value of the shares fell. After a verdict for Ps, the district court awarded damages measured "out-of-pocket": the difference between the price paid and the "value" of the stocks when bought. D appeals.

Issue. Whether damages for "inside trading" by tippees on an open market should reflect the plaintiff's "out-of-pocket" loss.

Held. No. Judgment reversed.

♦   Because the trading of a tipper or tippee on the basis of confidential information does not induce investors to trade in the opposite direction, such investors should not recover from such an inside trader their "out-of-pocket" loss.

♦   The "out-of-pocket" measure is likely to create insurmountable proof problems because it requires the calculation of a hypothetical figure, the "value" of the stock during the period of nondisclosure. One cannot assume that the tip is on a par with the later disclosure, and one cannot satisfactorily determine how the market would have reacted to the public release of the tipped information at an earlier time by its reaction to that information at a later time.

♦   The "out-of-pocket" measure may overdeter the insider by imposing exorbitant damages.

♦   Permitting recovery of damages caused by erosion of the stock's market price attributable to the wrongful trading would avoid windfall recoveries. But this "causation-in-fact" measure would deny recovery for the tippee's violation of his duty to disclose before trading. It would also impose on the uninformed trader the difficult, in many cases impossible, burden of proving the time when and the extent to which the integrity of the market was affected by the tippee's conduct.

◆ If a reasonable investor would have delayed his purchase or not purchased at all if he had possessed the tipped information, a court could allow the investor to recover any post-purchase share price decline occurring during the period from the time of purchase to discovery or public disclosure, but no more than the tippee's gain. This disgorgement measure would provide damages roughly commensurate to the actual harm caused by the tippee's wrongful conduct. It is the best measure for a case like this even though it: (i) makes the wrongdoer's gain prerequisite to recovery under rule 10b-5; (ii) partially duplicates similar remedies available in other proceedings; (iii) still permits windfalls, especially in depressed markets; and (iv) may so limit recovery that fewer suits would be brought.

─────────────

3) **The Insider Trading Sanctions Act of 1984.** This Act adds section 21(d)(2) to the 1934 Act, authorizing the S.E.C. to seek, and a federal court in its discretion to impose, a civil penalty up to treble the profit or loss avoided as a result of "inside trading." The S.E.C. may also seek, in addition, disgorgement, restitution, and criminal penalties.

4) **Controlling persons.** Not only does the Insider Trading and Securities Fraud Enforcement Act of 1988 embrace the measure of damages used in *Elkind*, as noted before, it also makes the civil penalty provisions of the Insider Trading Sanctions Act of 1984 applicable to "controlling persons" or employees who engage in "insider trading" for their own account. Under the Act, it is not clear who qualifies as a "controlling person." It is clear, however, that before the S.E.C. may obtain a civil penalty against a "controlling person," it must prove knowledge or reckless disregard of the fact that the "controlled person" was likely to engage in the act or acts constituting the violation before they occurred *or* knowing or reckless failure to "establish, maintain, or enforce any policy or procedure" required in order to institute and maintain an adequate system of supervision and internal controls to protect against securities law violations.

2. **Section 16(b) and "Short Swing" Profits.**

a. **Section 16.** Subsection (a) imposes filing requirements on officers, directors, and beneficial owners of more than 10% of any class of non-exempt equity security of corporations subject to the 1934 Act. These people must disclose their initial holdings and changes in them. Subsection (b) provides: "For the purpose of preventing the unfair use of information which may have been obtained by such beneficial owner, director, or officer by reason of his relationship to the issuer, any profit realized by him from any purchase and sale, or any sale and purchase, of any [non-exempt] equity security of such issuer . . . within any period of less than six months, unless such security was acquired in good faith in connection with a debt previously contracted, shall inure to and be recoverable by the issuer, irrespective of any intention on the part of such beneficial owner, director, or officer in entering into such transaction of holding the security purchased or of not repurchasing the security sold for a period of exceeding six months. Suit to recover such profit may be instituted . . . by the issuer, or by the owner of any security of the issuer in the name and in behalf of the issuer if the issuer shall fail or refuse to bring such suit within sixty days after request or shall fail diligently to prosecute the same thereafter. . . ."

b. **Who is covered?**

1) **Job title not determinative--**

Merrill Lynch, Pierce, Fenner & Smith, Inc. v. Livingston, 566 F.2d 1119 (9th Cir. 1978).

Facts. Merrill Lynch, Pierce, Fenner & Smith (P) employed Livingston (D) as a salesman. In recognition of his outstanding sales record, P awarded D the title of vice president. His job, however, did not change. He acquired no executive or policymaking duties. D did continue to receive information that P disseminated to its employees, but not the general public. D sold a total of 1,000 shares of stock and repurchased them within six months, realizing a profit of almost $15,000. P claimed that D thereby violated section 16(b). The district court found D liable, and D appeals.

Issue. Does section 16(b) reach any employee with the title of officer and access to information not generally available to the investing public?

Held. No. Judgment reversed.

♦ Job titles do not themselves trigger liability under section 16(b). Liability follows from the existence of a relationship with the corporation that makes it more probable than not that the individual has access to insider information.

♦ The title "Vice President" does no more than raise an inference that the title holder has executive duties and access to confidential information. But the record shows that D was simply a salesman, thus rebutting the inference.

♦ Information freely circulated among nonmanagerial employees is not insider information within the meaning of section 16(b), even if the general public does not have the same information.

♦ The record in this case clearly demonstrates that D was not privy to insider information. The information that he received was made available to all securities salesmen and did not supply a basis for liability.

2) Role is critical--

CBI Industries, Inc. v. Horton, 682 F.2d 643 (7th Cir. 1982).

Facts. Horton (D) served as a director of CBI Industries, Inc. (P) and as a co-trustee of a trust created by his mother for the benefit of his two sons, who were ages 19 and 22 during the relevant period. D sold 3,000 of his shares of CBI stock on the open market. Within six months, he had the trust buy 2,000 shares on the open market. The purchase price was lower than the sale price. P sued D under section 16(b) of the Securities Act and recovered $25,000. D appeals.

Issue. If, within a six-month period, a corporate director sells stock on the market and then has a trust in which his sons are the beneficiaries purchase it, is the difference in price a "profit realized by him" within the meaning of section 16(b)?

Held. No. Judgment reversed.

♦　　　Unless the trust was a sham, D could not realize a profit on any gains by the trust because he lacked the power to divert the income of the trust to himself. He could not even look to the trust to fulfill his legal obligation of support because, his sons being of age, his obligation had expired. That D would receive the trust proceeds if both of his sons predeceased him before reaching the age of 25 has little if any significance because of the law of probability of this contingency.

♦　　　Although "profit realized" could be read to include nonpecuniary gains, like the enjoyment of seeing one's children prosper, such a reading would result in placing greater restrictions on corporate insiders than Congress can plausibly be thought to have intended in 1934, when notions of conflict of interest were less exacting than they are today. One implication would be that no corporate insider could dare manage, control, or influence an investment portfolio that contained stock of his company, and the Supreme Court has refused to so hold.

♦　　　It would be arbitrary to use as a cut-off point the definition of beneficial owner in Rule 16a-8 because the purpose of this definition is unrelated to the issue in the present case. It is to figure out who has a large enough stake in the corporation to be deemed an insider, and for this purpose, the adding up of family interests is reasonable. But D is an insider by virtue of his directorship.

♦　　　Profit realized by a corporate insider means direct pecuniary benefit to the insider.

♦　　　P may be able to show that the trust was a sham or that D was able to use the assets of the trust to pay his personal expenses. D may benefit through an increase of the actuarial value of his contingent remainder, but P must show this on remand.

Comment. According to the casebook authors, this decision conflicts with earlier decisions and the long-standing position of the S.E.C.

---

3) Sales by former 10% holder not covered--

Reliance Electric Co. v. Emerson Electric Co., 404 U.S. 418 (1972).

Facts. Emerson Electric Co. (D) acquired 13.2% of the outstanding common stock of Dodge Manufacturing Co., in an unsuccessful attempt to take over Dodge. The shareholders of Dodge approved a merger with Reliance Electric Co. (P). D realized that any further attempts to take over Dodge were certain to fail and decided to dispose of its shares. On the advice of counsel, D decided to sell enough stock to bring its holdings under 10% and thereby immunize the remainder of their shares from liability under section 16(b). D sold 37,000 shares, which brought its holding to 9.96%. D then sold the remainder of the shares. Both transactions took place within six months of the purchase. After P demanded the profits realized in the sale, D sought declaratory judgment as to its liability under section 16(b). The district court held D liable for the total amount of the profits. The court of appeals affirmed as to the first sale but reversed as to the second. P appeals.

Issue. May an owner of 10% of a company's stock sell off the stock in two separate transactions, within six months, in an attempt to immunize the second transaction from liability under section 16(b)?

Held. Yes. Judgment affirmed.

♦ Liability cannot be imposed on D merely because it sought to avoid liability under section 16(b). The only question is whether the method used to avoid liability was prohibited by the statute.

♦ The statute provides that the owner must have 10% at the time of the purchase and of the sale. Congress may have regarded one with a long-term investment of more than 10% as more likely to have access to inside information than one who moves in and out of the 10% at the time of the second sale; therefore it does not fall within section 16(b).

♦ If the two-step sale does give rise to a danger that the statute was intended to prevent, Congress should amend the statute to deter those transactions.

Dissent (Douglas, Brennan, White, JJ.). The majority view allows section 16(b) to be easily circumvented. In doing so, the deterrent value and the wholesome purpose of the act are lost. The statute should be construed as allowing a rebuttable presumption that a series of dispositive transactions are part of a single plan of distribution. Such a reading would provide efficient administration of the statute, while retaining its original purpose.

---

4) **Effect of change in 16(b) status.** In *Foremost-McKesson, Inc. v. Provident Securities Co.*, 423 U.S. 232 (1976), the Supreme Court held that, "in a purchase sale sequence, a beneficial owner must account for profits only if he was a beneficial owner 'before the purchase.'" According to the Court, whether an officer or director had to hold her position at the time of both purchase and sale remained an open question. Earlier decisions of the second circuit had answered this question "no": one who was a director or officer at either time was subject to 16(b) liability.

5) **"Deputization theory."** In *Feder v. Martin Marietta Corp.*, 406 F.2d 260 (2d Cir. 1969), the court held an investor owning less than 10% liable under 16(b) on the theory that the investor had "deputized" an officer to represent it on the board. Imposing liability on this theory could deter large shareholders, including institutional investors, from participating actively in the selection of directors.

c. **Computing the "profit realized."** Customarily, the federal courts use the rule of "lowest price in, highest price out" to compute the profit realized.

d. **Exemptions.** The S.E.C. has used its power under section 16(b) to exempt a number of transactions from the reach of the statute. These transactions include qualified stock options and stock appreciation rights, squeeze out mergers and analogous transactions, and conversions of convertible securities.

e. **The definition of "purchase or sale."**

1) **The "pragmatic" (or subjective) approach--**

Kern County Land Co. v. Occidental Petroleum Corp., 411 U.S. 582 (1973).

Facts. On May 8, 1967, Occidental (D) made a tender offer for Kern County Land (P) stock. By June 8, D had acquired over 20% of P's outstanding common stock. In order to frustrate D's takeover attempt, P sought a merger with Tenneco, Inc., to be effectuated through an exchange of P stock for Tenneco preferred stock. Realizing that it would be stuck as a minority shareholder in Tenneco, D sold Tenneco an option to buy all of the Tenneco preferred stock to which D would become entitled as a result of the merger. For this option, Tenneco paid $8,866,230, which would apply to the purchase price if the option were exercised. Tenneco could exercise the option six months and one day after D's stock purchase (December 11, 1967). D did not oppose the merger, but did attempt, unsuccessfully, to have the closing enjoined until a later date. The merger closed August 30, 1967, whereupon D obtained the right to exchange its P stock for Tenneco preferred. Tenneco exercised its option on December 11, 1967. P filed suit under section 16(b) to recover the profits that D realized on the transaction. The district court granted summary judgment in favor of P. On appeal, the court of appeals reversed, granting summary judgment for D. P sought and obtained certiorari.

Issue. Did the sale of the option or the merger closing constitute a sale for section 16(b) purposes?

Held. No. Judgment affirmed.

♦ As the maker of a hostile takeover bid, which eventually failed, D never had access to material, nonpublic information about P. Even if D had planned to profit by selling its stake to a competing bidder, it would not have traded on such information.

♦ Treating the exchange as a sale would not advance the deterrent effect of section 16(b). There was no potential for speculative abuse in an involuntary exchange of stock. D did not engineer the merger, did not vote for it, and unsuccessfully attempted to enjoin its closing.

♦ Generally, granting an option does not constitute a sale under section 16(b). D wanted to escape minority shareholder status and Tenneco wanted to rid itself of a potentially troublesome minority shareholder. Since the terms of the option put the exercise date more than six months in the future and did not require Tenneco to purchase D's shares, D had no opportunity to trade on material, nonpublic information. The fixed price kept D from sharing in the rising price on the stock market. If anyone might have traded on material, nonpublic information, it was Tenneco.

Dissent (Douglas, Brennan, Stewart, JJ.). Section 16(b) encompasses all transactions, without regard to the actual use of inside information. The statute is intended to have a broad deterrent effect. Although it may occasionally snare someone who did not actually trade on inside information, it is in the public interest to have unrestricted operation of section 16(b). The majority's pragmatic view will require an ad hoc analysis of each transaction, which will be inefficient and costly. The prophylactic effect of the statute needs to be preserved, perhaps at the cost of someone being caught unwillingly.

---

2) **Scope of the "pragmatic" (or "subjective") approach.** The *Kern* majority's approach might signify simply a willingness to adopt a narrow definition of "a class of transactions in which the possibility

of abuse was believed to be intolerably great." Alternatively it might signify an insistence that the transaction in question could have lent itself to speculative abuse or even that it did.

f. **Indemnification.** In *Bunker Ramo-Eltra Corp. v. Fairchild Industries*, 639 F. Supp. 409 (D. Md. 1986), the court refused to enforce an agreement that the target of a hostile tender offer would indemnify its white knight from any section 16(b) liability.

3. **Common Law Liability to the Corporation.**

a. **Insider trading constitutes breach of duty to corporation--**

Diamond v. Oreamuno, 24 N.Y.2d 494, 248 N.E.2d 910, 301 N.Y.S.2d (1969).

Facts. Management Assistance, Inc. ("MAI") financed computer installations through sale and lease back arrangements. MAI's leases required it to repair and maintain the computers. Lacking the capacity to perform these services, MAI contracted with IBM to perform them. When IBM raised its service prices, MAI's earnings declined dramatically. Prior to the public announcement of these developments, MAI's chairman and president (Ds) sold 56,500 MAI shares at $28 per share. After the announcement, the price plummeted to $11. Claiming that this trading constituted a breach of Ds' fiduciary duty, Diamond (P), an MAI shareholder, brought a derivative suit seeking recovery of $800,000 allegedly realized by Ds. The trial court dismissed for failure to state a cause of action. The appellate court reinstated the complaint with respect to Ds, but otherwise affirmed. Ds appeal.

Issue. May a corporate officer be held liable in a derivative suit for the gain realized or loss avoided by trading his company's stock on the basis of material, nonpublic information?

Held. Yes. Judgment affirmed.

◆ A corporate officer breaches his fiduciary duty by trading his company's stock on the basis of material, nonpublic information whether or not his corporation suffered any damages as a result. As between MAI and Ds, MAI has a higher claim to the proceeds derived from the exploitation of such information.

◆ MAI may have suffered damage to its reputation for integrity, thereby reducing public acceptance of its stock.

◆ Permitting a derivative claim for trading on the basis of material, nonpublic information will not deter officers from investing in their corporation.

◆ Federal securities law does not preempt state regulation of this conduct. Rule 10b-5 does not provide an adequate remedy because of procedural/economic obstacles to suit and the limited resources of the S.E.C. Double recovery is unlikely and remediable by placing Ds' disgorged profits in a fund subject first to the claims of injured investors, with the residue payable to the corporation.

---

b. Insider trading not necessarily a breach of duty owed to corporation--

Freeman v. Decio, 584 F.2d 186 (7th Cir. 1978).

Facts. Freeman (P), a Skyline shareholder, filed a derivative suit against corporate officers (Ds) for making sales and gifts of Skyline stock on the basis of material, nonpublic information: that Skyline had overstated its earnings or that its reported earnings would decline. The district court dismissed on the ground that Indiana did not view such trading as a breach of fiduciary duty.

Issue. May a corporate officer be held liable in a derivative suit for the gain realized or loss avoided by trading his company's stock on the basis of material, nonpublic information?

Held. No. Judgment affirmed.

♦ Although most authorities still favor deterring insider trading, many now recognize that enforcing such a prohibition can adversely affect markets.

♦ Unlike traditional trust law, current corporation law does not bar an officer or director from profiting because of his position, beyond what he receives from the corporation. Not all information generated in the course of carrying on a business fits snugly into the corporate asset mold, and most information involved in insider trading does not. A corporation may have an interest in preventing such information from becoming public or in regulating the timing of the disclosure. Insider trading does not entail the disclosure of inside information, but rather its use in a manner in which the corporation itself is prohibited from exploiting it.

♦ The unfairness that is the basis of the widespread disapproval of insider trading is borne primarily by participants in the securities markets, rather than by the corporation itself. By comparison, the harm to corporate good will posited by the *Diamond* court pales in significance.

♦ Since *Diamond*, the rule 10b-5 class action has made substantial advances toward becoming the kind of effective remedy for insider trading that the court of appeals hoped that it might become.

VI. VOTING AND CORPORATE CONTROL

A. OVERVIEW: VOTING AND "SHAREHOLDER DEMOCRACY"

1. **Shareholder Voting and Service on the Board.** Shareholders collectively hold the power to choose and replace the board. They elect its members. Some, if not all, of the directors must stand for election annually. In most states, absent a contrary provision in the articles of incorporation, a majority of those shares voted at a meeting where a quorum is present may elect the entire board. Such a majority may also remove a director from the board, at least under some circumstances.

2. **Shareholder Voting and the Pursuit of Shareholder Interests.**

   a. **Berle and Means and the "separation of ownership and control."** Does the existence of the shareholders' collective voting power cause the board, and the officers serving at the board's pleasure, to pursue shareholder interests? In a famous and still influential book, *The Modern Corporation and Private Property* (1932), Berle and Means answered "no." According to them, "ownership is so widely scattered that working control can be maintained with but a minority interest." In the absence of "even a substantial minority interest. . . , control may be held by the directors or titular managers who can employ the proxy machinery to become a self-perpetuating body, even though as a group they own but a small fraction of the stock outstanding. . . ." Berle and Means argued that control over the proxy machinery gave management a nearly overwhelming advantage vis-a-vis insurgents. Management solicits proxies at the expense of the corporation while insurgents must finance not only their own solicitation, but, if they are to have any chance of prevailing, a political campaign as well.

   b. **Other mechanisms furthering "accountability" to shareholders.** Mechanisms other than voting may still cause officers and directors to pursue shareholder interests. These include incentive compensation plans, the market for managers, share sell-offs by unhappy holders (a sell-off leading to a drop in price could substantially reduce the wealth of officers and directors), and the market for corporate control.

   c. **Developments bearing on the Berle and Means argument.**

      1) **Federal proxy regulation.** The Securities Exchange Act of 1934 requires that, with respect to "reporting companies," proxy solicitors distribute to shareholders a statement disclosing their identity, background, and plans as well as the specific proposals to be voted on. The Act subjects these statements, and others made in connection

with the solicitation of proxies, to antifraud rules that are relatively plaintiff-friendly.

2) **The rise of institutional investors.** Institutional investors (notably pension funds) have acquired a commanding presence in the capital markets. In 1933, they owned about 8.5% of the stock traded on the New York Stock Exchange; today, they own or manage about 50% of all stock traded anywhere. This development may explain why recent empirical research on share ownership among Fortune 500 firms shows much less dispersal than Berle and Means observed. Institutional investors pressure management to pursue shareholder interests: indirectly through relatively frequent trading and directly through relatively aggressive monitoring and participation in shareholder votes.

3) **Takeovers.** Today's proxy contest is usually linked to a pending, prospective, or hoped-for takeover. Probably for this reason, institutional investors tend to support the insurgents in these contests more than others.

d. **Obstacles to collective shareholder action.**

1) **Information costs and "rational apathy."** Acquiring and analyzing information about corporate matters tends to be costly, especially in terms of forgone opportunities. Thus, a shareholder will usually engage in these activities only so long as they expect the costs of acquiring or analyzing a little more information to fall short of the gains. With respect to many corporate matters, a shareholder with modest holdings in a public corporation cannot expect to gain from any vote-related activities because his votes will not affect the outcome. He will engage in no such activities, remaining "rationally apathetic." (The calculus may vary depending on the matter at stake. Thus, shareholders are less likely to be rationally apathetic about takeover-related matters.)

2) **Free riding.** A shareholder with a substantial holding may find it cost-effective to devote significant resources to acquiring and analyzing information. Still, he will probably devote fewer resources than would be optimal from the perspective of all shareholders collectively. He will lack the incentive to do so, for the others may take a "free ride" on his efforts: share in the gains but not the costs. The shareholder may contract around this problem, but contracting can be costly. In some situations, the law permits a shareholder to "tax" others for his costs—bringing a successful derivative suit or waging a successful proxy fight.

3) **The market alternative.** In deciding whether to engage in more voting-related activities, shareholders will consider their alternatives.

For shareholders in widely held corporations, selling their stock will often be the alternative of choice.

4) **Conflict of interest.** Conflicting interests may cause some institutional investors to pursue shareholder interests less aggressively than one might have expected. For example, bankers might worry that a displeased management might switch corporate accounts to another bank.

B. THE SUBSTANTIVE LAW OF SHAREHOLDER VOTING

1. **Who Votes?** In almost all states, a corporation may allocate voting power among shareholders in any way that it wishes. The laws of a few states, including Delaware, even authorize bondholder voting. Despite this permissiveness, corporations typically enfranchise only their common shareholders, at least with respect to director selection.

2. **When Should a Shareholder Vote Be Required?** Not only does election to (and removal from) the board require a shareholder vote, but so too do "fundamental" changes, such as a merger, liquidation, sale of substantially all assets, or amendment of the articles of incorporation. (The board may also submit other transactions to a shareholder vote.) Why subject fundamental changes to shareholder approval? Economic analysis suggests that such changes, more than other transactions, will tempt directors to pursue their own interests at the expense of shareholders because such changes may well result in the departure of current directors from the board (what game theorists call the "end game" or "final period" problem). Perhaps this is why most states provide special rules for voting on fundamental changes that make approval more difficult to obtain. Some states require more votes for the approval of fundamental changes than for election to the board. These states may require (or permit the articles of incorporation to require) approval by a supermajority of all shares voting or by a majority of all shares outstanding. Many states enfranchise the holders of otherwise nonvoting shares when it comes to the approval of at least some fundamental changes. For example, quite a few of these states require that a merger obtain the approval of a majority of the holders of each class of shares, at least if the merger would likely change their rights, preferences, or privileges as would a charter amendment requiring such approval. (Most states also deny shareholders the power to initiate such transactions although they may nominate candidates for directorships.)

3. **Board May Set the Time for a Shareholder Meeting--**

Hilton Hotels Corp. v. ITT Corp. (Hilton I), 962 F. Supp. 1302 (D. Nev. 1997).

Facts. Under Nevada Corporation Law, annual meetings are required to be held to enable shareholders to elect directors and conduct other corporate business. Fearing that ITT Corporation's (D's) board of directors was delaying the annual meeting of D to frustrate a tender offer and proxy contest by Hilton Hotel Corporation and HLT Corporation (Ps), Ps' shareholders sought a preliminary injunction to force D to call its annual meeting within 12 months of its last annual meeting. Ps argued that "annual meeting" as used in the Nevada Revised Statutes and D's bylaws required a meeting to be conducted every 12 months. Alternatively, Ps argued that even if consistent with Nevada law and D's bylaws, failure to call an annual meeting within 12 months of its last annual meeting would constitute a breach of fiduciary duty by D's directors.

Issue. Should the shareholder class be able to force D to conduct its annual meeting within 12 months of its last annual meeting?

Held. No. Motion denied.

♦   The term annual meeting as used in the Nevada Revised Statutes and D's bylaws distinguishes between the regular meeting for the election of directors and other special meetings called by the board. If the Nevada Legislature or D intended that annual meetings be conducted every 12 months, they could have respectively provided through statute or in the bylaws.

♦   Failure to hold an annual meeting that has not been set and is not yet required to be set does not impede the shareholder franchise in breach of any fiduciary duty.

---

4.   **Evasions of the Voting Requirement.**

a.   **Restructuring--**

Hilton Hotels Corporation v. ITT Corp. (Hilton II), 978 F. Supp. 1342 (D. Nev. 1997).

Facts. In late January 1997, Hilton Hotels Corporation (P) announced both a $55 per share tender offer for the stock of ITT Corporation (D) and plans for a proxy contest at D's next annual meeting. In mid-February, D's board, consisting of nine outside directors and two inside directors, formally rejected the tender offer. The board then proceeded to sell several non-core assets and to oppose the takeover before Nevada, New Jersey, and Mississippi gaming regulators. In mid-July, the board announced its "Comprehensive Plan" to split D into three, assigning D's hotel and gaming business —about 93% of its then-current assets—to "ITT Destinations." Under the plan (i) D's board would become the board of ITT Destinations; (ii) the directors would serve three-year terms with one-third of the board standing for election each year; and (iii) repeal of this "staggered" or "classified" board scheme or removal of a director without cause would require a shareholder vote of 80%. The board announced that it would implement this plan without obtaining shareholder approval, which neither the Nevada statute nor D's governing documents expressly required (although in 1995, D's board submitted a planned division of the company to the shareholders for approval). Subsequently, the board adopted in large measure the business strategy advocated by P. Shortly after the board announced its Comprehensive Plan, P announced an amended tender offer of $70 per share, which the board rejected. At the meeting, the Goldman Sachs advisors hired by the board opined that the market valued D's shares under the Comprehensive Plan at $62 to $64. Subsequently, the board offered $70 per share for 26% of D's shares, using borrowed funds. In late August, P requested a preliminary and permanent injunction enjoining the Comprehensive Plan.

Issue. In the face of P's tender offer and proxy contest, could D's board implement its comprehensive plan without obtaining shareholder approval?

Held. No. Injunctive relief granted.

♦ Because this case involved both a tender offer and a proxy contest, the proper legal standard, in the absence of Nevada statute or case on point, is a *Unocal/ Blasius* analysis as articulated in *Stroud v. Grace, infra,* and *Unitrin, Inc. v. American General Corp., infra.* In assessing a challenge to defensive actions by a target corporation's board of directors in a takeover context, a court should evaluate the board's overall response, including the justification for each contested defensive measure, and the results achieved thereby, and when the defensive actions are inextricably related, a court must evaluate them collectively as a unitary response to the perceived threat.

♦ The board made no showing that P would pursue a corporate policy different than the board sought to implement through its Comprehensive Plan. During the months preceding the hearing, the board largely adopted P's proposed strategy. D did not show that P would be unable to run D or be ineffective in doing so. That some Sheraton franchise owners would be unhappy if P were to enter into certain management contracts was neither fundamental nor pervasive enough to constitute a "threat" to D's corporate policy or effectiveness.

♦ P's offer of $70 a share did not qualify as a "threat" because (i) contrary to D's claim, this price did reflect a control premium as evidenced by the Goldman Sachs opinion solicited by D's board that the market value D's shares under the Comprehensive Plan at $62 to $64 and (ii) D itself was offering to buy back about 26% of its stock at $70 a share, while planning to burden its remaining shares with much more debt.

♦ D's board failed to meet its burden under the first prong of the *Unocal* test of showing "good faith and reasonable investigation" of a threat to corporate policy or effectiveness. After P announced its tender offer, the board did not meet with P's representatives.

◆ Even in good faith, a board may not take ordinarily permissible actions if its primary purpose is to disenfranchise the shareholders in light of a proxy contest. The following circumstantial evidence, considered together, demonstrates that the primary purpose of D's Comprehensive Plan was to disenfranchise its shareholders.

The first bit of evidence is the *timing* of the plan. The board announced its Comprehensive Plan well after P's initial tender offer. The board did claim that it had contemplated a spin-off or asset sale earlier, but it made no such claim about the adoption of a classified board. The plan would have dramatically restructured D in little more than two months, two months before a scheduled annual meeting at which shareholders would have voted on an annually elected board.

The second piece of evidence is the *entrenchment* of the board the plan would offer. D's directors who approved the Comprehensive Plan in time to avoid the shareholder vote that otherwise would have occurred at D's 1997 annual meeting would take much more protected positions as directors of ITT Destinations.

The third piece of evidence is the board's *inconsistency*. The planned rapid implementation of the board's plan coupled with the board's opposition to P's tender offer is inconsistent with the board's argument defending its postponement of the 1997 annual meeting from May to November, which was that the delay would give shareholders more time to inform themselves and to consider the implications of their vote.

Finally, the last important piece of circumstantial evidence is the board's *past behavior*. The board did put its 1995 division of the company to a shareholder vote.

◆ Installing a classified board for ITT Destinations, a company that would encompass 93% of D's current assets and 87% of its revenues, would at least cause D's current shareholders to lose their existing right to replace a majority of D's incumbent board members for one year. Because of the inherent conflicts of interest that arise when shareholders are not permitted free exercise of their franchise, a board's unilateral decision to engage in defensive measures that purposefully deprive shareholders of their vote cannot pass muster under *Unocal* and *Stroud* without a "compelling justification." The board offered no such justification, stating only that it declined to seek shareholder approval of its plan to avoid market risks and other business problems as its advisors suggested. That the plan might generate additional benefits for shareholders did not remedy the fundamental flaw of board entrenchment. Thus, this defensive measure was preclusive and coercive under *Unitrin*.

◆ The right of shareholders to vote on directors at an annual meeting is a fundamental principle of corporate law, and it is not outweighed by the interests listed in

Nevada Revised Statutes section 78.138—interest related to non-shareholder constituencies.

---

b. **"Blank check" preferred stock.** In *Unilever Acquisition Corp. v. Richardson-Vicks, Inc.*, 618 F. Supp. 407 (S.D.N.Y. 1985), the board of a target corporation (Richardson-Vicks) responded to a hostile tender offer by creating a new class of preferred stock, each share of which would carry 25 votes per share unless transferred to a new holder, in which case it would carry only five votes per share. This practically precluded the hostile bidder from buying control so long as a significant minority fraction of the shareholders did not tender their shares. The district court ruled that such a fundamental change in voting rights required a shareholder vote, in part because it discriminated against incoming shareholders.

c. **The "de facto merger" doctrine.** An issue analogous to the one raised by *Unilever Acquisition Corp. v. Richardson-Vicks, Inc.*, *supra*, may arise when a transaction would function in a particular setting much like a merger, but is not listed as a "fundamental change" in the relevant statute. Some courts insist that shareholders be accorded the same voting and appraisal rights that they would have had had the transaction been structured as a merger; hence, the name of the doctrine. The California General Corporation Law codifies this result by conferring the same basic voting and appraisal rights on shareholders in all "reorganizations."

5. **What Voting Power Should a Share Carry? Rule 19C-4 and the One Shareholder/One Vote Controversy.**

a. **Exchange rules and issuing stock.** As a condition of listing, the New York Stock Exchange ("NYSE") requires companies to seek shareholder approval for issuing stock if issuing it could either work a change in control or increase outstanding common stock by 18.5%. From the 1920s to the mid-1980s, the NYSE refused to list a company's common stock unless each share of any class of such stock had exactly one vote. The American Stock Exchange and NASDAQ (the National Association of Securities Dealers automated quotation service) competed by accepting common stock listings from companies with shares having disparate voting rights (within limits). This competition seriously threatened NYSE revenues, however, only when the top management of many publicly held companies developed techniques for defeating or deterring takeovers which employed stock with limited voting rights or multiple votes. Against this background, General Motors's 1984 decision to finance its acquisition of Electronic Data Systems Corp. by issuing common stock with one-half vote per share prompted the NYSE to declare a moratorium on enforcement of its rule and appoint a committee to review "qualitative listing standards." Many companies then followed GM's example.

b. **Using disparate voting rights to thwart takeovers.** A board might permit only management and its allies to exchange one-vote common stock for the multi-vote kind, but such a decision would probably provoke a credible claim of self-dealing. The board could achieve the same end with less risk by distributing multi-vote stock to all holders that either (i) loses its extra votes upon transfer, at least for a period of time (a tenured voting plan), or (ii) cannot be transferred but can be converted into common stock possessing greater dividend rights (all holders except management and its allies would tend to convert). Alternatively, the board could adopt a "capped voting rights plan" limiting the number of shares any holder may vote.

Any of these techniques could fail for lack of shareholder approval. All would require amendment to the articles of incorporation unless the articles already empowered the board to issue "blank check" preferred stock, in which case shareholder approval might be required anyway under decisions like *Hilton Hotels Corporation v. ITT Corp. (Hilton II)*. Approval might be difficult to come by because it would reduce the chances that shareholders would receive an above-market price for their shares in a tender offer. This difficulty may explain why management usually employs in connection with one of these techniques some mechanism, like an extraordinary dividend, that will give the shareholders a "sweetener" upon approval.

c. **One-share/one-vote at the S.E.C.** A proposal by the NYSE to relax its one-share/one-vote rule triggered S.E.C. hearings addressed to the question of whether the S.E.C. should: (i) require the NYSE to retain its rule, (ii) make deviation from the rule conditional on supermajority approval or periodic reaffirmation, or (iii) impose a uniform one-share/one-vote rule on all exchanges and NASDAQ. Supporters of the NYSE proposal argued that disparate voting rights plans could serve a number of legitimate purposes, that empirical evidence did not show that such plans hurt share prices, and that state legislatures, rather than the S.E.C., should address matters of corporate governance like this one.

Opponents of the NYSE proposal argued that disparate voting plans could insulate incumbent management from the mechanisms of shareholder accountability, including the market for corporate control. But if the shareholders vote for such a plan, why prohibit it? Opponents of the NYSE proposal argued that often shareholder approval merely reflects the problems of collective action compounded by the offering of "sweeteners." When sweeteners are offered, shareholders know that approval of the plan will result in a prompt payoff, whereas disapproval may do no more than preserve whatever chance of displacing management that then exists. But if that's true, shouldn't disparate voting plans hurt share prices, contrary to the findings of the studies done to date? Opponents of the NYSE proposal argued that the studies: (i) focused on plans that did no more than perpetuate the incumbents' control; and (ii) did not capture the actual effect of these plans on stock price because they failed to compare the effect of disparate voting rights plans with the likely effect of their closest effective substitutes: the leveraged buyout or stock repurchase which typically provides holders with a premium substantially in excess of a "sweetener."

In 1988, the S.E.C. adopted Rule 19c-4 barring all exchanges and NASDAQ from listing (or quoting) stock of a domestic company that "issues any class of security, or takes other corporate action, with the effect of nullifying, restricting or disparately reducing the per-share voting rights of an outstanding class or classes of common stock." The rule exempted from its scope shares with multiple votes or limited voting that are sold in an initial public offering or were outstanding as of July 1988. [Note that in *The Business Roundtable v. Securities and Exchange Commission*, 905 F.2d 406 (1990), the D.C. Circuit Court of Appeals held that the Commission lacked the authority to promulgate the rule because it "directly controls the substantive allocation of powers among classes of shareholders."]

d. Where CEO-director-principal shareholder threatens to block beneficial transactions unless corporation adopts amendment, shareholder approval of plan is voidable--

Lacos Land Co. v. Arden Group, Inc., 517 A.2d 271 (Del. Ch. 1986).

Facts. The board of directors of Arden Group, Inc. proposed an amendment to the articles authorizing the board to issue a new class of shares, Class B Common Stock, which would be offered to all holders in a one-to-one exchange for their existing shares. Each Class B share would carry lower dividend rights and restrictions on transferability, but have 10 votes. Moreover, the class would elect 75% of the board. The directors acknowledged that they had fashioned the Class B shares so that they would be attractive mainly to its CEO and 21% shareholder, Briskin.

Briskin had become CEO in 1976 when Arden Group found itself in desperate condition. With Briskin at the helm, the price of Arden Group's publicly traded shares rose from less than $2 to around $25, with the latest rise occurring after the announcement of the proposed amendment. Apparently, Briskin instigated the amendment to protect his power over Arden Group's business future, but not in response to any specific takeover threat.

The proxy statement issued in connection with the amendment said that "Briskin . . . has informed the Company of his concern that certain transactions which could be determined by the Board of Directors to be in the best interests of all of the stockholders . . . might make the Company vulnerable to an unsolicited or hostile takeover attempt or to an attempt at 'greenmail,' and that he would not give his support to any such transactions for which his approval might be required unless steps were taken to secure his voting position in the Company." At the annual meeting, more than 1.4 million shares (64% of those outstanding) voted in favor of the amendment, with Briskin, his family, and a trustee, acting at the direction of Arden Group's management, casting about one million. About 325,000 shares voted "no." Lacos Land Co. (P) sued to block the issuance and exchange of the Class B stock, claiming that the proxy statement was materially misleading and that Arden Group's board breached its duty to the shareholders by approving the amendment.

Issue. Did the Briskin threat contained in the proxy statement render shareholder approval of the amendment voidable?

Held. Yes. Preliminary injunction granted.

♦ In making his threat, Briskin did not limit and could not be understood to have limited himself to exercising only stockholder power, as the proxy statement (some of the transactions identified would not require shareholder approval) and oral argument made clear.

♦ Regardless of his motivation, Briskin breached his duty of loyalty to the shareholders by making this threat. He put the board in a position where it had to approve the amendment so that it could even consider certain transactions that might threaten Briskin's control. The board, in turn, did the same to the shareholders.

Comment. It is not clear whether the outcome would have been any different if Briskin had only been a shareholder or if the amendment had been presented as a device for giving him an incentive to displace himself—issues to which the next main case, *Schreiber v. Carney, infra,* arguably speaks.

---

6. **Vote Buying.**

    a. **Statutory treatment.** Most, if not all, corporation statutes bar shareholders from selling their votes except in specified circumstances where the buyer will likely have similar incentives as a holder. For example, New York's Business Corporation Law section 609 provides that a "shareholder shall not sell his vote or issue a proxy to vote to any person for any sum of money or anything of value, except as authorized in this section and section 620 (Agreements as to voting. . .)." Section 609 then permits a shareholder to grant an irrevocable proxy to, among others, a pledgee or one who has agreed to purchase the sharcholder's shares. The exception for "agreements as to voting," which is implicit in many statcs' laws, may be a very broad one.

    b. **Vote buying legal where it benefits stockholders and it is ratified by a majority of independent stockholders after full disclosure--**

Schreiber v. Carney, 447 A.2d 17 (Del. Ch. 1982).

Facts. Texas International Airlines (D) and Texas Air entered into merger negotiations. D's controlling (35%) shareholder, Jet Capital Inc. ("JCI"), threatened to block the merger, citing adverse tax consequences that it would suffer unless it exercised certain D warrants prior to the merger. JCI claimed that it lacked funds necessary to exercise these warrants and that it could not afford to borrow from a third-party lender. To deal with this problem, D's board considered making a corporate loan to JCI. Because D and JCI had common directors, D's board formed a committee consisting of the three directors unaffiliated with JCI and empowered that committee to resolve the matter. With the assistance of its own lawyer and investment banker, the committee found that D should pursue the proposed merger and, to that end, should grant a loan to JCI bearing an interest rate just sufficient to reimburse D for dividends likely to be paid out prior to expiration of the warrants.

Accordingly, the loan agreement called for D to loan $3,335,000 at 5% until the 1982 expiration of the warrants and thereafter at the then-prevailing prime rate. D's directors unanimously approved the agreement conditional on approval by a majority of all outstanding shares and a majority of all shares voted by shareholders other than JCI, its officers, and directors. After full disclosure, the shareholders voted overwhelmingly in favor. Schreiber (P) filed suit to enjoin the loan, alleging that it constituted illegal vote buying and corporate waste.

Issue. May a corporation buy the votes of its principal holder in order to secure approval of a transaction expected to benefit all holders if the purchase is ratified by independent shareholders after full disclosure?

Held. Yes. Injunction is not granted.

- The loan constituted vote buying. However, since vote buying is simply a voting agreement supported by consideration personal to the stockholder, it is illegal per se only if its objective is to defraud or disenfranchise the other stockholders.

- Vote buying is not illegal simply because it deprives the other shareholders of the seller's personal judgment. In widely held corporations, this personal judgment is of no significance. Moreover, Delaware law permits shareholders wide latitude in decisions affecting the restriction or transfer of voting rights.

- Because vote buying is so easily abused, it must be subject to a test for intrinsic fairness. Since the object and purpose of the agreement was to further the interest of all D stockholders, ratification of the transaction by a majority of the independent stockholders, after a full disclosure of all germane facts with complete candor, precludes any further judicial inquiry of it.

Comment. It is not at all clear that there is a principled distinction between *Lacos* and *Schreiber*, although the voting plan challenged in *Lacos* would have given Briskin permanent control whereas the one challenged in *Schreiber* diluted JCI's voting power.

---

      c.   **Vote buying substitutes.** Vote pooling agreements, irrevocable proxies, "standstill agreements" (*i.e.*, potential tender offeror and target board agree that the potential offeror will abide by a ceiling on its share ownership), and charter amendments creating weighted voting may all function in a manner similar to vote buying.

C. VOTING PROCEDURES

    1.   **Record Dates.** Anyone registered on a corporation's stock ledger as a holder on the record date is entitled to vote at the next shareholders' meeting (and is entitled to timely notice of the meeting). The board of directors customarily sets the record date either through a bylaw or a resolution. The relevant corporation law, however, may limit the board's discretion. In any event, it usually requires the corporation to prepare and make available for inspection an alphabetical list of holders showing their addresses and share ownership. Post record date buyers may vote their shares by obtaining a proxy from the seller, which may be made irrevocable.

    2.   **Proxies.** Shareholders may, and generally do, vote by proxy. A shareholder may revoke a proxy at any time and for any reason unless she makes the proxy irrevocable. If the proxy is irrevocable, the proxy holder is the only one who is entitled to vote. Revocation of a ***revocable*** proxy may be accomplished simply by delivering a proxy with a later date. If the corporation reports under the Securities Exchange Act of 1934, every proxy expires one year after the shareholder grants it.

    3.   **"Street Name" Ownership.** Shareholders frequently leave their shares registered in the name of their broker or banker who uses a "street name"—an assumed name entered on the stock ledger for this particular purpose. This practice substantially relieves holders of recordkeeping chores and the risk of loss or theft. It also facilitates the creation and use of margin accounts. Most importantly, it reduces the need for the physical transfer of stock certificates, a time-consuming and costly process. To further minimize physical transfer, brokerage firms in cooperation with stock exchanges have established depository companies whose function is to hold master share certificates in which the brokerage firms have equitable interests.

      a.   **Effect on proxies.** This system of holding shares could make it difficult to solicit proxies. Stock exchange rules have long required brokerage firms to forward proxy materials and annual reports to beneficial owners and to vote as instructed, but these rules do not facilitate direct communication. S.E.C. rule 14b-1 requires brokerage firms to inform the corporation of the names, addresses, and holdings of customers who are beneficial owners (unless the beneficial owners object). A similar rule applies to banks acting as trustees.

4. **Stockholder Consents.** In some states, Delaware included (General Corporation Law section 228), shareholders may take action without notice, much less a meeting, via written consents.

    a. **Unless specified in the articles, directors may not forestall shareholder action by consent through unreasonable ministerial-type review of the legal sufficiency of the consents--**

Datapoint Corp. v. Plaza Securities Co., 496 A.2d 1031 (Del. 1985).

Facts. Asher B. Edelman, beneficial owner of more than 10% of the shares of Datapoint Corp. (D) and general partner of Ps, offered to acquire D. After D's board rejected the offer, Edelman renewed it and threatened to solicit consents to replace the incumbent directors with his own candidates. Four days later, D's board adopted bylaws to govern, for the first time, any attempt to take corporate action by written shareholder consent. On January 30, Edelman withdrew his offer and announced his intention to begin soliciting written consents. Ps then filed suit seeking injunctive relief against enforcement of the bylaw. Meanwhile, D's investment banker advised it that the board would need "at least 60 days . . . to achieve a transaction or series of transactions which would best serve the interests of all of [D's] shareholders." The board amended the bylaw to delay the effectiveness of action taken by shareholder consent to the later of: (i) 45 days after the record date, which the board would set 15 days after receipt of a shareholder's notice of intent to solicit consents (unless the soliciting shareholder requested more time); *or* (ii) the final termination of any court proceeding challenging the validity of the consents (unless and until the court determines that such proceeding is not being pursued in good faith). D then sued to invalidate any consents obtained by Ps. The Chancery Court enjoined D from enforcing the amended bylaw, and D appeals.

Issue. Does the amended bylaw conflict with the Delaware shareholder-action-by-consent statute (Del. Gen. Corp. Law section 228)?

Held. Yes. Judgment affirmed.

♦   Section 228 provides that, unless the articles provide otherwise, any action that could be taken at a shareholders' meeting may be taken by written consent "without prior notice and without a vote." It contains no language suggesting that such action may be lawfully deferred or thwarted on grounds not relating to the legal sufficiency of the consents obtained.

- D's bylaw is not designed simply to postpone the effectiveness of such action pending a ministerial-type review of the legal sufficiency of the consents. Rather, the bylaw is designed to provide the incumbent directors with time to defeat the shareholder action by seeking revocations (or proxies), and such action is contrary to section 228.

- The bylaw provision staying the effective date of any shareholder consent action until termination of any lawsuits challenging such action effectively gives the incumbent directors the power to stultify the shareholders' statutory rights.

----

  b. Setting the record date to undermine shareholder action by consent. In *Empire of Carolina, Inc. v. Deltona Corp.*, 514 A.2d 1091 (1986), the Delaware Supreme Court upheld a board's action in setting a record date for shareholder consents that gave the board enough time to issue a major new block of shares and sell them to one opposed to the shareholder action. According to the court, *Datapoint* did not speak to whether such action was permissible. The Delaware legislature subsequently amended the corporation statute (section 213(b)) to limit the discretion of the board in setting the record date for shareholder consents: the date must fall between the day the board sets it and 10 days later. (Absent a set record date, it becomes the first day on which a signed written consent setting forth the action taken or proposed is delivered to the corporation.)

  c. Board interference with shareholder consent action and the business judgment rule. *Blasius Industries, Inc. v. Atlas Corp.*, 564 A.2d 651 (Del. Ch. 1988), dealt with a consent solicitation seeking to expand the board from seven to 15 members, the maximum specified in the articles. When the target board proposed to exercise its power to expand its size to nine and fill the resulting vacancies, the consenting shareholder sought help in court. Despite finding that the board acted in good faith to further what it believed was the corporation's best interest, the court enjoined the board from acting on its proposal. Declaring that the business judgment rule was inapplicable, the court said that where the board's purpose was to prevent shareholders from resolving governance issues, the board had to show a "compelling justification" for its actions. The court then sapped some of the strength of its opinion by distinguishing board actions designed to further some other purpose, but having an "incidental" impact on the ability of shareholders to act by consent.

D. PROXY CONTEST EXPENSES

  1. Board May Reimburse Prevailing Insurgents for at Least Some of Their Proxy Contest Expenses--

Rosenfeld v. Fairchild Engine & Airplane Corp., 309 N.Y. 168, 128 N.E.2d 291 (1955).

Facts. Shareholders (P) brought a derivative action to get a return of money that Fairchild (D) reimbursed to the old management (unsuccessful in a proxy contest) ***and*** to the new management. The majority of the shareholders had ratified the reimbursement payments. The proxy contest had centered around the compensation paid to one director (who was also the chief executive officer). The lower court held for D and P appeals.

Issue. Is it lawful for the corporation, with the approval of a majority of the shareholders, to pay the expenses of the competing parties in a proxy contest?

Held. Yes. Judgment affirmed.

♦ In a contest over policy, as compared to a purely personal power contest, directors (current management) have the right to make reasonable and proper expenditures, subject to the scrutiny of the courts when duly challenged. To be reasonable and proper, these expenditures must be for the purpose of persuading shareholders of the correctness of their position and soliciting their support for policies that the directors believe, in good faith, are in the best interests of the corporation.

♦ There is no obligation on the corporation to reimburse the successful outside contestants. But the shareholders may vote to reimburse such contestants for the reasonable and bona fide expenses the contestants incur.

Comment. Insurgents face a free rider problem: they bear the costs of the proxy contest but share the gains with nonparticipating shareholders. Corporate reimbursement of successful insurgents ameliorates this problem. It does not solve it because, going into the contest, the insurgents must take into account the possibility that they will lose and receive no reimbursement. Corporate reimbursement of unsuccessful insurgents, however, might create perverse incentives to mount proxy contests likely to reduce shareholder welfare.

E. SPECIAL VOTING SYSTEMS: CUMULATIVE, CLASS, AND SUPERMAJORITY VOTING

1. Cumulative Voting.

a. **Distinguished from "straight" voting system.** Under a "straight" voting system, shareholders vote to fill each vacant directorship independently of the others. Thus, a majority of the shares voted may fill each vacancy. Under a cumulative voting system, shareholders vote to fill all vacancies at once, with each share casting the same number of votes as there are vacancies and allocating these votes in any way that the holder desires. A minority of the shares voted may fill at least one vacancy.

b. The formula.

$$X \quad = \quad Y \quad \times \quad N$$

(number of   (number of   (number of
shares needed   shares voting   directors de-
to elect a   <u>at meeting)</u>   <u>sired to elect)</u> + 1
given number   1 + N (total number of direc-
of directors)   tors to be elected)

For example: If a minority shareholder wishes to assure election of one director on an eight-person board, and there are 1,500 shares, with 900 expected to vote at the meeting:

$$X = \frac{900 \times 1}{1 + 8} + 1 = 101 \text{ shares required}$$

c. **Right to cumulative voting.** In some states, cumulative voting is mandatory. In other states, it is permissive. In some states, the right is given in the state constitution, and in others it is merely statutory.

d. **Reducing the impact.** Staggering the terms of directors, authorizing removal by majority vote, reducing the size of the board, and distributing stock with disparate voting rights will reduce the impact of cumulative voting. Many cumulative voting statutes limit "staggering" by placing a ceiling on the number of director "classes," a floor on the number of directors in each "class," or both. These statutes usually protect directors from removal by the majority, but then the matter of removal for "cause" becomes problematic.

e. **Value and use.** Whether cumulative voting makes the shareholders or even minority shareholders better off is subject to considerable controversy. Where state law does not mandate cumulative voting, few large corporations use it. Where state law does mandate it, shareholders of large corporations tend not to take advantage of it.

2. Class Voting. Many corporation statutes require that, in order to become effective, an amendment to the articles of incorporation that would adversely affect one or more classes of shares (preferred, for example) must be approved by a majority of those shares. For three reasons, this veto power provides only limited protection to holders of these shares. First, it gives holders the power to check, not initiate, actions. It would not prevent the directors elected by the common shareholders from declining to declare dividends payable to the preferred shareholders. Second, the scope of this veto power is uncertain. Third, a board could end-run the class approval requirement by merging the corporation into a newly formed "shell" corporation whose articles already contain the desired provisions. However, to discourage this "end run" many states, including New York, have enacted relevant corporation statutes that make such a merger subject to the same class approval requirement that the directors are trying to defeat.

F.   REMOVAL AND VACANCIES

1.   Directors.

a.   When to remove. At common law, shareholders could remove directors only for cause. A number of state corporation statutes are more permissive. Some authorize articles of incorporation and shareholder-adopted bylaws that provide for removal without cause. The Delaware and California statutes and the Revised Model Business Corporation Act take the next step: they simply authorize removal without cause. In the absence of a permissive statute, it is not clear whether a court would enforce a provision in the articles for removal without cause.

b.   How to remove. Generally, a director may be removed by a majority of the shares voted at a meeting called for this purpose. If the removal is for cause, a hearing must be held, but just what kind could or should be held is not at all clear.

c.   Filling vacancies. At common law, shareholders filled board vacancies. Modern corporation statutes generally permit the board to do so.

2.   Officers.
Generally, modern corporation statutes permit the board to remove officers without cause, but permit the removed officer to recover damages if the removal constitutes a breach of contract.

G.   JUDICIAL SUPERVISION OF ELECTION CONTESTS

1.   Changing the Date of the Annual Shareholder Meeting--

Schnell v. Chris-Craft Industries, Inc., 285 A.2d 437 (Del. 1971).

Facts. When the management of Chris-Craft Industries (D) learned that some dissident shareholders (Ps) had taken steps to wage a proxy contest, D's board amended the bylaws to move up the annual meeting by five weeks and failed to produce a list of holders. D's board took these actions to make it more difficult for Ps to solicit other holders. Ps sued to block the board's action. The Chancery Court refused to grant Ps an injunction. Ps appeal.

Issue. May a board of directors move up an annual meeting for the purpose of hindering a proxy contest by dissident holders?

Held. No. Judgment reversed and cause remanded to Chancery Court with instructions to set annual meeting on the date provided in the bylaws prior to amendment.

---

2. **Effect or Purpose.** Several federal courts, confronted with a maneuver similar to that of the Chris-Craft board, have focused on the likely effect of the maneuver rather than the board's purpose. Where the likely effect would have been to perpetuate management in office, these courts, applying ordinary duty of loyalty analysis, have placed the burden of proof on the board to show that its actions were justified by legitimate corporate objectives.

3. **Board-Interpreted Eligibility Requirements for Directorships--**

Stroud v. Grace, 606 A.2d 75 (Del. 1992)

Facts. At the beginning of 1989, Roger, Minot, and Gerrish Milliken (Ds) controlled more than 50% of the outstanding shares of privately held Milliken Enterprises, Inc. (D). Moreover, by virtue of a General Option Agreement ("GOA") subscribed to by more than 70% of the company's holders, the family and the company held a right of first refusal on stock offered to third parties. Roger, Minot, and Gerrish served as three of the four inside directors on a 10-person board.

In early 1989, the board considered amendments to the company's articles and bylaws. The two most controversial amendments were Article Eleventh (c) and Bylaw 3. Article Eleventh (c) defined three groups of directors and established the minimum or maximum number of directors who could belong to each group. A majority of the board had to qualify as category one directors: people who had "*substantial* experience in line (as distinct from staff) positions in the management of *substantial* private institutions" (emphasis added), but were not officers, employees, or stockholders of the company. At least three directors had to qualify as category two directors: beneficial stockholders of the company. Finally, no more than two directors could qualify as category three directors (unless they also qualified as category two directors): present or past CEOs, COOs, or presidents of the company.

Bylaw 3 (i) required a shareholder to provide a notice of nomination no later than 14 days prior to the date of the meeting for the election of directors (seven days if the board calls the meeting on less than 21 days' notice); (ii) required that the notice include information showing that the nominee possessed the requisite qualifications, including qualifications set forth in the applicable portion of Article Eleventh (c); and (iii) authorized the board, or if not feasible, the person presiding at the meeting of the stockholders, to determine whether a nominee has met the qualification requirements set forth in the articles.

The board voted unanimously (one outside director was absent) to recommend that the shareholders approve the amendments at the annual meeting. The notice of the meeting was accompanied by the resolution proposing the amendments and by copies of the articles and bylaws then in force. The notice stated, "These amendments are proposed in lieu of all amendments previously proposed upon which the stockholders have not acted." The notice did not explain the differences or similarities between the newly proposed amendments and those withdrawn, one of which contained a provision identifying a threat to control. The notice disclosed that management would not solicit proxies and expressly encouraged shareholders to attend the meeting at which the chairman, Roger Milliken, and others would "endeavor to answer questions concerning the matters to be voted upon, including the proposed amendments. . . ."

Ninety-three percent of the company's eligible voters, holding almost 98% of the shares entitled to vote, personally attended the annual meeting. Seventy-eight percent of the shares entitled to vote approved the proposed amendments.

The Strouds (Ps), owners of 17% of the company's stock, brought individual and derivative actions against Ds, claiming (i) the directors breached their duty of care and duty of loyalty by recommending the amendments, (ii) the directors failed to provide adequate notice, and (iii) the amendments were "unfair" to shareholders because they insulated the Milliken family from any future proxy contests. Ps moved for summary judgment. Scrutinizing the amendments under the "intrinsic fairness" test, the Vice Chancellor held that Bylaw 3 did not pass. He found that the "board could effectively disenfranchise voters because subsection (f), when read in conjunction with the subsection limiting the shareholder's right to submit its notice of nomination not less than 14 days before the election, gave the directors the unfettered discretion to disqualify the shareholders' candidates without recourse." With respect to all other claims he granted summary judgment for Ds, sua sponte. Both sides appeal.

Issues.

(i)   Must the conduct of D's board pass muster under the heightened judicial review standard of *Unocal Corp. v. Mesa Petroleum Co.* (*supra*) applicable to defensive measures taken in response to a perceived threat to control?

(ii)   Did shareholder approval cure any alleged breach of fiduciary duty in connection with the board's recommendation?

(iii)   Must the amendments pass muster under the test of "intrinsic fairness"?

(iv)   Do Article Eleventh (c) and Bylaw 3 pass muster under the test of "intrinsic fairness"?

Held. (i) No. (ii) Yes. (iii) No. (iv) Yes. Judgment reversed.

♦   *Unocal Corp. v. Mesa Petroleum* does not apply to the conduct of Ds' board because of the lack of any threat to the board's control and because of shareholder approval. Roger, Minot, and Gerrish Milliken control over 50% of the company's outstanding stock and hold the right of first refusal on most of the rest, so the company was "neither a takeover target nor vulnerable to one." Any defensive effects of the GAO—an example of commonly used contractual devices designed to preserve family ownership—and the amendments themselves were collateral at best.

♦ Ps offered no proof that Ds' disclosures were misleading or inadequate. Since Ps did not allege fraud or waste, shareholder approval cured any alleged breach of fiduciary duty in connection with the board's recommendation.

♦ Since the board did not face any threat to its control, it cannot be said that the primary purpose of the board's action was to interfere with or impede exercise of the shareholder franchise. More fundamentally, a fully informed majority of Milliken shareholders ratified the amendments. In these circumstances the "intrinsic fairness" test does not apply.

♦ Despite the use of "substantial" in Article Eleventh (c)'s category one qualifications, the article is not so vague as to render them "unfair" to shareholders. The board could define the term as long as it "exercised [its] discretion fairly." For the same reasons that this article is not "unfair" on its face, neither is Bylaw 3.

---

4. **Bringing *Blasius* Back: Board May Not Expand Its Size and Fill Resulting Vacancies to Thwart Election of Opponents--**

MM Companies, Inc. v. Liquid Audio, Inc., 813 A.2d 1118 (Del. 2003).

Facts. In October 2001, MM Companies, Inc. (P) took several steps toward acquiring Liquid Audio, Inc., (D), a publicly traded corporation. P sent a letter on behalf of a group that owned slightly more than 7% of D's stock, expressing an interest in acquiring D for $3 per share, which the board spurned as "inadequate." P also asked the board to call a special meeting of D's shareholders to fill two vacancies on D's five-member staggered board, but the board declined to do so and filled the vacancies with two of its allies. In November, P announced that it would nominate its own candidates for the two seats on D's board that were up for election at the next annual meeting. In December, P notified D's board that, at the annual meeting, P planned (i) to propose expansion of the board by four members, from five to nine, and (ii) to nominate candidates for these four positions. On June 10, 2002, P began soliciting proxies for D's annual meeting scheduled for July 1, 2002. Three days later, D's board announced a stock-for-stock merger transaction with Alliance Entertainment Corporation and the indefinite postponement of its annual meeting, pending a vote on the merger transaction. Subsequently, it became apparent that P's nominees for the board would be elected to fill the two vacancies. The board became concerned that this would prompt two of the incumbent directors to resign, thereby giving P control of D and jeopardizing the pending merger. To prevent that from occurring, the board amended its bylaws to increase the size of the board to seven members and then appointed two more allies to fill these positions. P sued, claiming that by taking these actions the members of D's board violated their fiduciary duties as set forth in *Blasius* and *Unocal* in that these actions frustrated P's attempt to gain a "substantial presence" on D's board for at least one year and guaranteed D's management such presence, if not control, for at least two years. The Court of Chancery entered judgment for D, and P appeals.

Issue. Did D's board violate its fiduciary duties by expanding its size from five to seven and filling the resulting vacancies?

Held. Yes. Judgment reversed.

♦ Not only did the board have to show that its conduct was proportionate and reasonable in relation to the threat to corporate policy posed by P (*Unocal, infra*) but because the board's actions "purposefully disenfranchise[d] its shareholders" in connection with "issues of control" (*Stroud, supra*), the board had to also show that it had a "compelling justification" for its conduct. [*Blasius, supra*] The board failed to show such a justification for increasing the size of the board and filling the resulting vacancies.

Comment. The result might have been different had the shareholders previously approved a limitation on their own voting authority as they had in *Stroud, supra*.

---

5. **Defensive Tactics in Proxy Contests.** It has become standard practice to structure "poison pills" (*see* IX.C.2.e., *infra*) so that a proxy contestant qualifies as the beneficial holder of any stock that the contestant may vote, whether directly or indirectly, except pursuant to revocable proxies given in response to a proxy solicitation. [*See S*tahl v. Apple Bancorp., Inc., Fed. Sec. L. Rep. (CCH ¶ 95,412 (Del. Ch. Aug. 9, 1990)] The bylaws of many public corporations now contain provisions requiring that would-be insurgents give notice of their plans and regulating the use of written consents.

H. SHAREHOLDERS' RIGHT OF INSPECTION

1. **Introduction.** Pursuit of shareholder interests may practically require inspection of some corporate records, especially the list of shareholders. At common law a shareholder had a right to inspect his corporation's books and records if he had a "proper purpose." All corporation statutes regulate this matter. They may speak to the "proper purpose" requirement as well as to a number of other issues such as the type of books and records subject to inspection, shareholder qualification, the mechanics of demanding, court enforcement, and penalties for failure to permit.

2. **Delaware Law.** Section 220(b) of the Delaware Corporation Code provides in pertinent part: "Any stockholder, in person or by attorney or other agent, shall, upon written demand under oath stating the purpose thereof, have the right during the usual hours for business to inspect for any proper purpose the

corporation's stock ledger, a list of its stockholders, and its other books and records, and to make copies or extracts therefrom. A proper purpose shall mean a purpose reasonably related to such person's interest as a stockholder." Section 220(c) provides that ". . . [t]he court may, in its discretion, prescribe any limitations or conditions with reference to the inspection. . . ."

3. Credible Basis to Find Probable Wrongdoing on the Part of Corporate Management Justifies Tailored Inspection of Books and Records--

Security First Corp. v. U.S. Die Casting and Development Co., 687 A.2d 563 (Del. 1997).

Facts. Security First Corporation (D), a bank holding company whose shares traded on NASDAQ, entered into a merger agreement with Mid Am, Inc., a larger bank holding company. After the announcement of the merger, the price of D's stock increased significantly.

Section 9.05 of the merger agreement permitted the board of either company to terminate the agreement, provided that, in the event of certain contingencies arising in the 12 months thereafter, D would pay a termination fee of $2 million and would reimburse Mid Am for certain expenses up to $250,000. Three months after striking the agreement, the merger fell through—according to D's officers and directors, because of "the realization that Mid Am's management philosophy and direction were fundamentally different from its own." None of the contingencies specified in section 9.05 had occurred, but D and Mid Am entered into a termination agreement pursuant to which D reimbursed Mid Am for $275,000 in expenses and agreed to pay an additional $2 million contingent on the occurrence of an event listed in section 9.05 within 18 months of the effective date of the termination agreement. D did not request any documentation for expenses. Counsel for U.S. Die Casting and Development Corporation (P), owner of approximately 5% of D's common stock, wrote to D's chairman and CEO, Charles Valentine, stating: "This either takes the company 'out of play' or diminishes the amount payable to the stockholders if it is sold. In either event, the agreement seems inappropriate and destructive to stockholder values." Upon disclosure of the termination agreement, the price of D's common stock dropped significantly and did not bounce back.

Following the termination, D increased dividend payments to its stockholders. According to the court of chancery, "[a] thoughtful stockholder might look at this dividend increase as an effort to ameliorate dismay about the Board of Directors' abandonment of a seemingly beneficial merger for [D's] stockholders."

P then made a demand to inspect the most recent list of stockholders and the merger agreement; all minutes, notes, records, memoranda, writings, correspondence, telephone messages, or the like that in any way directly or indirectly deal with or discuss either the agreement or the payment of $275,000 to Mid Am or a penalty to be paid if D or its assets are sold to another in the future; minutes of all proceedings of directors or committees of directors from January 1, 1994; all press releases relative to the agreement; any and all documents or records discussing the relationship between the employees of D after the completion of the merger contemplated by the agreement; any and all bank or savings and loan regulatory applications and amendments thereto related to the agreement; and any and all correspondence with federal or state bank or savings and loan regulatory agencies in connection with the agreement. Concerning the stockholder list, P stated that it wished "to communicate with the shareholders of [D] with respect to [D's] business, particularly the failed merger with Mid Am, Inc."

When D refused to honor P's demand, P sought an order compelling inspection pursuant to section 220 of the Delaware Corporation Code. After a hearing, the chancellor found that according to the amended complaint and P's trial brief and P's post-trial reply brief, P's purpose for requesting an inspection of D's books and records was to investigate the possibility of corporate mismanagement. The chancellor accepted P's written proffer that the payment of $275,000 alone represented a specific transaction raising the plausibility of more than speculative, general mismanagement. At the hearing, David Slyman, P's president, chief executive officer, and sole stockholder, testified that he had no idea what he would do with the stockholder list. The court of chancery ordered D to comply with P's demand. D appeals.

Issues.

(i)   Is a stockholder entitled to inspect corporate books and records if he shows a credible basis to find probable corporate wrongdoing?

(ii)   Does the purpose of the inspection limit its scope?

(iii)   Is a stockholder entitled to a stockholder list if he admits that he has no idea what he would do with the list?

Held. (i) Yes; (ii) Yes; (iii) No. Judgment affirmed in part, reversed in part, and remanded.

♦   Once a stockholder proves by a preponderance of the evidence that a credible basis exists to find probable wrongdoing on the part of corporate management—not that wrongdoing actually occurred—he becomes entitled to inspection of corporate books and records.

♦   The credible basis may take the form of documents, testimony, or logic. Here the basis includes (i) D's payment of $275,000 to Mid Am when D never broke the merger agreement; (ii) D's failure to request that Mid Am document the expenses purportedly justifying the $275,000 payment, which exceeded by $25,000 the amount for expenses provided in the merger agreement; (iii) D's promise to pay Mid Am $2 million in the event certain contingencies arose within 18 months of the termination agreement when D had promised in the merger agreement to pay Mid Am $2 million in the event that the same contingencies arose within 12 months, and (iv) disclosure of the termination agreement was followed by a significant drop in the price of D's common stock from which it did not recover prior to the hearing, while D has increased its dividends.

- The difference between the vice chancellor's finding that "a specific transaction rais[ed] the plausibility of more than speculative, general mismanagement" and the requirement that "[t]here must be some evidence of possible mismanagement as would warrant further investigation" is merely semantic.

- Section 220(c) provides that "[t]he Court may, in its discretion, prescribe any limitations or conditions with reference to the inspection." A section 220 proceeding should result in an order circumscribed with "rifled precision" to satisfy the stockholder's stated purpose. The stockholder bears the burden of proving that each category of books and records is essential to the accomplishment of the stockholder's articulated purpose for the inspection.

- Under section 220(c), once a stockholder has made a demand to obtain a stockholder list that otherwise comports with the statutory requirements, the corporation bears the burden of proving that the stockholder's purpose is improper. On appeal, the court reviews de novo the propriety of the purpose. Slyman's admission that he had no idea what he would do with such a list shows that P's purpose amounted to no more than idle curiosity, which does not qualify as a proper purpose.

Comment. The court did note that, after a material change of circumstances, P could make a new demand and, if necessary, file a new proceeding to obtain the stockholder list if P then has a bona fide purpose to inspect the list.

---

4. Purpose of Inspection Controls Its Scope--

Saito v. McKesson HBOC Inc., 806 A.2d 113 (Del. 2002)

Facts. In 1998, three days after McKesson Corporation ("McKesson") entered into a stock-for-stock merger agreement with HBO & Company ("HBOC"), Saito (P) purchased McKesson stock. After the merger transaction was consummated in January 1999, HBOC became a wholly-owned subsidiary of McKesson and the combined company was renamed McKesson HBOC ("D"). From April through July, McKesson HBOC then announced a series of financial restatements triggered by its year-end audit process, all of which McKesson HBOC attributed to HBOC accounting irregularities. The restatements triggered a number of derivative claims, to one of which P was a party. The court of chancery dismissed his complaint but suggested that P review the books and records of the companies pursuant to 8 Del. C. section 220 in order "to obtain information necessary to sue derivatively." P sought to do just that in order (i) to further investigate breaches of fiduciary duties by the boards of directors of HBOC, McKesson, and McKesson HBOC related to their oversight of their respective company's accounting procedures and financial reporting; and (ii) to investigate potential claims against advisors engaged by McKesson and HBOC to the acquisition of HBOC by McKesson. Finding credible evidence of possible wrongdoing, the court of chancery held that P's purpose was "proper" within the meaning of section 220, but the court only compelled inspection of McKesson HBOC documents that were dated after P acquired McKesson stock. The court refused to compel inspection of HBOC documents. It also refused to compel inspection of McKesson HBOC documents relating to claims against third-party advisors. P appeals.

Issues.

(i)   Pursuant to section 220, may a stockholder inspect documents dated before the stockholder first acquired the corporation's stock?

(ii)   Pursuant to section 220, may a shareholder inspect documents in a corporation's possession which were prepared by third parties?

(iii) Pursuant to section 220, may a stockholder of a parent company inspect a subsidiary's documents?

Held. (i) Yes. (ii) Yes (iii) Yes. Judgment affirmed in part and reversed in part.

♦   Section 220 gives a stockholder the right to inspect books and records for a "proper purpose" "reasonably related" to the stockholder's interest. The court of chancery's finding of credible evidence of possible wrongdoing establishes that P's purpose was proper.

♦   A stockholder who demands inspection for a proper purpose should be given access to all of the documents in the corporation's possession, custody or control that are necessary to satisfy that proper purpose, including documents dated before the stockholder acquired his stock. Such documents might relate to a continuing wrong that both predates and postdates the stockholder's purchase date, or the alleged post-purchase-date wrongs may have had their foundation in events that transpired earlier (such as McKesson's apparent failure to learn of HBOC's accounting irregularities until months after the merger transaction closed).

♦   Under section 220, a parent corporation's stockholder does not have the same right to inspect a subsidiary's books and records as he does the parent's. So P does not have the right to inspect HBOC's books and records that were never provided to McKesson or McKesson HBOC. But P does have the right to inspect relevant documents that HBOC gave to McKesson before the merger, or to McKesson HBOC after the merger, which P would need in order to understand what McKesson or McKesson HBOC's directors knew, and why they failed to recognize HBOC's accounting irregularities prior to the closing of the merger transaction.

---

5.   **List of Stockholders vs. Other Books and Records.** Courts have received requests to inspect stockholder lists more hospitably than requests to inspect

other books and records. Delaware shifts the burden of proof with respect to proper purpose. New York gives shareholders an unqualified right to inspect annual balance sheets and profit and loss statements, but it makes inspection of all other records conditional on a showing of good faith and proper purpose. Mandamus is the usual remedy for refusal to permit inspection.

6. **Beneficial Owners.** Some courts now honor requests for lists not only of share-holders, but also for beneficial owners known to the corporation. Courts have generally declined, however, to honor inspection requests from beneficial owners.

7. **State Inspection Rights/Federal Proxy Rules.** Under federal proxy rule 14a-7 a security holder, or tender offeror, may insist that the issuer either provide her with a list of security holders or mail her communications to them (at the holder's expense). Courts have rejected the claim that this rule preempts state inspection laws.

I. FEDERAL LAW

1. **Securities Exchange Act of 1934.**

   a. **Basic proxy provision of the Act.** Section 14(a) of the Act provides:

   > It shall be unlawful for any persons, by the use of the mails or by any means or instrumentality of interstate commerce or of any facility of a national securities exchange or otherwise, in contravention of such rules and regulations as the Commission may prescribe as necessary or appropriate in the public interest or for the protection of investors, to solicit or to permit the use of his name to solicit any proxy or consent or authorization in respect of any security (other than an exempted security) registered pursuant to Section 12.

   b. **Rules adopted by the S.E.C.** Under the authority given by section 14 of the Act, the S.E.C. has adopted several rules for the regulation of proxy solicitation. These rules prescribe a disclosure document—the proxy statement—that a solicitor generally must furnish to each person solicited before or at the time of solicitation.

      1) **Disclosure required.** Rule 14a-3, in conjunction with Schedule 14A, prescribes the contents and the format of the proxy statement and the annual report that must precede it. Rule 14a-4 governs the contents and the format of the proxy itself.

      2) **Contested elections.** Rule 14a-7 requires the issuer to either furnish the insurgents with an accurate, up-to-date list of shareholders or mail the insurgents' proxy solicitation materials (at the insurgents' expense). Rule 14a-11 requires every participant in the contested elec-

tion, including anyone contributing $500 or more, to file a disclosure statement.

3)   **Shareholder proposals.** Rule 14a-8 requires management to include certain proposals submitted by shareholders in its own proxy solicitation materials and to place these proposals on the agenda of the meeting for a vote.

4)   **Prohibition on "fraud."** Rule 14a-9 prohibits "fraud" in connection with proxy solicitations in a manner analogous to rule 10b-5.

2.   **Communications to Which Rules Apply.**

a.   **Solicitations to which rules apply.** Rule 14a-1 defines "solicit" and "solicitation" to include:

(i)   Any request for a proxy, whether or not accompanied by or included in a form of proxy;

(ii)   Any request to execute or not to execute, or to revoke, a proxy; or

(iii) The furnishing of a form of proxy or other communication to security holders under circumstances reasonably calculated to result in the procurement, withholding, or revocation of a proxy.

This language is so broad, it would probably reach a telephone call from one shareholder to another to suggest attendance at a shareholders' meeting to vote against a stock option plan for executives. If so interpreted, the rule would aggravate, rather than ameliorate, the problems shareholders face in taking collective action. It might also raise serious First Amendment concerns. Rule 14a-2 mitigates, but does not eliminate, these problems. It exempts certain communications from all of the proxy rules except the prohibition on "fraud." Exempt communications include: (i) certain solicitations of 10 or fewer holders; (ii) impartial requests by a record owner to the beneficial owners requesting a proxy; and (iii) "advice by any person to any other person with whom the advisor has a business relationship" if the advisor communicates in the ordinary course of business, receives no payment from a proxy solicitor for giving the advice, and discloses to the shareholder any significant relationship with the corporation.

b.   **The proxy rules apply to solicitations of written shareholder consents.**

3.   **Reform of the Nomination and Election Process.** In a 2003 staff report, the S.E.C.'s Division of Corporate Finance labeled two considerations fundamental in proposing any shareholder access rule: (i) when the rule may be used and (ii) by whom. The division argued that, if the S.E.C. made availability of the

rule depend on triggering events, then the triggering events should relate to evidence of ineffectiveness in the proxy process.

4. **What Must Be Disclosed.**

   a. **Depends on context.** Under rule 14a-3, Schedule 14A dictates the contents of the required disclosure, and Schedule 14A provides that what must be disclosed depends in large part on the context.

   b. **Board elections.** When management solicits proxies to vote for directors, its proxy statement must be preceded or accompanied by an annual report containing prescribed financial information. The statement must disclose information about all transactions and relationships between each director and the corporation and the operation of the board and its committees (Item 6).

   c. **Contested elections.** Rule 14a-11 in conjunction with Schedule 14B requires extensive and intrusive disclosure by insurgents. They must bear the cost of making them whereas management may look to the corporate treasury. Rule 14a-11 requires that insurgents make a Schedule 14B filing five business days prior to a solicitation, which could make it even more difficult for an insurgent to contact like-minded holders.

5. **Filing with the S.E.C.** All documents that a solicitor must deliver to shareholders and many other documents prepared in connection with a solicitation must be filed with the S.E.C.

6. **The Regulatory Costs of Shareholder Activism.** Even if institutional investors gained direct access to the corporate proxy machinery, they might decline to use it for fear that such use would subject them to significantly greater regulation under sections 13(d) or 16(b) of the Securities Exchange Act.

   a. **Management's incentive to delay.** Rule 14a-7(b)(2) reduces this incentive by requiring management to mail an insurgent's proxy materials "prior to the earlier of: (i) a day corresponding to the first date on which the registrant proxy soliciting material was related to security holders in connection with the last annual meeting of shareholders, or (ii) the first day on which solicitation is made on behalf of the registrant."

   b. **Mailing vs. shareholder list.** Insurgents almost always prefer to obtain the list. The list facilitates communication with holders and avoids the need to give management a look at the insurgent's materials before shareholders see them.

7. **Shareholder Proposals.** Rule 14a-8 requires management to include in its proxy solicitation certain proposals made by shareholders. The rule permits management to exclude proposals on a variety of grounds. The two grounds most often

invoked are (c)(5) ("not significantly related to the registrant's business") and (c)(7) ("ordinary business operations").

a. Promotion of causes; ordinary business affairs--

Medical Committee for Human Rights v. Securities and Exchange Commission, 432 F.2d 659 (D.C. Cir. 1970).

Facts. The Medical Committee for Human Rights (P) wrote a letter in 1968 requesting that a resolution be placed in the proxy statement for the 1968 annual meeting of Dow Chemical Company's shareholders advocating that the certificate of incorporation be amended to prohibit the sale of napalm to any buyer using it against human beings. P's main concern was human welfare, but P also expressed concern that napalm manufacture was hurting Dow's business and the company's ability to recruit young people into employment. Dow answered that the proposal was too late for 1968, but in 1969 again refused to permit the resolution to be included. P then suggested that the resolution be changed to one totally banning the manufacture of napalm. Dow still refused. P appealed to the S.E.C. and the S.E.C. indicated that it would take no action if Dow excluded the resolution. P appeals the S.E.C.'s order.

Issues.

(i)   Is a "no-action" response by the S.E.C. appealable to the circuit courts?

(ii)   Is it clear that Dow's management had a proper basis for excluding P's resolution?

Held. (i) Yes. (ii) No. Judgment reversed and remanded.

♦   No-action responses by the S.E.C. are reviewable by the circuit courts. The purpose of section 14 is to protect investors, and many small investors have no other response than to appeal to the S.E.C. (rather than bringing private actions).

♦   Dow's bases for excluding P's proposal are not clear. For that reason the case is remanded.

> There is an exception allowed where the matter relates to the "ordinary" business operations of the company. The S.E.C. simply accepted Dow's argument on this point, with no independent findings. The burden of proof is on the company to show why the proposal is not a proper subject. Delaware law provides that the articles may be amended to change the nature of the company's business.

> There is also an exception where the proposal is based primarily on a shareholder's sponsorship of general political, moral, or social causes. Here, Dow has listed prior such issues that have been presented to it and the S.E.C. has listed no independent basis for its decision. Yet shareholders have the

right under state law to indicate where they wish to have the corporation's assets deployed; also, the company has indicated that it manufactures napalm despite the business results thereof (for political and patriotic reasons). If this is the case, then shareholders have as much right to dispute this company policy as management has to espouse it.

---

b.   Private cause of action/"policy" vs. "implementation"--

Roosevelt v. E.I. Du Pont de Nemours & Co., 958 F.2d 416 (D.C. Cir. 1992).

Facts. Prior to Du Pont's (D's) 1991 annual meeting, Friends of the Earth Oceanic Society submitted a shareholder proposal on behalf of Roosevelt (P). The proposal would have (i) established January 1, 1995, as the latest target date for the phase-out of D's chlorofluorocarbon ("CFC") and halon production; and (ii) required, within six months, detailed reports to shareholders about research and development efforts to develop CFC substitutes and plans for marketing the substitutes. D declined to include the proposal in its proxy materials on the ground that it "relat[ed] to the conduct of [D's] ordinary business operations" and so was excludable under rule 14(a)-8(c)(7). D notified the S.E.C. of its decision as required by rule 14(a)-8(d), and, in due course, the S.E.C. staff issued a "no-action letter," citing the same ground as D had. P sought a temporary restraining order and an injunction.

When the litigation began, D had set a phase-out target date of "as soon as possible, but at least by the year 2000." Subsequently, D changed "the year 2000" to year-end 1995. The trial judge found D's "as soon as possible" policy credible because D had expended more than $240 million to develop CFC substitutes and had shut down the world's largest CFC production plant. The trial judge entered judgment for D and found that, to implement the phase-out safely, D had to use "'business and technical skills' day-to-day that are not meant for shareholder debate and participation."

Issues.

(i)   When a company declines to include a shareholder's proposal in its proxy materials, may the shareholder bring a private action under section 14(a) of the 1934 Act to enforce rule 14(a)-8(c)(7)?

(ii)   Did Roosevelt's proposal deal with matters "relating to the conduct of [D's] ordinary business operations" within the meaning of rule 14(a)-8(c)(7)?

Held. (i) Yes. (ii) Yes. Judgment affirmed.

♦   A shareholder may bring a private action under section 14(a) of the 1934 Act to enforce rule 14(a)-8(c)(7).

In *J.I. Case Co. v. Borak* (*supra*), the Court held that a shareholder could sue privately under section 14(a) to enforce the rule 14a-9 ban on misleading statements in proxy limitations. This rule thus vests a shareholder with the "right to accurate information." This right is in harmony with, but discrete from, a right to be informed that rule 14a-8 affirms. Section 14(a) shelters use of the proxy solicitation process as a means by which stockholders may become informed about management policies and may communicate with each other. Therefore, it provides just as much support to an implied private right of action to enforce rule 14a-8.

The relief sought by a rule 14a-8 plaintiff—a declaration or injunction requiring inclusion of the shareholder's proposal in management's proxy materials—creates none of the causation problems that an award of damages for a rule 14a-9 violation might create (problems about which the court expressed considerable concern in *Virginia Bankshares* (*supra*)).

It would be demonstrably inequitable to shareholders with claims comparable to those previously recognized to deny the right to sue asserted here. [Virginia Bankshares] Such a denial would upset long-standing administrative arrangements and shareholder expectations.

♦   Roosevelt's proposal dealt with matters "relating to the conduct of [D's] ordinary business operations" within the meaning of rule 14(a)-8(c)(7).

The parties agree that CFC production must be phased out, that substitutes must be developed, and that both should be achieved sooner rather than later. D has undertaken to eliminate the products in question by year-end 1995, and has pledged to do so sooner if "possible," a pledge that the trial judge found credible. Given the necessary complexity of the phase-out, D must carry it out safely, using "business and technical skills" day-to-day that are not meant for shareholder debate and participation. The proposal's target date for elimination differs from D's by only one year. In these circumstances, what is at stake is the "implementation of a policy," "the timing for an agreed-upon action." Even the S.E.C. has generally focused on five-year intervals in classifying timing questions as involving "fundamental business strategy" or "long-term goals."

Roosevelt has not shown that the detailed research and development or marketing information she seeks implicates significant policy issues, and not merely implementation arrangements.

Comment. Because of the significance that the court seems to attach to the "size" of the parties' disagreement—here the latest target date for the phase-out of CFCs—the opinion provides little certainty for managers, shareholders, or their lawyers.

---

      c.   **Employment matters, especially discrimination.** Amidst much lobbying, the S.E.C. has flip-flopped on the question of whether employment decisions, especially decisions that might become subject to employment discrimination claims, qualify as "ordinary business" decisions.

      d.   **Shareholder proposals to amend bylaws.** To strengthen the argument that a proposal must be submitted to the shareholders, proponents have taken to framing them as amendments to a corporation's bylaws. In *Brotherhood of Teamsters General Fund v. Fleming Co., Inc.*, 975 P.2d 907 (Okla. 1999), the Oklahoma Supreme Court required submission to the shareholders of a bylaw amendment proposed by a pension fund that would have nullified the corporation's poison pill. The court did observe that Oklahoma law did not expressly authorize a board to adopt a poison pill.

8.   **Anti-Fraud Liability Under Rule 14a-9.**

      a.   **Culpability required.** Courts and commentators have split on the question of whether negligence suffices for liability under rule 14a-9.

      b.   **Standing.** Only a shareholder subject to the allegedly faulty solicitation may sue, but she may sue regardless of how she actually voted.

9.   **Causation.**

      a.   **In suit to enjoin voting of proxies, proof of material misstatement or omission was sufficient causation--**

Mills v. Electric Auto-Lite Co., 396 U.S. 375 (1970).

Facts. Shareholders (Ps) brought a derivative suit to enjoin Electric Auto-Lite Co. (D) from voting proxies it had solicited to approve a merger into Mergenthaler Linotype Co. ("M"). Proxy materials did not disclose that M controlled 54% of D and D's board of directors. The merger was already carried out; suit was to set it aside based on the false or misleading statements in the proxy materials. A two-thirds vote of the shareholders was necessary to approve the merger, so that to approve it the votes of shareholders other than M were required. The district court found that the proxy statements were deficient. The court of appeals agreed but reversed on the question of causation.

Issue. If the plaintiff proves that the proxy solicitation contained materially misleading statements of fact, must the plaintiff also prove that he relied on the contents of the proxy statement and that such reliance caused his injury (*i.e.,* caused the plaintiff to vote as he did)?

Held. No. Judgment vacated and case remanded.

♦   The proxy solicitation omitted material information.

- The defect must be material—*i.e.,* it must have a significant propensity to affect the vote on the issue voted on (that is, it must be considered important by a reasonable shareholder). Where this is shown, it does not also have to be shown that the misleading statement was the cause of the shareholders' voting as they did (*i.e.,* that they relied on it). It must be shown, however, that the proxy solicitation was necessary to the transaction that resulted in the detriment to Ps.

- Section 29 of the Act makes void all contracts made in violation of the Act. But this does not mean that all such contracts are unenforceable. Courts of equity look at all of the circumstances in determining the appropriate remedy (and one factor in rescission is the fairness of the terms of the merger). Recovering damages is also a possibility and depends on whether actual damage can be shown. The case must be remanded to the district court for findings on these issues.

- A successful plaintiff in a case of violation of section 14a is entitled to reasonable costs and attorneys' fees when the action is brought on behalf of a class and benefits all members of the class. This is a court-made rule. The class is all shareholders of the defendant. The benefit is the exposure of the deceit practiced on all of the shareholders.

Comment. The real issue here is whether a court will review the "fairness" of the transaction. The argument was made that, to show causation, the plaintiff had to show that the disclosure of the material fact would have changed the shareholder vote and therefore the court could look at the fairness of the merger transaction (since presumably, if it was fair, then the shareholders would have approved it anyway, despite the nondisclosure). The court here held that it will not look into fairness—that even if a transaction is "fair," this does not excuse materially misleading statements in the proxy materials. Hence, "materially" misleading statements are enough for a violation where the proxy solicitation was necessary to approve the transaction. ***Actual causation need not be shown*** (D argued that since the transaction was fair, there was no causation). In effect, the court indicates that it will leave to the shareholders the issue of approving or disapproving the transaction. The "fairness" of the transaction, however, will be considered in determining the measure of damages for the violation.

---

b.   **No cause of action for shareholders whose approval was not required--**

Virginia Bankshares, Inc. v. Sandberg, 501 U.S. 1083 (1991).

Facts. *See supra.*

Issue. When a transaction does not require the votes of minority shareholders, can one of them prove damages compensable under section 14(a) if her approval is solicited?

Held. Judgment reversed. Such statements may qualify as "materially misleading" within the meaning of section 14(a), but a member of a class of minority shareholders whose votes are not required to approve a transaction cannot prove damages compensable under section 14(a).

♦ To prove damages compensable under section 14(a) a plaintiff must establish the "essential link" between the proxy solicitation and the transaction as required by *Mills v. Electric Auto-Lite Co. (supra)*.

♦ That FABI and VBI may not have proceeded with the planned merger absent approval by the minority shareholders should not suffice as this "essential link." Permitting it to suffice would pose the same threats that prompted the Court in *Blue Chip Stamps v. Manor Drug Stores* (*supra*) to limit the availability of the rule 10b-5 cause of action: "speculative claims and procedural intractability. . . . Causation would turn on inferences about what the corporate directors would have thought and done without the minority shareholder approval," thus requiring a trial in every case. Reliable evidence would seldom exist. Well-counseled directors would make statements about plans to proceed regardless of minority shareholder approval. Plaintiffs would use discovery to search for conversations at odds with official pronouncements, in hopes of finding support for ex post facto guesses about how much heat the directors would have stood in the absence of such approval.

♦ Minority shareholder approval might have protected the merger from voidability (and the Bank's directors from liability) due to the undisclosed conflict of interest, but that does not suffice as the "essential link" here because, under Virginia law, such approval provides no such protection if secured without disclosure of the conflict or with materially misleading statements.

Concurrence and dissent (Stevens, Marshall, JJ.). (Concurring in Parts I and II of the Court's opinion (addressing the materiality issue) but dissenting from Part III.) Because the jury found the merger unfair, the interest in providing a remedy is stronger than in *Mills*, while the interest in avoiding speculative controversy is the same, and, in any event, can be taken into account at the remedy stage. That management found it necessary—whether for "legal or practical reasons"—to solicit proxies from minority shareholders to obtain their approval of the merger should suffice as the essential link required by *Mills*.

Concurrence and dissent (Kennedy, Marshall, Blackmun, Stevens, JJ.). (Concurring in Parts I and II of the Court's opinion but dissenting from Part III.) Those who lack the strength to vote down a proposal have more need of disclosure. The voting process involves not only casting ballots but also the formulation and withdrawal of proposals, the minority's right to block a vote through court action or the threat of adverse consequences, or the negotiation of an increase in price. The likelihood that causation exists supports elimination of any requirement that the plaintiff prove the material misstatement or omission caused the transaction to go forward when it otherwise would have been halted or voted down. The merit of the essential link formulation is that it rests upon the likelihood of causation and eliminates the difficulty of proof, which, if anything, is greater where the minority lacks sufficient votes to defeat the proposal. Any causation inquiry under section 14(a) requires a court to consider a hypothetical universe in which adequate disclosure is made.

---

    c.   **What if the suit seeks damages?** Even if the proxy statement contains a material misrepresentation or omission, the plaintiff may find it very difficult to show that she suffered any loss as a result of it.

10. **Remedies.** Damage judgments may prove elusive because of the problem of proving that the defective statement caused the loss. Injunctions may not be forthcoming because judges may worry about the harm that might be done if a transaction is held up or undone. The S.E.C. may be more successful than private plaintiffs in securing injunctive relief because some courts have held that the S.E.C. need not show irreparable harm, but only likelihood of future violations.

VII. ORGANIZATION FOR THE SMALLER ENTERPRISE: PARTNER-SHIPS, CLOSE CORPORATIONS, LIMITED LIABILITY COMPANIES, AND OTHER NON-CORPORATE FORMS

A. INTRODUCTION

The principals of relatively small enterprises often find that the corporate organizational form does not suit them nearly as well as the general partnership, limited liability partnership ("LLP"), limited partnership, or limited liability company ("LLC") forms. But courts increasingly permit people to adapt the corporate form, in particular its decisionmaking rules, to their partnership-like needs (while sometimes imposing partnership-like fiduciary duties on corporate officers and directors). And many states have enacted special "close corporations" statutes providing for different rules and, in some instances, more flexibility (at least in theory).

B. PARTNERSHIPS

When two or more people conduct a business as co-owners, a court will usually treat them as partners even if they did not so consider themselves, with each "partner" possessing the power to bind the business and bearing personal liability for its debts. In most states, some version of the Uniform Partnership Act ("UPA") governs partnerships. In a few states, the Revised Uniform Partnership Act of 1993 ("RUPA"), which makes some major changes in the UPA, governs. A partnership is a tax-reporting but not a tax-paying entity.

1. The Nature of Partnership: Aggregate or Entity?

a. **Generally.** It is often convenient to refer to a business by its trade name, as if it were an "entity" separate from the individuals involved in it. Some sections of the Uniform Partnership Act do likewise, but many refer to a partnership business as an aggregation of the partners. Whether the law should treat a partnership as a "jural entity," like a corporation, or as an aggregation of the partners may depend on what is really at stake. For most purposes, the Revised Uniform Partnership Act seems to suggest "entity" treatment.

b. **Impact of a change in partners on obligations of third parties--**

Fairway Development v. Title Insurance Co. of Minnesota, 621 F. Supp. 120 (N.D. Ohio 1985).

Facts. Fairway Development (P), a three-person partnership formed to acquire and develop real estate, bought title insurance from Title Insurance Co. of Minnesota (D). Two of the partners later sold their interests to the remaining partner and a third party who continued and expanded the business. Subsequently, D refused to honor the terms of the insurance policy. P sued for breach of contract and moved for summary judgment. D also moved for summary judgment on the ground that the partnership with which it had contracted had dissolved upon the departure of the two partners.

Issue. Absent an agreement, does a party contracting with a partnership remain liable on the contract after a change in the identity of the partners?

Held. No. D's motion for summary judgment granted.

♦ Ohio's version of the Uniform Partnership Act provides that a change in the identity of the partners dissolves their partnership even if one of them continues the business. A party that contracted with the original partnership does not remain liable to the new one.

Comment. Many, perhaps most, courts would have reached the opposite conclusion under the UPA. Section 201 of the RUPA requires the opposite conclusion.

---

2. **Formation: When Is an Association a Partnership?** People interested in associating in a business often wish to form the relation of co-owners, which the law views as partnership. Under both the UPA and the RUPA, associates may do this without taking any formal steps. But it is not always easy to distinguish this relationship from others like employer/employee or creditor/borrower, especially if the "employee" receives a share of the "employer's" profits or if the "creditor" possesses unusual control over the "borrower's" business decisions. Thus, disputes may arise about whether the law of partnership governs a business relationship or whether business associates ought to be treated as partners for the purpose of some other law. RUPA section 202 does not appear to make any significant change in this portion of the UPA or to reduce the attendant uncertainty.

a. **The approach of the Uniform Partnership Act.** Section 7 provides:

   1) Except as provided by section 16, persons who are not partners as to each other are not partners as to third persons.

   2) Joint tenancy, tenancy in common, tenancy by the entireties, joint property, common property, or part ownership does not of itself es-

tablish a partnership, whether such co-owners do or do not share any profits made by the use of the property.

3) The sharing of gross returns does not of itself establish a partnership, whether or not the persons sharing them have a joint or common right or interest in any property from which the returns are derived.

4) The receipt by a person of a share of the profits of a business is prima facie evidence that he is a partner in the business, but no such inference shall be drawn if such profits were received in payment:

   a) As a debt by installments or otherwise,

   b) As wages of an employee or rent to a landlord,

   c) As an annuity to a widow or representative of a deceased partner,

   d) As interest on a loan though the amount of payment varies with the profits of the business, or

   e) As the consideration for the sale of goodwill of a business or other property by installments or otherwise.

b. **Profit sharing + "intent" = partnership--**

Vohland v. Sweet, 433 N.E.2d 860 (Ind. Ct. App. 1982).

Facts. In 1956, Sweet (P) began working for Paul Vohland's (D's) father as an hourly employee in the father's nursery business. When the father retired in 1963, D took over the business, refocused it on landscape gardening, and agreed to pay P 20% of the net profits as a "commission." D handled all of the finances and books and most of the sales. He borrowed money solely in his own name for business purposes, including the purchase of his siblings' interest in the business, operating expenses, bid bonds, motor vehicles, taxes, and purchases of real estate. P managed the physical aspects of the nursery and supervised the care of the nursery stock and the performance of the contracts for the customers. No partnership income tax returns were filed. D and his wife filed a joint return on which was reported on Schedule C, under D's name, the revenues from the business and the money paid to P as an expense. P filed as a self-employed salesman.

The business necessarily depleted the nursery stock. D claimed that he was contractually bound to replenish it, but P disputed this claim. Replenishing the stock required planting and maintenance. The cost of these activities was deducted from "profits" before calculating P's 20%. According to P, the two talked about this and D assured P that D "was going to take . . . [P] in and that . . . [P would have] a piece of the action." Although D denied that this conversation had taken place, he acknowledged that P had refused to permit a similar deduction for a truck unless P's name appeared on the title.

In 1979, P sued for dissolution of an alleged partnership and for an accounting. The trial court awarded P $58,733, which was 20% of the value (according to P) of the nursery stock purchased with earnings. D appeals.

Issue. Were the parties partners in the landscape gardening business?

Held. Yes. Judgment affirmed.

♦ Sharing profits is prima facie evidence of partnership.

♦ One who furnishes skill and labor in lieu of money or property still may be a partner.

♦ The agreement, conversation, and other conduct of the parties (resolving factual disputes in favor of P, who prevailed at trial) support the conclusion that the parties intended to form a partnership in the sense that they intended to do the things that constitute a partnership. While P's 20% was characterized as a "commission," these non-lawyer parties may well have used this term to refer to a share of the profits.

♦ The evidence also supports the finding that "profits" included payments for replenishing nursery stock.

---

c. **Creditor with unusual control--**

Lupien v. Malsbenden, 477 A.2d 746 (Me. 1984).

Facts. In March 1980, Lupien (P) entered into a written agreement with Cragin, doing business as York Motor Mart ("York"), for the construction of a kit car. The purchase order and bill of sale, signed by Cragin, identified the seller as York Motor Mart. Malsbenden (D) had invested $85,000 in the kit car segment of York's business (Cragin carried on an unrelated car repair business at York). D characterized this investment as a no-interest loan. Much of the loan took the form of day-to-day payments for kits and other parts, equipment, and the salary of at least one employee. Repayments of principal were due on the sale of kits rather than at fixed times.

After P signed the contract, he visited York Motor Mart an average of once or twice a week to check on the progress of his kit car. During these visits P generally dealt with D because Cragin was not present. On one such visit D required P to sign over ownership of P's pickup truck as payment for the balance due under the contract. D provided P with a rental car, and later a "demo," to use while waiting for the kit car. After discovering that the "demo" belonged to a third party who had entrusted it to York for resale, D bought it for P's use.

D participated in the control of York Motor Mart on a day-to-day basis, opening it each morning, ordering parts and equipment. After Cragin "disappeared" in May, D had physical control of York's premises. He continued to dispose of assets there through the time of trial (1983). When P failed to receive a new kit car as provided in the contract, P brought a breach of contract claim against D as a partner of Cragin. The trial court found for P.

Issue. Were Cragin and D partners in the business?

Held. Yes. Judgment affirmed.

♦ Vis-a-vis a third party, D's financial interest in York combined with his participation in its day-to-day business made him a partner even if he and Cragin considered themselves creditor and borrower.

---

3. **Powers of Partners.**

   a. **Powers of an agent.** An agent's actions bind the principal if they were (i) requested by the principal or (ii) reasonably understood to be necessary to do that which the principal wanted done. In legalese, the agent has ***actual authority*** to engage in such actions. This authority is ***express*** when the principal requested the actions and ***implied*** otherwise.

   Even if an agent lacks actual authority, her actions may still bind the principal. They will bind the principal if the principal has manifested to a relevant third party that the agent is acting on the principal's behalf and the third party does not know any better. Again in legalese, the agent has ***apparent authority*** to engage in such actions. Simply putting the agent in a particular position may constitute a "manifestation"—even if the relevant third party is unaware that the person with whom she is dealing is an agent.

   b. **A partner's agency powers.**

      1) **Mutual agency.** UPA section 9(1) provides for mutual agency in a partnership: "Every partner is an agent of the partnership for the purpose of its business, and the act of every partner, including the execution in the partnership name of any instrument for apparently carrying on in the usual way the business of the partnership of which he is a member, binds the partnership, unless the partner so acting has in fact no authority to act for the partnership in the particular matter, and the person with whom he is dealing has knowledge of the fact that he has no such authority." Courts have interpreted section 9(1) as diminishing the need for written authority even when the Statute of Frauds would otherwise require it.

2) **Limitation on agent's powers.** UPA section 9(2) limits a partner's agency powers: "An act of a partner which is not apparently for the carrying on of the business of the partnership in the usual way does not bind the partnership unless authorized by the other partners." Section 9(3) generally requires unanimous consent for a partner to engage in certain extraordinary transactions, like selling all of the key assets of the partnership's business. Under RUPA section 303, partners may limit the power of one or more partners by filing a "statement of partnership authority" with the secretary of state, but section 303(e) provides that, other than in real property transactions, "a person not a partner is not deemed to know of a limitation on the authority of a partner merely because the limitation is contained in a filed statement."

4. **Liabilities of Partners.** UPA section 15 makes all partners "jointly and severally" liable for all tort liabilities "chargeable to the partnership," but only "jointly" liable for "all other debts and obligations of the partnership." *Note:* Under section 13, a partnership bears liability for the "wrongful act or omission of any partner acting in the ordinary course of the business of the partnership." Between the partners each bears responsibility for the partnership's losses in proportion to the partner's share of the profits. The impact of the tort/contract distinction is largely procedural; in some states a plaintiff seeking a judgment on a contract claim against all partners must join them. RUPA section 306 makes each partner jointly and severally liable for all claims against the partnership, and section 307 permits claimants to name the partnership as the defendant.

5. **Partnership Governance.** UPA section 18 provides:

   (g) No person can become a member of a partnership without the consent of all the partners.

   (h) Any difference arising as to ordinary matters connected with the partnership business may be decided by a majority of the partners; but no act in contravention of any agreement between the partners may be done rightfully without the consent of all the partners.

   Absent an agreement to the contrary, each partner is entitled to an equal share of the partnership profits.

6. **Fiduciary Duties.**

   a. **Scope of fiduciary duty--**

Meinhard v. Salmon, 249 N.Y. 458, 164 N.E. 545 (1928).

Facts. Gerry leased a hotel to Salmon (D) for 20 years; D was obligated to spend $200,000 in improvements. Shortly thereafter D entered a joint venture with Meinhard (P) for P to pay one-half of the money needed to alter and manage the property, receiving 40% of the net profits for five years and 50% thereafter. D had the sole power to manage the property; D's interest in the lease from Gerry was never assigned to P. Gerry owned a substantial amount of adjoining property and near the end of the lease term tried to put together a deal to level all of the property and put up one large building. Failing that, Gerry approached D, and they entered a lease on all of the ground (renewable for a period up to 80 years), eventually calling for the destruction of the hotel and the building of a new, larger building. P found out about the new lease and demanded that it be held in trust as an asset of their joint venture. The lower court held that P was entitled to a half interest in the new lease and must assume responsibility for half of the obligations. D appeals the judgment.

Issue. Does the new lease come within D's fiduciary obligation to his joint venture partner as a joint venture "opportunity"?

Held. Yes. Judgment for P affirmed.

♦ Joint venture partners have the highest obligation of loyalty to their partners. This includes an obligation not to usurp opportunities that are incidents of the joint venture. The duty is even higher of a managing coadventurer.

♦ There was a close nexus between the joint venture and the opportunity that was brought to the manager of the joint venture, since the opportunity was essentially an extension and enlargement of the subject matter of the old one.

♦ Since D was to control the project, he should receive 51 shares of the corporation that holds the lease on the new project, and P should have 49 shares.

Dissent (Andrews, J.). This is not a general partnership. It is a joint venture, entered into by D to get financing for his project. There was no expectancy of a renewal of the lease, and no intention that P be part of D's business forever. He, for example, never received an assigned interest in D's lease with Gerry; and he could not have renewed the lease had there been a renewal provision. It was a limited venture for a specific term. So the new opportunity was not an extension of the old one.

---

b. **RUPA.** The RUPA purports to limit the fiduciary duties of partners and appears to make at least some of them unwaivable. [Note the italicized portions.]

Section 404. General standards of partner's conduct.

(a) The *only* fiduciary duties a partner owes to the partnership and the other partners are the duty of loyalty and the duty of care set forth in subsections (b) and (c).

(b) A partner's *duty of loyalty* to the partnership and the other partners is *limited* to the following:

(1) To account to the partnership and hold as trustee for it any property, profit, or benefit derived by the partner in the conduct and winding up of the partnership business or derived from a use by the partner of partnership property, including the appropriation of a partnership opportunity.

(2) To refrain from dealing with the partnership in the conduct or winding up of the partnership business as, or on behalf of, a party having an interest adverse to the partnership; and

(3) To refrain from competing with the partnership in the conduct of the partnership business before the dissolution of the partnership.

(c) A partner's *duty of care* to the partnership and the other partners in the conduct and winding up of the partnership business is *limited* to refraining from engaging in grossly negligent or reckless conduct, intentional misconduct, or a knowing violation of law.

(d) A partner shall discharge the duties to the partnership and the other partners under this [Act] or under the partnership agreement and exercise any rights consistently with the obligations of good faith and fair dealing.

(e) A partner *does not violate* a duty or obligation under this [Act] or under the partnership agreement *merely because the partner's conduct furthers the partner's own interest.*

(f) A partner may lend money to and transact other business with the partnership, and as to each loan or transaction, the rights and obligations of a partner are the same as those of a person who is not a partner, subject to other applicable law.

[Emphasis added]

Section 103. Effects of partnership agreement; nonwaivable provisions.

(b) The partnership agreement *may not*:

(1) *Vary the rights and duties under Section 105 except to* eliminate the duty to provide copies of statements to all of the partners;

(2) Unreasonably restrict the right of access to books and records under Section 403(b);

(3) *Eliminate the duty of loyalty* under Section 404(b) or 603(b)(3), *but*:

(i) The partnership agreement *may identify specific types or categories of activities that do not violate the duty of loyalty, if not manifestly unreasonable;* or

(ii) all of the partners or a number of percentage specified in the partnership agreement may authorize or ratify, after full disclosure of all material facts, a specific act or transaction that otherwise would violate the duty of loyalty;

(4) *Unreasonably reduce the duty of care* under Section 404(c) or 603(b)(3);

(5) Eliminate the obligation of good faith and fair dealing under Section 404(d), *but* the partnership agreement *may prescribe the standards by which the performance of the obligation is to be measured, if the standards are not manifestly unreasonable.*

[Emphasis added]

7. **Partnership Dissolution.**

a. **Process of ending the relationship of partners.** This process has three conceptual stages: "dissolution," "winding up," and "termination." Dissolution begins when a partner ceases her association in the carrying on of the partnership's business. Dissolution may trigger a number of consequences, the most important being a winding up. Winding up may take the form of a liquidation, but it may also take the form of a buyout of the dissociating partner's interest, in which case the remaining partners carry on the business. The partners can provide for this outcome expressly, or otherwise avoid a winding up by entering into a continuation agreement. In many jurisdictions, however, the partners cannot avoid a dissolution and the other consequences that a dissolution triggers.

b. **RUPA.** The RUPA uses the same terms, but defines them differently. For example, it defines "dissolution" as the termination of the business. The RUPA does not significantly change the substance of this aspect of the UPA, although it does make explicit that any "dissociation" will trigger either a buy-out of the partner's interest in the firm or a termination and winding up of the business.

C. CLOSE CORPORATIONS

1. Introduction.

a. **Major attributes.** The major attributes of close corporations include: few shareholders, all of whom ordinarily take an active role in the business; shares not traded publicly and usually not at all; typically, scope of operations and amount of invested capital limited.

b. **Similarity to partnership.** Close corporation shareholders prefer to deal with each other like partners. Because they usually work with one another daily, they almost always want to have control over who becomes a decisionmaker in the business. Because they usually look to the business for their livelihoods and cannot easily sell their interests, they usually prefer more say in management than they would have under the traditional corporate approach of majority rule. Of course, the more say each shareholder has, the more likely is deadlock. As a result, close corporation shareholders have just as much interest in providing for dissolution as do partners.

c. **Close corporation shareholders' preferences and the law.** Initially, the devices and procedures adopted by close corporation shareholders met with judicial hostility. This hostility gradually ebbed, at least in cases where the challenged device or procedure had had no significant adverse impact on a third party. In the past 30 years, about one-half of the states have enacted statutes authorizing at least some of the devices and procedures preferred by close corporation shareholders. Defining the close corporation for the purpose of such statutes has presented a significant issue on which the various state legislatures have split. Some of these statutes require a formal election appearing in the articles.

2. Restrictions on Transfer of Shares.

a. **Why close corporation shareholders want restrictions on transfer of shares.** The principal reasons that close corporation shareholders want restrictions on the transfer of shares include: (i) to guarantee a say in the choice of their fellow workers and decisionmakers; (ii) to preserve the initial allocation of control; or (iii) to secure favorable treatment under a close corporation statute, the income tax laws, or the securities law. On the flip side, these shareholders may want to provide themselves some liquidity with a buy out provision.

b. **Forms.** Transfer restrictions range from prohibition to consent to a right of first refusal.

c. **Enforceability.** Generally, the more onerous the restriction, the less likely it is that a court will enforce it or interpret it broadly.

1)   Disparity between option price and current value--

Allen v. Biltmore Tissue Corp., 2 N.Y.2d 534, 141 N.E.2d 812, 161 N.Y.S.2d 418 (1957).

Facts. Biltmore (D) provided, in its bylaws, that if a shareholder wished to sell his shares, the corporation or other shareholders had a 60-day option to purchase them at the price for which the corporation originally sold them. If the shareholder died, the option period was 90 days. Kaplan, a shareholder, was considering selling his shares and wrote the corporation asking what price it would pay him for them. Five days later, he died. Letters testamentary were issued 53 days after his death. Kaplan's executors (Ps) contacted D approximately three and one-half months after his death. The attorney for the executors asked D to issue a new stock certificate in the name of the estate. D's directors decided to exercise the purchase option and informed the attorney that they would pay an amount somewhat higher than the original price of the shares, but not as high as market value. Ps brought this action to compel D to issue a new certificate. They contended that the purchase option was an unreasonable restraint on the alienability of Kaplan's property. D filed a counterclaim for specific performance of the estate's alleged obligation to reconvey the stock to D. The trial court found for D. The appellate court reversed and found for Ps. D appeals.

Issue. Is a bylaw valid which allows the corporation an option to repurchase shares from its shareholders at the price for which it sold them?

Held. Yes. Judgment of the appellate court reversed and that of the trial court reinstated.

◆   If a bylaw made it impossible for a shareholder to sell to anyone except the corporation at whatever price it wished to pay, this court would strike it down as illegal. In this case, D's right was limited; it had to purchase within 90 days. If it did not, the shareholder's estate could sell to whom, and for what price, it desired.

◆   Confusion often arises around stock repurchase options because of the contract nature of the option, which puts a binding obligation on the stock purchaser, and the property nature of the stock, which militates against restraints on alienation. But it is clear that the law will allow reasonable restrictions on alienation so long as they do not amount to prohibitions against it.

◆   The appellate court thought the price specified in the bylaw was unfair. If we accepted the appellate court's reasoning, we would seriously damage the ability of close corporations to restrict their membership in the way partnerships restrict theirs. We recognize a social utility in this characteristic of close corporations and do not wish to impair it by throwing every pricing formula other than fair market value into question. When the shareholder purchased the stock, he and the corporation both agreed to be bound by the price formula and the other restrictions of the option.

Comment. Although the court does not specifically say so, its decision implies that the option period did not begin to run against the corporation until it received notice that a legal representative of the shareholder's estate had been appointed.

---

2) Absolute restrictions invalid--

Rafe v. Hindin, 29 A.D.2d 481, 288 N.Y.S.2d 662 (1968), *aff'd*, 23 N.Y.2d 759, 244 N.E.2d 469, 296 N.Y.S.2d 955 (1968).

Facts. P and D formed a corporation for the purpose of developing a parcel of real estate. Each had a stock certificate for 50% of the shares. The certificate, on its face, was not transferable without the consent of the other shareholder. Four years later, P was in financial difficulty and found a buyer for the stock at $44,000. P offered the stock to D for that price. D refused to buy the stock and refused to consent to its transfer. P sued to have the restriction canceled. The trial court denied P's motion for summary judgment.

Issue. Is an absolute restriction on the transfer of the stock of a for-profit corporation invalid as against public policy?

Held. Yes. The order denying P's motion for summary judgment is reversed.

- ♦ In a small business corporation, due to the personal nature of the relationship involved, we have held that it is permissible to restrict transfer of the stock without the consent of the shareholders so long as it is stated that consent will not be unreasonably withheld.

- ♦ Some courts have struck down absolute restrictions on transfers on the ground that they are a restraint on alienation. Since, in this state, stock is personal—not real— property, we cannot follow this line of cases.

- ♦ We hold that the restriction involved is unreasonable and against public policy. It could allow someone in D's position to buy the stock at whatever price he chose.

- ♦ D contends that it was orally agreed between P and D that consent would not be unreasonably withheld. (D claimed he reasonably withheld consent.) Such parol evidence is inadmissible.

---

3) Factors considered by the courts.
In determining whether to uphold a restriction or transfer of shares, the court will consider factors such as the corporation's size, the degree of restraint, the duration of

restriction, the method for determining price, the procedure used to adopt restriction, the relationship to pursuing corporate objectives, and the risk of harm presented by a hostile shareholder.

    4)   **State regulation.** Many states now regulate transfer restrictions and buy out provisions, but do so in a variety of ways.

3.   **Special Agreements Allocating Authority.**

    a.   **Shareholder agreements respecting election of directors.**

        1)   **Agreement to secure investment enforceable--**

E.K. Buck Retail Stores v. Harkert, 157 Neb. 867, 62 N.W.2d 288 (1954).

Facts. Harkert (D) was in financial difficulty and his company owed money to Buck (P). P, in exchange for stock in D's company and an agreement, canceled the debt and gave the company $53,625. The agreement called for P and D to both have the right to appoint two directors (there was a total of four directors). P sued to enforce the agreement. The trial court found for P and D appeals.

Issue. May shareholders agree between themselves as to the appointing of corporate directors?

Held. Yes. Judgment affirmed.

♦   D contends that public policy prohibits a shareholder from bargaining away his right to vote for directors. D errs.

♦   Applicable law prevails over private agreements between shareholders. We find no law that makes this particular agreement improper.

♦   The provisions of this agreement were for the benefit of the corporation. It was not invalid per se since there was sufficient consideration to support it (canceling the debt and putting in over $50,000). Following this agreement the business operated successfully for over 11 years. It was implied in the agreement that this agreement would be valid only so long as P held stock in the corporation.

---

        2)   **Arbitrator to break deadlocks--**

Ringling v. Ringling Brothers-Barnum & Bailey Combined Shows, Inc., 29 Del. Ch. 318, 49 A.2d 603 (1946).

Facts. Ringling (P) owned 315 shares, Haley (D) 315, and North 370 of Ringling Brothers-Barnum & Bailey Combined Shows, Inc. P and D entered an agreement for 10 years that they would act jointly in exercising their voting rights and that, if they could not agree, the decision would be made by an arbitrator. At a shareholder meeting, they could not agree and D voted his shares rather than following the direction of the arbitrator. P sues for specific performance of the contract.

Issue. May two of the three shareholders of a corporation agree that they shall vote together and that if they cannot agree an arbitrator shall decide how they should vote?

Held. Yes. Judgment for P.

♦   The agreement has sufficient consideration in the mutual promises.

♦   The agreement is not a voting trust, since the shareholders vote their shares, and only give up this right to an arbitrator if they cannot agree.

♦   Such shareholder agreements are not invalid due to public policy, if the agreement has valid objectives and is not part of a fraudulent scheme.

♦   The theory is that an irrevocable proxy (a proxy coupled with an interest) has been given. The willing party becomes the agent of the resisting party for the purpose of casting the vote.

----

3)   On appeal--

Ringling Bros.-Barnum & Bailey Combined Shows v. Ringling, 29 Del. Ch. 610, 53 A.2d 441 (1947).

Facts. *See* preceding case. D appeals the lower court decision.

Issue. *See* preceding case.

Held. Judgment for P reversed as to remedy given by the trial court.

♦   The agreement did not provide that on violation either party could vote the shares of the other, or that the arbitrator could vote them. It simply provided that in case of disagreement the arbitrator would make a decision as to how the votes should be made. If one party refused to vote in accord with the arbitrator, it simply means that these votes should not be counted. Thus, the six persons elected directors by the votes of the other two shareholders should hold office, and the remaining director should be elected at the next shareholder meeting.

Comment. The two major issues associated with pooling agreements are: (i) whether such agreements are void as against public policy, and (ii) if they are valid, how and against whom will they be enforced. Courts have split in the situation represented by the *Ringling Brothers* cases. Some have indicated that a vote cannot be split from its shares and have refused to uphold such agreements.

> **b.** **Voting trusts.** In the case of a voting trust the owner of the stock transfers legal title to a trustee who, since he has legal title, has the right to vote the stock. The agreement must be in writing and is usually irrevocable during the duration of the agreement.
>
> **1)** **Illegal voting trusts--**

Abercrombie v. Davies, 36 Del. Ch. 371, 130 A.2d 338 (1957).

Facts. Davies and nine other oil companies formed a corporation (American) to develop foreign oil rights. Davies and several of the other companies then formed a committee of eight persons (Ds); together, they owned 54% of the stock and could elect eight directors. These companies agreed that Ds could determine how their shares would be voted; each shareholder transferred to Ds endorsed blank stock certificates, together with written irrevocable proxies for a period of 10 years. The stock was placed in escrow. There was cumulative voting on the shares. The transfers of the stock were not made on the corporation's books. Ds' decisions were made by a vote of seven out of eight Ds. An arbitrator was authorized to break any deadlocks. At any time, Ds could vote to change the arrangement to a voting trust. Then Ds elected themselves directors. The plan worked until two Ds broke the agreement. When Davies threatened to enforce the agreement, shareholders of the corporation who were not part of the arrangement (Ps) sued to invalidate the agreement. The lower court found for Ds on the basis that it was a valid voting agreement since the group had advanced funds to the corporation based on the validity of the voting agreement (an "interest"), and irrevocable proxies were necessary if the agreement was to work. Since the stock ownership did not pass to Ds and Ds still could be removed by the shareholders who appointed them, the lower court held that there was no voting trust.

Issue. Is this agreement a legal voting trust?

Held. No. Judgment for Ps.

◆ Most of the elements of a voting trust are present here. It makes no difference that the shareholders had no intent to create a voting trust, nor that the ownership of the shares was not actually transferred on the books of the corporation.

◆ Here, the stock certificates with irrevocable proxies were transferred to Ds. Also, although the shareholders could remove Ds from the committee, the shareholders parted with control of their votes, since seven out of eight votes controlled the vote of all Ds. Thus, all of the elements of a voting trust were present (divorce of voting rights from ownership, vote transferred to an agent, a period of 10 years, and the object of the agreement being to gain control over the corporation).

♦ The agreement did not comply with the statutory requirements for a valid voting trust. The stock was not registered in the names of the trustees, and the agreement was not filed with the corporation's office. Thus, a secret trust was created, which is unlawful.

---

2) Creating a new class of nonvoting stock does not create a voting trust--

Lehrman v. Cohen, 43 Del. Ch. 222, 222 A.2d 800 (1966).

Facts. The Cohen family (Ds) and Lehrman (P) owned equal voting power in the Giant Food Corporation (each owning different classes of common stock). Each elected two directors to a four-person board. At the time P acquired all of the AL class of stock, Ds (who owned the AC class of stock) insisted that a new class of stock be created (one share of AD voting stock, with no dividends or redemption rights but with the power to elect a fifth director) in order to break the voting deadlock. The AD stock was issued to Danzansky, the company lawyer, who elected himself the fifth director. Cohen then resigned as president, and Danzansky was elected president at a stockholders meeting (AC and AD stock voting in favor) with a large salary and stock options and an employment contract. Danzansky then resigned as a director and elected another person in his place. The board then ratified his election as president and the employment contract (the AL directors voting against it). P (owner of the AL stock) then sued on the basis that: (i) the AD stock arrangement was an illegal voting trust since in effect it gave a portion of the AL and AC stock voting power (10% from each) to AD (like a trustee) and the AD stock had no other rights except voting, and (ii) that stock having only voting rights but no other rights is illegal under state law. The lower court granted summary judgment for Ds; P appeals.

Issue. Does creation of a new class of voting stock (without any other rights) create an unlawful voting trust?

Held. No. Judgment for Ds affirmed.

♦ The first test for a voting trust is whether the voting right is separated from the other incidents of ownership. AC and AL owners retained all of their rights.

♦ The rationale of the voting trust statute is to avoid secret uncontrolled combinations of shareholders from acquiring voting control of the corporation. This is prevented by requiring that voting trusts be disclosed to the corporation. P's rationale is not supported by this purpose, since creation of a new class of voting stock is fully disclosed.

♦ State law does not require that each class of stock created have voting and all the other rights of each other class. Specifically, state law allows creation of stock having no voting rights.

---

c. **Agreements respecting actions of directors.** Close corporation shareholders usually have vital interests in matters ordinarily resolved by directors—for example, the selection of officers and their compensation. Efforts to protect these interests may seem to conflict with the nearly universal corporation law provision that the business and affairs of a corporation shall be managed by or under the authority of the board of directors.

1) **Less than unanimous shareholder agreements as to how they will act as directors are invalid--**

McQuade v. Stoneham, 263 N.Y. 323, 189 N.E. 234 (1934).

Facts. The corporation had 2,500 shares outstanding. Stoneham and McGraw (Ds) had 1,306 shares and 70 shares, respectively; McQuade (P) had 70 shares. Ds and P agreed to use their best efforts to elect themselves directors and officers, to take salaries and to perpetuate themselves in office (and further, not to amend the articles, bylaws, etc., as long as any of the three owned stock). Stoneham appointed the other four directors. Three years later, at a directors meeting, Ds refused to vote, thus allowing the other four directors to outvote P in removing him as an officer. At a later shareholder meeting, P was removed as a director (he had gotten into personal differences with Stoneham). P sued for specific performance of the shareholder agreement. The trial court found for P and Ds appeal.

Issue. May shareholders agree among themselves as to how they will act as directors in managing the affairs of the corporation?

Held. No. Judgment for P reversed.

♦ Shareholders may not agree to control the directors in the exercise of their independent judgment. They may combine to elect directors, but they must let the directors manage the business, which includes the election of officers.

Concurrence. The contract is itself valid. It is unenforceable because the employment is illegal. Directors owe a high duty of care to all shareholders.

---

2) Unanimous shareholder agreements as to how they will act as directors generally are valid--

Clark v. Dodge, 269 N.Y. 410, 199 N.E. 641 (1936).

Facts. Dodge (D) owned 75% of two corporations, and Clark (P) owned the remaining 25%. P ran the business and knew the secret formula that was used. P and D entered into a written contract which provided that D, during his lifetime and after his death through a trustee, would vote his stock and vote as a director that P should: (i) continue to serve as a director; (ii) continue to serve as general manager so long as P should be faithful, efficient, and competent; (iii) receive one-fourth of the net income of the corporation during his life; and (iv) that no unreasonable or incommensurate salaries should be paid to other officers or agents which would affect P's profits. P agreed to disclose the formula to D's son, which he did. D then fired P and P sued for specific performance of the contract. The trial judge dismissed P's complaint on the ground that, in so far as the agreement purported to bind D in his role as director, it could not be enforced because it was inconsistent with the corporation statute vesting the board of directors with the power to manage the business. P appeals.

Issue. Was the agreement between P and D enforceable in so far as it purported to bind D in his role as director?

Held. Yes. Judgment reversed.

♦ This agreement impinges only slightly upon the powers of the board and could not harm the shareholders, all of whom were parties, the creditors of the corporations, or the public.

Comment. Compare the *McQuade* case. The rationale (other than the factual difference that here all shareholders agreed) is different; *i.e.,* whether or not there is any injury to interested parties from such a mild interference with the management role of the board. In effect, this case represents the modern view of how to treat the close corporation; do not hold it to the statutory formalities of state corporation law, but do what makes sense in the factual context of a close corporation.

d. Agreements implied by majority's fiduciary duty.

1) Freeze out--

Wilkes v. Springside Nursing Home, Inc., 370 Mass. 842, 353 N.E.2d 657 (1976).

Facts. Wilkes (P) had an option to purchase a building and lot where a hospital had once been located. Riche, Quinn, and Pipkin (Ds) joined with P in forming a close corporation to run a nursing home on the property. Each invested an equal amount of cash and purchased an equal number of shares. It was understood that each would be a director and receive money from the corporation in equal amounts as long as each actively assumed his share of the burden of operating the business. Pipkin sold his shares to Connor (D), now deceased. Quinn wanted to buy part of the corporate property. P convinced the other shareholder-directors to sell the property at a higher price than Quinn had anticipated paying. From that point, the relationship between Quinn and P deteriorated. Ds voted to put themselves on salary from the corporation. They did not give P a salary. Later, they voted P out of his office and his directorship. P brought an action for declaratory judgment against the other shareholders for breach of the incorporation agreement and for breach of their fiduciary duty. The trial court found for Ds, and P appeals.

Issue. Did the majority shareholders breach their duty of good faith and loyalty to P when they cut P out of both the position of a director and a salary?

Held. Yes. Judgment reversed and remanded for a determination of the damages P has suffered.

♦　　The rule in this state is that shareholders in a close corporation have the same duty toward each other that partners have; that is, the utmost good faith and loyalty. If several shareholders combine to "freeze out" another shareholder by removing him from all decisionmaking roles and denying him a return on his investment, they have breached their fiduciary duty to him.

♦　　We recognize that an untempered application of the strict good faith standard would hamper the ability of the controlling group to manage the corporation for the good of all concerned. The rights of this group must be balanced against its duty to minority shareholders. Therefore, when the control group can show a legitimate business purpose for its actions, no breach will be found.

♦　　In this case, there was no valid business purpose in taking P's directorship, management position, and salary from him. He was at all times ready to perform his responsibilities to the corporation. His damages will not be diminished by Ds' claim that they performed his duties during the time they refused to let him perform them.

---

2)　**No need to give a closely held corporation the opportunity to purchase its own stock--**

Zidell v. Zidell, Inc., 277 Or. 423, 560 P.2d 1091 (1977).

Facts. Action for seizing corporate opportunity. Arnold Zidell (P) and Emery Zidell (D) each owned 37.5% of Zidell, Inc. Rosenfeld owned the remaining 25%. Rosenfeld sold his stock to D. P sued, contending that the corporation was entitled to buy the stock and hence that D breached his fiduciary duty when he bought the stock for himself. The trial court found for D and P appeals.

Issue. Does a corporate director of a closely held corporation have the duty first to give the corporation the opportunity to buy corporate stock before doing so himself?

Held. No. Judgment affirmed.

♦ Absent a corporate policy to the contrary, there is no special corporate interest in the corporation's purchasing its own shares.

♦ Here, there is no corporate policy to the contrary. Furthermore, there are no disinterested board members who could make the decision to purchase the stock. We do not believe that it is necessary to protect minority shareholders in situations such as this one. If P wanted to be specially protected he should have sought such protective provisions when the corporation was organized. P has also failed to prove that the welfare of the corporation requires the sale of the Rosenfeld stock to the corporation.

---

e. **Directors' delegation of management authority by contract.**

1) **Contracting away power to fire--**

Kennerson v. Burbank Amusement Co., 120 Cal. App. 2d 157, 260 P.2d 823 (1953).

Facts. Kennerson (P) was hired by Burbank (D) to be general manager of a theatre. The employment contract stated that it could be canceled by a vote of 80% of the original stockholders, even if they subsequently sold the stock. P was discharged and he sued. D defended claiming that the contract impermissibly delegated the control of the corporation to people other than the board of directors. The trial court upheld the contract, holding for P. D appeals.

Issue. May corporate powers to hire or fire be delegated so that the board of directors no longer has control of such matters?

Held. No. Judgment reversed.

♦ California recognizes that the board of directors cannot delegate its function to govern. The contract involved here did delegate such powers. Hence the contract was void and unenforceable.

---

2)   Impact of statutes on delegable and nondelegable duties--

Pioneer Specialties, Inc. v. Nelson, 161 Tex. 244, 339 S.W.2d 199 (1960).

Facts. Nelson (P) brought suit against Pioneer (D) for damages for breach of his contract of employment as president of that corporation for a period of two years. D moved for summary judgment. In April 1957, P was elected president of D. D's bylaws provided that corporate officers "shall be elected for one year," and P's term was for that period. But on August 1, 1957, P was employed (by contract) to be president for two years such that, although his elected term ended in April 1958, his employment contract did not end until July 31, 1959. On December 15, 1957, P was discharged as president by the board of directors. It was assumed, for purposes of consideration of the motion for summary judgment, that P's discharge was not for just cause. The trial court sustained D's motion, denying P any recovery. The court of civil appeals reversed that judgment and held that, although the bylaws provided for election for only one year, neither the bylaws nor any statutes prohibited employment for longer than one year. P was entitled to prove damages at trial if he could.

Issues.

(i)   Did the appellate court err in holding that the bylaws, which provide for the election of a president for one year, did not prohibit the employment of a person as president for two years (or more) in light of the Texas Corporation Code and other statutes?

(ii)   When a president of a corporation is removed without just cause before his elected term expires, does he have any contractual remedies?

Held. (i) Yes. (ii) Yes. Judgment of the appellate court reversed in part and affirmed in part.

♦   Although this is a case of first impression in this jurisdiction, the decision may be found in the corporation's bylaws and the Texas statutes regulating corporations. The appropriate bylaw states that the president "shall be elected for one year." Article 1327 of Revised Civil Statutes of Texas states, in part: "Contracts of employment may be entered into by the corporation with any of its officers . . . for such period of time as . . . not prohibited by the corporate charter or bylaws . . . ."

♦   We hold that the bylaw by necessary implication prohibits employment of a president for longer than one year. In this sense we modify the appellate decision.

♦   Section 2.43 of the Texas Business Corporation Act provides, in part: "Any officer . . . elected by the board of directors may be removed . . . whenever . . . the best interests of the corporation will be served thereby, but such removal shall be without prejudice to the contract rights, if any, of the person so removed. . . ."

♦   We therefore affirm the court of appeals in remanding the case for trial to give P an opportunity to prove a violation of his rights, if any, as well as resulting damages arising from his removal in December, 1957 up to the close of the one year for which he was elected president.

Dissent. I would affirm the trial court's decision. It is anomalous to say that an officer may be removed at any time by the board of directors but that such action can be made the basis of an award for damages for breach of its contract to employ an elected officer for a definite period of time. Since P was employed only to act as president and has been legally removed, he should have no cause of action for breach of contract.

---

4.   **Resolution of Disputes and Deadlocks.**

   a.   **Introduction.** Because holders of close corporations shares cannot readily turn to a market to extract the value of what they have put into and expect from the business, internal disputes may threaten the wealth and livelihood of one or more of these holders, the profitability of the business, or both. As these holders tend to divide shares evenly or adopt procedures and devices that give each of them a veto over at least some important decisions, deadlock may readily occur. Devices for coping with disputes and deadlocks include: (i) arbitration; (ii) judicial appointment of a receiver, provisional director or custodian; and (iii) dissolution.

   b.   **Irreparable harm not required for appointment of custodian--**

Giuricich v. Emtrol Corp., 449 A.2d 232 (Del. 1982).

Facts. Giuricich and another (Ps) and Continental formed Emtrol Corp. (D). Ps supplied technical expertise to the new venture and Continental supplied the capital. Continental received 80% of the new company's stock and the right to elect three of the five directors, while Ps received 20% and the right to elect two directors. Ps also received options to each acquire an additional 15% of D in the first year it became profitable. When Ps exercised their options, thus becoming 50% holders of Emtrol, they demanded that the board be restructured to reflect their holding even though their agreement with Continental made no provision for it. The board rejected the demand, amended the bylaws to expand the board to seven, and filled the vacancies with Continental allies. Its principal purpose was to give itself the governing hand in upcoming negotiations with Ps about executive compensation. The shareholder deadlock has prevented the election of successor directors indefinitely and led to numerous disputes about such matters as control and disbursement of corporate funds, corporate dividends, officers compensation, and bonuses. Ps petitioned for the appointment of a custodian. The Court of Chancery denied the petition on the ground that "there has been no injury to any vital interests of plaintiffs as shareholders, nor has Emtrol suffered any apparent injury. . . ," citing Delaware Code section 226(a)(2). Ps appeal.

Issue. May a custodian be appointed to break up a shareholder deadlock, without a showing of irreparable harm?

Held. Yes. Judgment reversed and remanded.

♦ Section 226(a)(1) applies to shareholder deadlock. By providing for the appointment of a custodian with more limited powers than a receiver, the legislature intended to create a more liberal and readily available remedy for shareholder deadlock. It manifested an intent by the Delaware legislature to "ease the onerous burden of proof under prior case law which made the appointment of a receiver for a solvent corporation almost hopeless, despite a potentially permanent shareholder deadlock."

♦ The courts will carefully scrutinize the willful perpetuation of a shareholder deadlock and the resulting entrenched board of directors. Here, D's board acted in pursuit of an "unworthy" purpose, creating a situation "violative of corporate democracy."

♦ The statute states that the Court of Chancery "may" appoint a custodian upon stated circumstances. While this action is within the discretion of the trial court, the trial court should have granted Ps' petition for the appointment of a custodian for Emtrol. Thus, its denial constituted an abuse of discretion.

Comment. One might argue that Ps demanded a restructuring of the board of directors for the same "unworthy" purpose that the board expanded its own size.

---

    c.   **Dissolution.**

        1) **Introduction.** Many modern statutes authorize courts to order dissolution on petition of those owning less than a majority of a corporation's shares. Many courts today take the position that, even in the absence of an authorizing statute, they may remedy abuse, dissension, or deadlock by appointing a receiver and winding up a corporation.

        2) **Shareholders' voluntarily abstaining from benefits for which corporation was formed is not reason for involuntarily dissolving the corporation--**

Nelkin v. H.J.R. Realty Corp., 25 N.Y.2d 543, 255 N.E.2d 713, 307 N.Y.S.2d 454 (1969).

Facts. Action for involuntary dissolution of a corporation. H.J.R. (D) was a corporation organized in 1941 for the sole purpose of owning and managing a building in New York.

The tenants were the only shareholders when the corporation was formed. They were Chatham Metal Products, Inc. (P), National Machinery Exchanges, Inc. ("National"), and Henry Nelkin, Inc. (P). The shareholders were to be charged a reduced rent. That part of the property not used by the shareholders was to be rented to other tenants at fair market value. In time all of the shareholders but National moved out. National continued to enjoy below fair market rate rent. In 1968, Ps petitioned for the involuntary dissolution of D. The lower court dismissed Ps' complaint.

Issue. Will a corporation be dissolved if, due to their voluntary action, the shareholders no longer enjoy the benefits for which the corporation was formed?

Held. No. Judgment affirmed.

♦   There are no charges that National is wrongfully diverting corporate assets, engaging in a fraud, or anything of that nature. Ps contend that D exists solely for the benefit of National and that as a matter of "judicial sponsorship" the corporation should be dissolved.

♦   Since there are no allegations of wrongdoing there can be no statutory dissolution. That is why Ps invoke the judicial sponsorship doctrine.

♦   The corporation is being operated for the original purpose and in accordance with the procedures set forth in the original shareholders' agreement. The fact that Ps, through their own voluntary action, no longer benefit from the agreement does not of itself entitle them to judicial dissolution. We affirm the dismissal of Ps' complaint.

Dissent. The situation contemplated by the original incorporation has changed dramatically. Ps no longer benefit from the corporation. Since changing circumstances have rendered impossible the achievement of the corporate objective, judicial dissolution should be granted.

---

3)   Protection of "reasonable expectations"--

Meiselman v. Meiselman, 309 N.C. 279, 307 S.E.2d 551 (1983).

Facts. The Meiselman brothers' deceased father gave 70% of the shares of several family businesses to his son Ira Meiselman (D) and 30% to his son Michael (P). Both worked in the businesses until a corporate action effectively excluded P from management. P sued, and D fired P. P then sought dissolution or a "buy-out at fair value." The trial court denied relief, and P appeals.

Issue. Under a statute authorizing a court to liquidate an incorporated business when "reasonably necessary for the protection of the rights or interests of the complaining shareholder," should a court grant equitable relief to protect the reasonable expectations of a shareholder in a close corporation?

Held. Yes. Judgment reversed and remanded.

♦ Shareholders in a close corporation customarily have "reasonable expectations" not fully reflected in the articles, bylaws, or side agreements between them. While in theory the holders might negotiate for protection of these expectations, in practice, they are unlikely to do so. When a shareholder receives his shares in a close corporation as a gift, as P did, he never has the opportunity to negotiate.

♦ To determine whether a holder's expectations are reasonable, a court must consider the situation at the inception of the business as well as changes in that situation and the course of dealing between the holders in conducting the affairs of the corporation. The expectations must be embodied in understandings, express or implied, among the holders.

♦ These reasonable expectations—if substantial—are part of a close corporation shareholder's "rights or interests," which a court may protect through liquidation if reasonably necessary. [N.C. Gen. Stat. §55-125(a)(4)] In this case, they may include secure employment, fringe benefits, and meaningful participation in the management of the family business.

♦ If a complaining shareholder establishes that one or more of his substantial reasonable expectations has been frustrated, through no fault of his own and in a manner largely beyond his own control, he may be entitled to dissolution or other equitable relief under section 55-125.1. This section provides that, in any shareholder action seeking dissolution, the court may grant such other relief as it deems appropriate, including: canceling or altering charter provisions and bylaws as well as resolutions and other corporate actions, and compelling buyouts. The shareholder need not show egregious wrongdoing on the part of management or controlling shareholders. In deciding whether to grant any such relief, the court must consider its costs and benefits for all of the shareholders.

Concurrence. In deciding whether to grant equitable relief, the court should consider what the complaining shareholder might have done to prompt the challenged action, whether the defendants engaged in oppression, and the circumstances under which the plaintiff came to be a holder. (Here, P became a holder as a result of his father's gift, which could indicate that P could reasonably expect only a locked-in-minority interest in a family corporation.)

———————————

4) **What is at stake.** Shareholder actions for dissolution rarely result in dissolution, even if they are successful. What is at stake in these actions is usually the bargaining position of the antagonistic holders.

D. LIMITED PARTNERSHIPS

Except for Louisiana, the states have provided for the organization of limited partnerships under either the Uniform Limited Partnership Act of 1916 ("ULPA") or the Revised Uniform Limited Partnership Act ("RULPA") of 1976 or 1985.

1. **Formalities and Limited Liability.** People wishing to organize a business as a limited partnership must follow certain formalities, one of which is filing a notice with some designated public office, usually the secretary of state. Failure to file can result in unlimited liability. RULPA section 304, however, provides that a person who "erroneously but in good faith" believed himself to be a limited partner can reduce this risk by making the appropriate filing or by withdrawing from future equity participation in the partnership. Once one of these steps is taken, only an outsider who transacted business with the partnership earlier can recover without limit and then only if the outsider believed that the person was a general partner when the transaction occurred.

2. **Limited Partners' Control and Limited Liability.** A limited partner risks losing only what he has invested as long as he exercises only his statutory rights and powers. These rights and powers are relatively minor because the limited partnership laws of the various states vest no formal decisionmaking authority in the limited partners, except a veto over the admission of new partners, and deny them the power to bind the limited partnership by their actions. In contrast, general partners possess the same rights and powers as they possess under the UPA.

Under section 7 of the ULPA, one who "takes part in the control of the business" becomes liable as a general partner. The courts have interpreted this "control rule" broadly. The 1976 RULPA provides more protection for limited partners by forcing creditors to meet a knowledge test. To recover under section 303 of this act, a creditor must show (i) the limited partner participated in control in ways "substantially the same as the exercise of the powers of a general partner," and (ii) the creditor knew this when he transacted business with the limited partnership. This section also created a safe harbor: a limited partner does not become liable as a general partner "solely" by engaging in one or more listed control-like activities, such as serving as an agent of the limited partnership. The 1985 RULPA provides even more protection by substituting a reliance test for the knowledge test. To recover under this act's section 303, a creditor must show that he "transact[ed] business with the limited partnership reasonably believing, based upon the limited partner's conduct, that the limited partner was a general partner." This section also brings within the safe harbor voting by limited partners on any matter related to the limited partnership's business that the written "partnership agreement states . . . may be subject to the[ir] approval or disapproval. . . ."

3. **Contractual Amendment of General Partner's Fiduciary Duty--**

Miller v. American Real Estate Partners, L.P., 2001 WL 1045643 (Del. Ch.)

Facts. Limited partners (P) in American Real Estate Partners, L.P. ("the partnership") (D), a limited partnership whose units are publicly traded, claimed that Carl Icahn (D) had breached his fiduciary duties by (i) acquiring the general partner interest in the limited partnership; (ii) using the general partner to make a rights offering that would enable one of his other investment vehicles to acquire a majority of American Real Estate's units, thereby insulating the general partner from removal; (iii) and cutting off all distributions so that he could devote the limited partnership's available cash to investments in which some of his other investment vehicles had a stake. Ds moved to dismiss the claim on the grounds that the limited partnership agreement ("the agreement") relieved the Ds of the fiduciary duties that P alleged had been breached.

Section 6.13(d) of the agreement provided that the general partner had sole and complete discretion to make or withhold distributions:

> Whenever in this agreement the general partner is permitted or required to make a decision (i) in its "sole discretion" or "discretion," with "absolute discretion" or under a grant of similar authority or latitude, the general partner shall be entitled to consider only such interests and factors as it desires and shall have no duty or obligation to give any consideration to any interest of, or factors affecting, the partnership, the operating partnership or the record holders, or (ii) in its good faith or under another express standard, the general partner shall act under such express standard and shall not be subject to any other, or different, standards imposed by this agreement or any other agreement contemplated herein.

Section 6.01 of the agreement provided that the sole purpose of the limited partnership was to make investment:

> Except as otherwise expressly provided or limited by the provisions of this agreement . . . the general partner shall have full, exclusive and complete discretion to manage and control the business and affairs of the partnership, to make all decisions affecting the business and affairs of the partnership, and to take all such actions as it deems necessary or appropriate to accomplish the purposes of the partnership as set forth herein. . . . The general partner shall use reasonable efforts to carry out the purposes of the partnership and shall devote to the management of the business and affairs of the partnership such time as the general partner, in its sole and absolute discretion, shall deem to be reasonably required for the operation thereof. . . .

Section 6.14 exempted the general partner and its directors and officers from liability except for liability (i) for a breach of the duty of loyalty, "as such duty may be set forth in or modified by this agreement, (ii) for acts or omissions not in good faith or which involve intentional misconduct or knowing violation of law or (iii) for any transaction from which such person derived an improper benefit."

Section 6.12 provided that:

> In addition to transactions specifically contemplated by the terms and provisions of this agreement, the partnership is expressly permitted to enter into other transactions with the general partner or any of its affiliates, including, without limitation, buying and selling properties from or to the general partner or any of its affiliates, subject to the limitations contained in this agreement, the Delaware Act *and in the Registration Statement* [emphasis added].

The registration statement provided that:

> The general partner is accountable to the partnership and the unitholders as a fiduciary and, consequently, must exercise good faith and integrity in handling partnership affairs.

Issue. Did the terms of the partnership agreement relieve Ds of the fiduciary duties that they allegedly violated?

Held. No. Judgment for P.

♦   Because general partners of publicly traded limited partnerships almost always draft their governing agreements, limits on something as important as fiduciary duties must be set forth clearly and unambiguously.

♦   Section 6.13(d) does not provide that the default provisions of limited partnership law must give way if they hinder the general partner's ability to act under the sole discretion, but rather that the sole discretion standard trumps other standards in the agreement. That the section expressly trumps conflicting provisions of the agreement and of other contracts suggests that it was not supposed to trump limited partnership default rules.

♦   The exculpatory provision in section 6.14 would have little, if any, significance if section 6.13(d) relieved Ds of the fiduciary duties that they allegedly breached.

♦   The provision in the registration statement that "[t]he general partner is accountable to the partnership and the unitholders as a fiduciary and, consequently, must exercise good faith and integrity in handling partnership affairs" also indicates that section 6.13(d) did not relieve Ds of the fiduciary duties that they allegedly breached.

E. LIMITED LIABILITY COMPANIES

1.   **Overview.** Every state has adopted a limited liability company ("LLC") statute. Each one of them cloaks "members"—as the principals of an LLC are usually known—with limited liability. No LLC statute contains a "control rule."

In fact, all but a handful of these statutes vest partnership-like decisionmaking authority in the members—absent a provision to the contrary in the articles of organization or the operating agreement. Indeed, the LLC was designed for key actors seeking (i) the opportunity to participate in day-to-day management, (ii) limited liability, and (iii) partnership "flow-thru" tax treatment. Until the late 1980s, efforts to combine these features in a noncorporate organizational form failed because the IRS took the position that limited liability precluded classification of an enterprise as a partnership for tax purposes. The legislative rush began when the IRS reversed this long-held position. *Note:* It is possible to combine these features in a corporate organizational form by electing Subchapter S status if the principals, their business activities, and the organization of their enterprise qualify for this status. A corporation does not qualify if it has: (i) more than 35 shareholders, (ii) a corporate shareholder, (iii) a nonresident alien shareholder, or (iv) more than one class of stock.

Many of the statutes (most patterned after RULPA) reflect a determined effort by their drafters to insure "flow-thru" tax treatment under the IRS "Kitner" rules for classifying business organizations for tax purposes as "partnerships," which received such treatment and "corporations," which did not. To insure this classification, an LLC statute had to resolve the control and duration issues so that a limited liability company would possess no more than two of the following three "corporate characteristics:" (i) centralized management; (ii) free transferability of interests; and (iii) continuity of [the enterprise's] life. The IRS has rescinded these rules and now simply permits members to choose "flow-thru" treatment.

2.   **No Limited Liability for LLC Members Who Fail to Disclose Existence of Their Business Organization to Third Parties--**

Westec v. Lanham and Preferred Income Investors, LLC, 955 P.2d 997 (Colo. 1998).

Facts. Larry Clark (D), a manager and member of Preferred Income Investors, LLC ("P.I.I.") (D), a limited liability company organized under the Colorado Limited Liability Company Act, ("LLC Act"), contacted Westec (P) about doing some engineering work for a development project. During preliminary discussions, Clark gave P's representatives his business card, which contained an address and, above the address, the letters "P.I.I." The address was that of Donald Lanham (D), another member of P.I.I. and its primary manager; the same address was listed as the principal office and place of business of P.I.I. in its articles of organization filed with the secretary of state. After further negotiations, Clark entered into an oral agreement with P's representatives and instructed them to send a written work proposal to Lanham. They did so in April 1995. In August, they sent Lanham a proposed contract along with a request that Lanham sign it and return it to P. P never received it, but in mid-August, Clark orally authorized them to begin work. When the work was done, P sent a bill for $9,183.40 to Lanham, but P received no payment. P sued Clark and Lanham individually as well as P.I.I. P.I.I. admitted liability.

The county court found that P's representatives understood Clark to be Lanham's agent and so dismissed Clark from the suit. The county court also found that P's representatives "did not have knowledge of any business entity" and dealt with Clark and Lanham "on a personal basis," so the court entered judgment against Lanham as well as P.I.I. Lanham appealed. The district court reversed principally on the grounds that, since Clark's business card contained the letters "P.I.I.," P had constructive notice that it was dealing with a limited liability company under the notice section of the LLC Act (section 7-80-208), which provides: "The fact that the articles of organization are on file in the office of the secretary of state is notice that the limited liability company is a limited liability company and is notice of all other facts set forth therein which are required to be set forth in the articles of organization." The district court also cited P's failure to investigate or request a personal guarantee. P appeals.

Issue. Is a member-manager of an LLC personally liable on a contract entered into by another member-manager and a third party if the third party lacks knowledge of the business entity and believes that the member-manager with whom he dealt was acting as an agent for the other member-manager?

Held. Yes. Judgment reversed and remanded.

♦ While Lanham was an agent of P.I.I., the trier of fact found that he failed to fully disclose his principal to a third party with whom his agent dealt, and, under agency law, this failure rendered him liable on the contract with the third party.

♦ The notice section of the LLC Act does not address the issue presented.

> To interpret the notice section as providing that the filing of an article of organization puts third parties who deal with a member of an LLC on constructive notice of the LLC's limited liability status even if they lack knowledge of the LLC's existence would invite sharp practices and outright fraud. Such an interpretation would permit an agent of an LLC to mislead a third party into believing that the agent would make good on a contract, conduct that the legislature did not mean to protect.

> A more plausible interpretation is that notice of an LLC's name puts a third party who deals with someone that he knows is a member of an LLC on constructive notice of the LLC's limited liability status and that managers and members bear no liability simply because of their status. This interpretation is consistent with the sections of the LLC Act that (i) require the name of an LLC to include the words "Limited Liability Company" or the initials "LLC" and (ii) expose members to individual liability when they engage in "improper actions" or fail "to observe the formalities or requirements relating to the management of its business and affairs when coupled with some other wrongful conduct."

> Courts should interpret statutes in derogation of the common law narrowly, particularly when a broad interpretation would depart radically from the settled

rules of agency and create uncertainty about accepted rules that govern business relationships.

When Lanham received the proposed contract from P that demonstrated that P believed that Lanham was the principal, he could have easily corrected P's mistake.

---

3. Piercing the Corporate Veil of an LLC--

Bastan v. RJM & Associates, LLC, 2001 WL 1006661 (Conn. Super. Ct.)

Facts. Bastan (P) paid a deposit to RJM & Associates, LLC (D), pursuant to a contract, to build a house. P sued D to recover the deposit and sought to recover from Robert Moravek, (D) the sole member of the LLC, claiming that Moravek had treated D's funds as his own by paying virtually all of his personal expenses from the account of the LLC.

Issue. May the limited liability veil of an LLC be pierced?

Held. Yes. Judgment for P.

♦ State corporation law section 34-133(b) provides that the personal liability of a member of an LLC "shall be no greater than that of a shareholder who is an employee of a corporation formed under chapter 601" and such a shareholder is subject to liability by "piercing the corporate veil." That the LLC statute expressly allows members to manage their LLCs does not preclude piercing; a person who ignores the intended separation between the individual and the company ought to be no better off than the sole shareholder who ignores corporate obligations.

F. LIMITED LIABILITY PARTNERSHIPS

Registering a partnership as an LLP—by filing a "registration statement" with the secretary of state—typically gives the partners limited liability in connection with "debts and obligations of the [LLP] arising from negligence, wrongful acts, or misconduct . . . by another partner or an employee, agent, or representative of the partnership" unless that "person [is] under his direct supervision and control." [Del. Code Ann., tit. b, ch. 15, 1515 (1992)]

VIII. SHAREHOLDERS' SUITS

A. INTRODUCTION

1. **Direct and Derivative Suits.** A shareholder may sue to enforce management's duties. The suit may be direct or derivative depending on the nature of the claim. If the claim is that management's breach reduced the residual value of the business (*e.g.,* shirking or self-dealing), the shareholder must sue derivatively in the name of the corporation. If the claim is that management's breach deprived the shareholder of some other right (other than her contingent right to that residual value, *e.g.,* right to inspect shareholder list), the shareholder must sue directly in her own name. It is sometimes difficult to distinguish the two types of claims, especially because direct suits may be brought as class actions.

2. **The Threat of Derivative "Strike" Suits.** A person with a relatively small stake in the residual value of a business might be tempted to bring a derivative suit for the primary purpose of being bought off. Requiring the defendants to make payment to the corporation reduces this temptation for the complaining shareholder. But it makes little difference to the complaining shareholder's attorney, who is usually the real party in interest. The attorney for a prevailing shareholder suing derivatively may obtain his fee from the corporation. He may therefore legitimately demand some payment in connection with a settlement.

3. **Limits on the Derivative Action.**

   a. **Generally.** In an effort to limit "strike" suits, and otherwise protect against overdeterrence, virtually all corporation statutes limit the shareholders who may bring derivative suits, and about one-third of them require at least some of these shareholders to provide security against the corporation's expenses before proceeding. All corporation statutes regulate settlement of derivative claims as well as requiring the complaining shareholder to exhaust internal remedies before bringing suit. Typical of these statutes is Rule 23.1 of the Federal Rules of Civil Procedure.

   b. **Federal Rule of Civil Procedure 23.1.** "In a derivative action. . . , the complaint shall be verified and shall allege . . . that the plaintiff was a shareholder . . . at the time of the transaction of which he complains or that his share thereafter devolved on him by operation of law. . . . The complaint shall also allege with particularity the efforts, if any, made by the plaintiff to obtain the action he desires from the directors or the reasons for his failure to obtain the action or for not making the effort. The derivative action may not be maintained if it appears that the plaintiff does not fairly and adequately represent the interests of the shareholders . . . similarly situated in enforcing the right of the corporation. . . . The action shall not be dismissed or compromised without the approval of the court, and notice of the proposed dismissal or compromise shall be given to shareholders . . . in such manner as the court directs."

B. EXHAUSTION OF INTERNAL REMEDIES

1. **The Issues.** Under what circumstances must the complaining shareholder demand that the directors or shareholders take action? If either group rejects the demand in whole or in part, what, if anything, may the complaining shareholder do to pursue her claim?

    a. **The Delaware approach.** Delaware's demand requirement parallels Federal Rule of Civil Procedure 23.1. Interpreting the "futility" exception to this requirement in *Aronson v. Lewis,* 473 A.2d 805 (Del. 1984), the Delaware Supreme Court held that a plaintiff would have to allege particularized facts that would create a reasonable doubt about the independence or disinterestedness of the directors or whether the challenged transaction is "otherwise the product of a valid exercise of business judgment."

    b. **"Universal demand."** Some critics of the Delaware approach have advocated "universal demand." The American Law Institute ("ALI"), for example, would require a written demand unless "the plaintiff makes a specific showing that irreparable injury to the corporation would otherwise result." [2 ALI, Principles of Corporate Governance: Analysis and Recommendations §7.03(b) (1992)] If a board rejects a demand, however, the ALI would subject the board's decision to "an elaborate set of standards that calibrates the deference afforded the decision of the directors to the character of the claim being asserted." The Model Business Corporation Act section 7.42 (1) (1995 Supp.) requires demand, but permits the derivative plaintiff to file suit within 90 days of the demand unless the demand is rejected earlier and to file even earlier if the corporation would otherwise suffer irreparable injury. [Model Business Corporation Act §7.42(2)] The legislatures of 12 states—Arizona, Connecticut, Florida, Georgia, Michigan, Mississippi, Montana, Nebraska, New Hampshire, North Carolina, Virginia, and Wisconsin—have adopted a universal demand requirement.

    c. **The New York approach.** The New York Court of Appeals interpreted demand futility in *Barr v. Wackman*, 36 N.Y.2d 371, 329 N.E.2d 180, 368 N.Y.S.2d 497 (1975), which arose in connection with the decision by the board of Talcott National Corporation ("Talcott") to reject a merger proposal from Gulf & Western Industries ("Gulf & Western") in favor of a cash tender offer from Associates First Capital Corporation, a Gulf & Western subsidiary. Under the merger proposal, Talcott holders would have received for each share $17 in cash and 0.6 of a warrant to purchase Gulf & Western stock, worth approximately $7; pursuant to the cash tender offer, Talcott holders received $20 per share. Talcott's board consisted of 13 outside directors, a director affiliated with a related company, and four interested inside directors. The derivative plaintiff claimed that the board abandoned the merger proposal after the four "controlling" inside directors received pecuniary and personal benefits from Gulf & Western in exchange for ceding control of Talcott on terms less favorable to Talcott's shareholders. The plaintiff also claimed that the outside directors failed "to do more than passively rubber-stamp the decisions of the active managers," whereas, had they discharged their duty of care, they would have been "put on notice of the claimed self-dealing of the affiliated directors." The court held that futility excused demand. The court said, however, that "[i]t is not sufficient merely to name a majority of the directors as parties defendant with conclusory allegations of wrongdoing or control by wrongdoers" to justify failure to make demand.

2.   Conflict of Interest and the Demand Requirement--

Marx v. Akers, 88 N.Y.2d 189, 644 N.Y.S.2d 121, 666 N.E.2d 1034 (1996).

Facts. Without making a demand on IBM's board of directors (Ds), Marx (P) filed a shareholder derivative suit alleging that the board had wasted corporate assets by awarding excessive compensation to IBM's executive officers and to its outside directors. The complaint alleged that during a five-year period, Ds increased their compensation rates from a base of $20,000 plus $500 for each meeting attended to a retainer of $55,000 plus 100 shares of IBM stock. The complaint also alleged that "[t]his compensation bears little relation to the part-time services rendered by the Non-Employee Directors or to the profitability of IBM. The board's responsibilities have not increased, its performance, measured by the company's earnings and stock price, has been poor yet its compensation has increased far in excess of the cost of living." The appellate division dismissed P's complaint for failure to make a demand, and P appeals.

Issues.

(i)   When a majority of a board consists of outside directors, does futility excuse a derivative plaintiff shareholder from making a demand in connection with claims of excessive compensation paid to *executive officers*?

(ii)   When a majority of a board consists of outside directors, does futility excuse a derivative plaintiff shareholder from making a demand in connection with claims of excessive compensation paid to *outside directors*?

(iii)   Does a claim that the compensation paid to outside directors "bears little relation to the part-time services rendered by [them] . . . or to the profitability of [the company]" and that the compensation increased in excess of the cost of living during a period when the "board's responsibilities [had] not increased [and] its performance, measured by the company's earnings and stock price, ha[d] been poor" state of cause of action?

Held. (i) No. (ii) Yes. (iii) No. Judgment affirmed.

♦ The demand requirement (i) creates a form of alternative dispute resolution by providing corporation directors with opportunities to correct alleged abuses, (ii) helps insulate directors from harassment by litigations on matters clearly within the discretion of directors, and (iii) discourages "strike suits" commenced by shareholders for personal gain rather than for the benefit of the corporation. The "futility" exception to the demand requirement permits shareholders to bring claims on behalf of the corporation when it is evident that directors will wrongfully refuse to bring such claims.

♦ The futility exception would swallow the rule if conclusory allegations of wrongdoing against each member of the board excused demand. To qualify for the futility exception, a shareholder must allege with particularity that (i) a majority of the board of directors is interested in the challenged transaction, by virtue of self-interest in the transaction or "control" by a self-interested director, (ii) that the board of directors did not fully inform themselves about the challenged transaction to the extent reasonably appropriate under the circumstances; or (iii) that the challenged transaction was so egregious on its face that it could not have been the product of sound business judgment of the directors.

♦ P's claim of excessive executive compensation did not show futility since P's allegations that less than a majority of the directors received such compensation indicate that the board was not interested, and P's conclusory allegations of faulty accounting procedures used to calculate executive compensation levels do not qualify as allegations of particular facts that the board failed to deliberate or exercise its business judgment in setting those levels.

♦ P's claim of excessive outside director compensation did show futility because P's allegation that outside directors comprised a majority of the board indicates that a majority of the board was self-interested.

♦ P's claim of excessive compensation of outside directors did not state a cause of action because P did not allege compensation rates excessive on their face or other facts that would have called into question whether the compensation was fair to the corporation when approved, the good faith of the directors setting those rates, or that the decision to set the compensation could not have been a product of valid business judgment. P's conclusory allegations are not factually based allegations of wrongdoing or waste that would, if true, sustain a verdict in P's favor.

---

3. The Board's Authority to Terminate the Suit.

    a. Where demand is required--

Levine v. Smith, 591 A.2d 194 (Del. 1991).

Facts. In 1984, General Motors ("GM") acquired 100% of the stock of Electronic Data Systems Corporation ("EDS"), a company founded by H. Ross Perot, its chairman. In return for his EDS stock, Perot received GM stock and became a member of the GM Board of Directors. EDS became a wholly owned subsidiary of GM, with Perot remaining as the EDS chairman.

Numerous disputes arose between Perot and GM management about the management and operation of EDS. Perot became more and more critical of GM's management and the quality of GM products, views reported widely in the media. Perot demanded that GM either buy him out or allow him more autonomy to run EDS as he saw fit. After an aborted effort by GM to sell EDS to American Telephone and Telegraph in 1986, GM began negotiations with Perot for a repurchase of his stock. An agreement was reached, and on November 30, 1986, a three-person subcommittee of outside, nonmanagement GM directors unanimously recommended approval of the repurchase plan. The next day, the plan received unanimous approval from the full GM board, which consisted of seven inside (management) directors, 14 outside directors, and Perot (who did not participate).

Ten days later, GM shareholder Levine (P) demanded, in writing, that the board rescind the repurchase. About four weeks later the board responded with a letter stating, "following review of the matters set forth in your . . . letter, the Board . . . unanimously determined that an attempt to rescind, or litigation . . . concerning [the repurchase] would not be in the best interests of the Corporation." P filed suit, claiming that GM's board "failed to exercise due care and to reach an informed business judgment in refusing his demand." He alleged that the board refused to hear an oral presentation from his lawyer and that the board "did not undertake an investigation" and "did nothing." GM moved to dismiss on the grounds that P's complaint did not comply with the particularity requirements of Rule 23.1. P requested discovery to substantiate his claim of wrongful refusal. The Court of Chancery denied his request and granted GM's motion. P appeals.

Issues.

(i)   When a board that has refused a shareholder's demand moves to dismiss his derivative suit pursuant to Rule 23.1, does the shareholder plaintiff have the right to discovery to substantiate his claim of wrongful refusal?

(ii)   When a board has refused a shareholder's demand, does the shareholder's derivative complaint necessarily comply with Rule 23.1 if it "alleges legally sufficient reasons to call into question the validity of the [b]oard['s] . . . exercise of business judgment"?

(iii)   When a board has refused a shareholder's demand, does a Rule 23.1 motion to dismiss the shareholder's derivative complaint require an inquiry into board disinterest and independence as well as application of the traditional business judgment rule—just as it would if demand had been excused?

(iv)   Did P's amended complaint allege with sufficient particularity to withstand a Rule 23.1 motion to dismiss that GM's board failed to act on an informed basis when it rejected his demand?

Held. (i) No. (ii) No. (iii) No. (iv) No. Chancery's dismissal of the complaint affirmed.

♦   The rationale for permitting discovery in a demand excused/*Zapata* context— when a board appoints a special litigation committee, it implicitly concedes that some directors are interested in the transaction and that it cannot invoke the protection of the business judgment rule—does not apply in a "demand refused" case such as this.

♦   Rule 23.1's particularity requirements apply not only to the making of demand, but also to the reason(s) that the board refused it.

♦   By making demand, a shareholder tacitly concedes the independence of a majority of the board to respond, leaving the board's good faith and the reasonableness of its investigation as the only matters for judicial scrutiny.

♦   The business judgment rule accords directors the presumption that they acted on an informed basis. The refusal of GM's board to hear an oral presentation from P's lawyer does not, as a matter of law, rebut this presumption. The board's letter rejecting P's demand refers to a "review of the matters set forth in [P's] . . . letter." This contradicts P's conclusory allegations that the board "did not undertake an investigation" and "did nothing."

Comments.

♦   The rationale for requiring demand on the board is not identical to the rationale for deferring to the board's judgment. Moreover, the consequences of requiring demand and deferring to the board's judgment are radically different. For these reasons, many courts purport, at least, to give less deference to a board's decision to terminate a derivative suit than to other decisions, even in a situation where demand is required.

♦   In the court's opinion in *Rales v. Blasband*, 634 A.2d 927 (Del. 1993), it noted "many avenues available to obtain [the] information" needed to comply with the particularity requirements of Rule 23.1, including: the media, government agencies, such as the S.E.C., and corporate records accessible to shareholders pursuant to their "right of inspection" under Delaware law.

---

   b.   Where demand is excused.

      1)   Termination by a special litigation committee--

Zapata Corp. v. Maldonado, 430 A.2d 779 (Del. 1981).

Facts. Maldonado (P), a stockholder in Zapata Corp. (D), instituted a derivative action on D's behalf. The suit alleged breaches of fiduciary duty by 10 of D's officers and directors. P brought this suit without first demanding that the board bring it, on the grounds that the demand would be futile since all directors were named as defendants. Several years later, the board appointed an independent investigating committee. By this time, four of the defendants were off the board, and the remaining directors appointed two new outside directors. These new directors comprised the investigating committee. After its investigation, the committee recommended that the action be dismissed. Its determination was binding on D, which moved for dismissal or summary judgment. The trial court denied the motions, holding that the "business judgment" rule is not a grant of authority to dismiss derivative suits, and that a stockholder sometimes has an individual right to maintain such actions. D filed an interlocutory appeal.

Issue. Did the committee have the power to cause this action to be dismissed?

Held. Yes. Trial court interlocutory order reversed; case remanded for proceedings consistent with this opinion.

♦ A stockholder does not have an individual right, once demand is made and refused, to continue a derivative suit. Unless it was wrongful, the board's decision that the suit would harm the company will be respected as a matter of business judgment. A stockholder has the right to initiate the action himself when demand may be properly excused as futile. However, excusing demand does not strip the board of its corporate power. There may be circumstances where the suit, although properly initiated, would not be in the corporation's best interests. This is the context here.

♦ The court must find a balancing point where bona fide stockholder power to bring corporation causes of action cannot be unfairly trampled on by the board, but where the corporation can rid itself of detrimental litigation. A two-step process is involved. First, the court must recognize that the board, even if tainted by self-interest, can legally delegate its authority to a committee of disinterested directors. However, the court may inquire on its own into the independence and good faith of the committee and the bases supporting its conclusions. If the court is satisfied on both counts, the second step is to apply its own business judgment as to whether the motion to dismiss should be granted. Thus, suits will be heard when corporate actions meet the criteria of the first step, but where the result would terminate a grievance worthy of consideration.

2) Issues left open by *Zapata*.

a) **Its scope.** To what extent, if any, does the *Zapata* two-step approach apply *where demand is required?* To a decision to terminate a *claim arising under federal law?*

b) **Should the amount of deference a court gives to a board or committee decision not to sue vary?** Should a court show more deference where the alleged principal culprits comprise only a minority of the board? Where the suit involves a claim against an employee who is neither a director nor a senior officer of the corporation? An outsider to the corporation? Should the answer depend in part on the nature of the alleged harm?

c) **Step two.** Must the court proceed to the second step where it applies its own business judgment? If it does proceed, under what circumstances may a court conclude that a decision to terminate litigation satisfied step one criteria, but not their "spirit"? Should the court consider evidence not before the board or the committee?

d) **Which costs count?** When reviewing a board or committee decision to terminate litigation, which costs should the court consider in deciding whether the likely recoverable damages discounted by the probability of a finding of liability are less than the likely costs that the corporation will incur by continuing the litigation? In *Joy v. North*, 692 F.2d 880 (2d Cir. 1982), the court answered: ". . . attorney's fees and other out-of-pocket expenses related to the litigation and time spent by corporate personnel preparing for and participating in the trial. The court should also weigh indemnification which is mandatory under corporate bylaws, private contract or [state] law, discounted of course by the probability of liability for such sums. We believe that indemnification the corporation may later pay as a matter of discretion should not be taken into account. . . . The existence . . . of insurance should not be considered, . . . [but it] is relevant to the calculation of potential benefits. Where, having completed the above analysis, the court finds a likely net return to the corporation which is not substantial in relation to shareholder equity, it may take into account two other items as costs[:] . . . the impact of distraction of key personnel by continued litigation [and] . . . potential lost profits which may result from the publicity of a trial. . . . We are mindful that other less direct costs may be incurred, such as a negative impact on morale and upon the corporate image. Nevertheless, we believe that such factors, with the two exceptions noted, should not be taken into account. . . ."

Alford v. Shaw, 320 N.C. 465, 358 S.E.2d 323 (1987).

Facts. Alford and other minority shareholders (Ps) charged the board of directors of All American Assurance Company ("AAA") with mismanagement. In response, AAA's board elected two theretofore unaffiliated men to the board, and designated them as a special investigative committee. The board authorized the committee to determine whether bringing suit against those implicated in any wrongdoing uncovered by the investigation would be in the best interests of AAA and its shareholders. Before the investigation was completed, Ps filed a shareholder's derivative suit against the controlling shareholders of AAA and a majority of its directors (Ds) alleging breach of fiduciary duty through fraud, self-dealing, and negligent acquiescence, which amounted to a looting of corporate assets for the benefit of Ds. Upon completion of the investigation, the committee filed a report with the trial court recommending a specified settlement of two of Ps' claims and dismissal of the rest. Based on this report, Ds moved for summary judgment and approval of the settlement agreement. Invoking the business judgment rule, the trial court granted the motion. The appellate court reversed, holding that defendant directors in a derivative suit cannot confer upon a special committee the power to bind the corporation with respect to the litigation. Ds appealed. In the supreme court's first decision in the case, it reversed, requiring substantial deference to the committee's recommendation.

Issue. Must a court defer to a special litigation committee's recommendation to terminate a minority shareholder's derivative suit against corporate directors?

Held. No. Judgment affirmed with modifications.

♦ A court ought not give great deference to the decision of a corporate committee whose institutional symbiosis with the corporation necessarily affects its ability to render a decision that fairly considers the interest of plaintiffs forced to bring suit on behalf of the corporation.

♦ The language of N.C. Gen. Stat. section 55-55 directs a court to determine whether the interest of any shareholder will be substantially affected by the discontinuance, dismissal, compromise, or settlement of a derivative suit. It would be difficult for the court to determine whether the interest of shareholders or creditors would be substantially affected without looking at the proposed action substantively. Thus, a court should scrutinize the merits of the committee's recommendation in the manner suggested by *Zapata*, and it should do so whether demand is excused or required.

♦ To make the required assessment of the committee's recommendation, the court must evaluate the adequacy of materials prepared by the corporation that support the corporation's decision to settle or dismiss a derivative suit along with the plaintiff's forecast of evidence. Upon remand, Ps shall be permitted to develop and present evidence, such as:

That the committee, though perhaps disinterested and independent, may not have been *qualified* to assess information supplied by those within the corporate structure who would benefit from decisions not to proceed with litigation;

That false and/or incomplete information was supplied to the committee because of the nonadversarial way in which it gathered and evaluated information; and

In light of these and other problems that arise from the structural bias inherent in board-appointed special litigation committees, that the committee's decision eviscerates Ps' opportunities as minority shareholders to vindicate their rights under state law.

---

4. **Demand on Shareholders.**

   a. **Introduction.** Many states explicitly require only a demand on the board, but more states follow the approach of Rule 23.1 in mentioning demand on the shareholders. Statutes like Rule 23.1 raise several difficult issues:

      1) Under what circumstances, if any, must a demand on the shareholders be made? Must a demand be made if the shareholders lack the authority to ratify the challenged transaction? Should it make any difference if the claim is fraud or self-dealing rather than negligence or mismanagement? Should an otherwise mandatory demand on the shareholders be excused if compliance would be very expensive due to widespread shareholding?

      2) If a demand must be made, should the complaining shareholder or the board make it?

      3) What action must be demanded?

      4) If the shareholders decide to do nothing, what are the consequences? Render judgment for the defendants? Allocate the burden of persuasion on the fairness question to the plaintiff? Somehow take the shareholders' decision into account in adjudicating the merits?

   b. **Shareholder demand not necessary when fraud alleged--**

Mayer v. Adams, 141 A.2d 458 (Del. 1958).

Facts. A shareholder (P) brought an action on behalf of the corporation (Phillips Petroleum) against the directors (Ds) for fraud. She did not first make demand on the directors, nor upon the shareholders—on the basis that since fraud was involved, shareholders could not ratify fraud, and since there were 100,000 shareholders, it would be too expensive and futile to poll them. The state statute indicated that the person bringing the suit had to state the efforts made to contact the shareholders and the reasons for not doing so. The trial court granted Ds' motion to dismiss.

Issue. When the ground for a derivative suit is fraud, is a demand on the shareholders necessary?

Held. No. Judgment reversed.

♦ In a *fraud* case there is nothing to be gained by making prior demand on the shareholders. Shareholders cannot by corporate law ratify fraud; so even if they disapprove, the shareholder may still bring an action.

♦ The position of Ds that the Rule allows shareholders to decide whether an action shall be brought is disapproved. The state rule is that demand on directors prior to suit is enough.

♦ There may be cases where prior demand on shareholders is required. We do not enumerate these here.

C. QUALIFICATIONS OF PLAINTIFF-SHAREHOLDER

1. Shareholder Must Own Stock at Time of Wrongdoing to Sue or Benefit from Suit--

Courtland Manor, Inc. v. Leeds, 347 A.2d 144 (Del. 1975).

Facts. Leeds (D) and his accountant (London) planned to construct a nursing home. A corporation was formed to run the nursing home and a limited partnership to construct it. Widder (P) and others invested $70,000 in the corporation. The anticipated construction costs were $900,000. The limited partnership was to rent the building to the corporation for 12.5% of the construction costs per year. Some of the stockholders were also limited partners. Construction costs went up as did the rent. After the home was completed and patients accepted, the corporation experienced a severe cash shortage. D was severed from the corporation. P and two others acquired control of the corporation by purchasing most of the outstanding stock for $4,000. Additional shares were issued and purchased by P and his partners. For a total of $19,000 they wound up with almost all of the stock and hence controlled what wound up being a $90,000 investment. P and the corporation (Courtland) sued D on the ground that the profit from the rent netted the limited partnership $30,000+ annually instead of the contemplated $7,000 and that this amounted to mismanagement of the corporation to the benefit of the limited partnership.

Issue. If a shareholder purchases stock from a known wrongdoer, may he subsequently sue the wrongdoer for the wrongful acts?

Held. No. Judgment for D.

♦   It is a settled equitable principle that a shareholder may not complain of acts of corporate management if he acquired his shares from those who either participated in or acquiesced to the wrongful transaction. The rationale for this rule is that where shareholders have purchased substantially all of the shares for the corporation at a fair price they have not sustained any injury from the wrongs that occurred prior to the sale. To hold otherwise permits the shareholders to purchase the stock at a low price and then garner a windfall when they sue the wrongdoers. There is no reason to let the shareholder in such a case recoup a substantial part of a fair purchase price.

♦   In one case, shareholders purchased 99% of the stock for $5 million and then turned around and sued the former shareholders for corporate mismanagement in the sum of $7 million. This would have allowed them to recoup their purchase price and $2 million. This is unfair.

♦   P has purchased a $90,000 investment for $19,000. If P was permitted to now recover for the wrongs committed, there would be a windfall profit. We cannot in equity allow that.

----

2.   Date of Wrong--

Goldie v. Yaker, 78 N.M. 485, 432 P.2d 841 (1967).

Facts. Yaker and Moscow (Ds) purchased on contract several acres of land for $15,000 ($500 down). Subsequently, Ds incorporated Intermountain Development Corporation ("Intermountain"). Ds sold to Intermountain 49 acres of the land in exchange for stock; Intermountain assumed the balance due on the contract. Intermountain was also to pay certain development costs. Goldie (P) subsequently became a stockholder in Intermountain. P sued Ds derivatively, claiming that the land was given an excessive value when transferred to Intermountain. Ds contended that P was not a stockholder at the time Intermountain entered into the contract and hence could not maintain an action. The trial judge found for Ds on this point and dismissed the complaint. P appeals.

Issue. Is the date of contracting the controlling date?

Held. Yes. Judgment affirmed.

♦   P claims that since a substantial portion of the land was transferred to Intermountain after P became a stockholder, he can maintain this action. P errs. The controlling date is the date the contract was executed, not the date of the transfer.

- P does not charge that the land deal was a fraud perpetrated upon future stockholders. Since there was no plan to defraud future stockholders, P cannot maintain the action.

D. SECURITY FOR EXPENSES

1. **Introduction.** In order to discourage "strike suits," many states have enacted statutes requiring the plaintiff-shareholder in a derivative suit, under certain circumstances, to post a bond or other security to indemnify the corporation against certain of its litigation expenses in the event that the plaintiff loses the suit.

2. **When Security Must Be Posted.** There is great variety in the requirements of state statutes.

    a. Some say that the plaintiff must post security if she owns less than a specified percentage of stock.

    b. Other states say that security is discretionary with the court (and it is demanded only when there is no reasonable possibility that the action could benefit the corporation).

3. **Who Is Entitled to Security?** In most states, only the corporation may demand security and only its expenses may be paid. Other states allow officers and directors to demand security and to receive reimbursement.

4. **Covered Expenses.** Normally, all expenses, including attorneys' fees, are covered. Also covered may be expenses of officers and directors that the corporation is obligated to pay because it has indemnified them (it may indemnify officers and directors for actions taken in good faith and pursuant to their business judgment, but normally not for fraudulent actions).

E. DEFENDING AGAINST DERIVATIVE SUITS

1. **Conflicting Interests of Defendants--**

Otis & Co. v. Pennsylvania Railroad, 57 F. Supp. 680 (E.D. Pa. 1944), *aff'd*, 155 F.2d 522 (3d Cir. 1946).

Facts. Otis (P), an investment banking house, and a shareholder in Pennsylvania Railroad (D), sued derivatively to recover $1 million from certain of D's officers and directors. The complaint alleged that a bond issue was improperly privately placed. The method of placing the bond issue was consistent with the way most railroads placed similar bond issues. D filed an answer to the complaint. P filed a motion to strike D's answer and to remove counsel on the ground that D, being the corporation on whose behalf P was suing, could not file an answer.

Issue. May a corporation file an answer in a derivative action if it is not alleged that the directors perpetrated a fraud?

Held. Yes. P's motion denied.

♦   It is a legal fiction that a corporation is a separate legal entity. Courts have struck an answer of the corporation in cases such as this, and in other cases the answer has been upheld. A hard and fast rule one way or the other is undesirable in this area. The choice must be based on the particular case before the court.

♦   In this case, there is no assertion of fraud or that the directors had a personal interest in the transaction. In cases like this, where it is a matter of corporate policy that is involved, it seems proper to allow the corporation to answer the complaint.

Were this a case involving charges of director fraud, self-interest, etc., the corporation would not be permitted to answer.

Comment. The court felt that this case involved stockholders on one side of a corporate policy and management on the other.

---

2.   **Conflicting Interests of Defendants' Counsel--**

Cannon v. U.S. Acoustics Corp., 398 F. Supp. 209 (E.D. Ill. 1975), *aff'd in part*, 532 F.2d 1178 (7th Cir. 1976).

Facts. Cannon and others (Ps) brought a shareholder's derivative action against U.S. Acoustics Corp., Perlite, Inc., and other individuals (Ds). All Ds were represented by the same legal counsel. Cannon was a former attorney for the corporations and the individual Ds. Ps moved to require the corporations to retain counsel independent from the counsel for the individual defendants, and Ds moved to have Cannon struck as a party plaintiff because of his former representation of Ds in matters related to the present action.

Issues.

(i)   Must the corporation retain counsel who is independent from that of the individual defendants, who are the alleged malefactors?

(ii)   Must an attorney who represented Ds in matters related to the present action withdraw as a party plaintiff?

Held. (i) Yes. (ii) Yes.

- Since there is a potential conflict of interest between the corporations and the individual defendants if any improper conduct on the part of the individuals is found, the corporations should retain independent legal counsel from the outset.

- Cannon must withdraw. Cannon cannot use information he gained as an attorney for defendants to later prosecute a shareholder's derivative suit against them, so he must withdraw.

F. DISMISSAL, DISCONTINUANCE, AND SETTLEMENT

Rule 23.1 requires court approval of dismissal, discontinuance, or settlement of derivative suits and notice to the shareholders of the proposed action, and most states have adopted similar laws. In some states, courts have permitted nonapproved settlements on the condition that such settlements do not bar other shareholders from pursuing the compromised claim.

G. INTERVENTION AND CONSOLIDATION

Federal law and the law of almost all states grant courts considerable discretion to permit shareholders to intervene in derivative suits and to consolidate derivative claims related to the same course of conduct.

H. CHARACTERIZATION OF THE SUIT

1. Characterization and Remedy--

Grimes v. Donald, 673 A.2d 1207 (Del. 1996).

Facts. Grimes (P), a shareholder in DSC Communications Corp., claimed that the board of directors had failed to use due care, committed waste, approved excessive compensation, and unlawfully delegated its duties and responsibilities by entering into an agreement with the CEO, Donald (D), which provided that D was entitled to damages if the board of directors "unreasonably interfered" with D's management of the company. P sought a declaration that the delegation provision was invalid. The court of chancery analyzed the claim as a direct claim, and D appeals.

Issue. May a shareholder proceed directly on an "abdication" claim when he seeks only a declaration that an agreement between the board and its CEO is invalid?

Held. Yes. Judgment affirmed.

- Whether a claim may proceed as a direct or a derivative action depends on the nature of the wrong alleged and the relief sought. Claims seeking injunctive or prospective relief, such as P's abdication claim, are more likely to qualify as direct.

Comment. The court's focus on the nature of the relief sought is consistent with the idea that the function of the shareholder derivative claim mechanism is to avoid the problems of fashioning compensatory relief that would plague a class action claim.

---

2. **A.L.I. Principles of Corporate Governance.** Section 7.01(d) of the A.L.I. Principles of Corporate Governance suggests that when a shareholder in a closely held corporation brings a suit raising derivative claims, a court should have discretion to exempt the suit from the restrictions and defenses applicable only to derivative suits and order an individual recovery *if* the court finds that doing so will *not* (i) unfairly expose the corporation or the defendants to a multiplicity of actions, (ii) materially prejudice the interests of creditors of the corporation, or (iii) interfere with a fair distribution of the recovery among all interested persons.

3. **Characterization and the Closely Held Corporation--**

Barth v. Barth, 659 N.E.2d 559 (Ind. 1995).

Facts. Robert Barth (P), owner of almost 30% of the shares of a three-shareholder corporation, sued Michael Barth (D), owner of 51% of the shares, alleging that D (i) paid excessive salaries to himself and to members of his immediate family; (ii) used corporate employees to perform services on his and his son's homes without compensating the corporation; (iii) dramatically lowered dividend payments; and (iv) appropriated corporate funds for personal investments. P brought his suit directly. The trial court dismissed on the grounds that the suit could only be brought derivatively. The court of appeals reversed on the ground that P could have satisfied the requirements for bringing a derivative action and that none of the reasons for requiring a suit like P's to be brought derivatively applied.

Issue. May a shareholder in a closely held corporation bring directly what would ordinarily be a derivative suit if the shareholder could have complied with the requirements applicable to derivative suits and the reasons for requiring certain claims to be brought derivatively were inapplicable?

Held. Yes. Judgment affirmed.

♦ When a shareholder claims that those in control of an incorporated business have engaged in actions that have reduced, or will reduce, the residual value of the business, requiring the claim to be brought derivatively rather than directly prevents one or more minority shareholders from damaging corporate creditors and the other shareholders. When the corporation is closely held, however, such claims often do not raise these concerns.

♦   Moreover, the relationship between shareholders in a closely held corporation is more like that of director to shareholder in a publicly held corporation.

Comment. Because a corporate recovery in a derivative action will benefit creditors while a direct recovery by a shareholder will not, the protection of creditors' principle could well be implicated in a shareholder suit against a closely held corporation with debt.

I.   REIMBURSEMENT OF PLAINTIFF'S EXPENSES

1.   Successful Plaintiffs Sometimes Entitled to Be Recompensed for Legal Expenses--

Fletcher v. A.J. Industries, Inc., 266 Cal. App. 2d 313, 72 Cal. Rptr. 146 (1968).

Facts. Fletcher (P), a shareholder, brought a shareholder derivative action against A.J. Industries and members of the board of directors, including Ver Halen and Malone (Ds), seeking several forms of relief against the corporation and the individual Ds. P charged Ds with corporate mismanagement. The matter was settled by stipulation (the board was reorganized, Malone was ousted, Ver Halen's employment contract was amended), but there was no monetary award at that time. P sought to recover for his attorneys' fees. After the trial court awarded P his fees, Ds appeal.

Issue. Should California adopt the "substantial benefit" rule and disregard the "common fund" doctrine?

Held. Yes. Judgment affirmed.

♦   Generally, attorneys' fees cannot be awarded unless authorized by statute or if the parties so provide in an agreement.

♦   An exception to this rule is the "common fund" doctrine. Under this doctrine, if a plaintiff undertakes litigation for a class of people (such as shareholders) and is successful, then part of the award is a fund for the benefit of the class members, and equity demands that the plaintiff be reimbursed for his attorneys' fees from the common fund. The rationale for this is that it is inequitable for the members of the class to enjoy the benefit of the fund without the responsibility of paying their share of the plaintiff's expenses. However, this doctrine cannot be applied where, as here, there is no common fund.

♦   We choose to adopt the "substantial benefit" rule. Under this rule, a variant of the common fund rule, a plaintiff can recover his expenses even if there is no common fund created so long as the class benefits from the litigation. As applied to shareholder's actions, this means that if the litigation results in a substantial benefit to the corporation, the suing shareholder can recover his attorneys' fees. We find that in this case P's litigation substantially benefited the corporation. It is not significant that the benefits were achieved by settlement rather than a final judgment, especially since, due to the nature of derivative actions, the trial court is in a position to scrutinize the fairness of the settlement.

Dissent. There was no common fund created by the litigation. It is for the legislature, not the judiciary, to determine if California should adopt the substantial benefit rule.

---

2. **Benefit to Whom?** Especially when the derivative action yields no monetary judgment for the corporation, controversy may surround the question of whether the suit benefited "the corporation."

3. **Attorneys' Fees.** Courts have used two approaches in setting attorneys' fees: (i) "salvage value"—award a percentage of the total recovery and (ii) "lodestar"—multiply time by hourly rate and adjust this lodestar figure to reflect risk and work quality. These two approaches provide attorneys with different incentives. The incentives provided by the lodestar methodology may well induce behavior somewhat inconsistent with the shareholders' collective welfare.

J. INDEMNIFICATION OF DEFENDANTS

1. **Introduction.** Absent the prospect of indemnification by the corporation, the threat of liability might deter able people from accepting high managerial positions at acceptable salaries. Of course, entitlement to indemnification under all circumstances could easily lead to underdeterrence. All states regulate indemnification, but the statutes vary significantly. Some statutes purport to be exclusive, providing the sole grounds and processes for indemnification. Others are clearly permissive, at least up to a point. In all states, a defendant who prevails on the merits is entitled to indemnification. The states differ in how they deal with defendants who settle or lose. Generally, statutes make it easier for settling defendants to obtain indemnification than losing ones (in some states, an adverse judgment on the merits precludes indemnification). Many statutes distinguish between amounts paid to satisfy claims and the costs of defense. Many regulate the board's decisionmaking process with respect to indemnification, and subject the board's decision to varying levels of judicial review.

2. **Indemnification Requires Good Faith--**

Waltuch v. Conticommodity Services, Inc., 88 F.3d 87 (2d Cir. 1996).

Facts. Waltuch (P) was a trader in silver futures and worked for Conticommodity Services, Inc. (D). In the 1980s, both P and D were the subject of several lawsuits filed by silver speculators alleging fraud, market manipulation, and antitrust violations. These lawsuits were settled, with D paying over $35 million in damages. P was dismissed from the suits with no settlement contribution. As a result of the litigation, P personally incurred $1.2 million in legal fees. P was also the subject of an enforcement proceeding brought by the Commodity Futures Trading Commission ("CFTC"), charging him with fraud and market manipulation. The proceeding was settled, and P was required to pay a fine and was banned from buying or selling futures for six months. P incurred another $1 million in legal fees in defending himself in the CFTC proceeding. P sued D for indemnification of his $2.2 million in legal fees. P claimed that D's articles of incorporation require D to indemnify him for his expenses in both actions. D argued that P's claim is barred because section 145 of Delaware's General Corporation Law permits indemnification only if the corporate officer acted in good faith. The district court agreed with D that P could recover only if he could demonstrate good faith. P appeals.

Issues.

(i)   Does section 145 require a corporate officer to have acted in good faith in order to be reimbursed?

(ii)   Must D reimburse P for legal fees P spent in defending both actions?

Held. (i) Yes. (ii) Yes. Judgment affirmed in part and reversed in part.

♦   The relevant provision of D's articles of incorporation contains no requirement of good faith for indemnification. However, D correctly notes that section 145(a) of Delaware's General Corporation Law *does* contain a good faith requirement. D therefore argues that its article is invalid under Delaware law to the extent that it requires indemnification of officers who have acted in bad faith. P contends that section 145(f) expressly allows corporations to indemnify officers in a manner broader than that set out in section 145(a).

♦   Section 145(f) states that the indemnification "provided by, or granted pursuant to, the other subsections of this section shall not be deemed exclusive if any other rights to which those seeking indemnification . . . may be entitled under any by-law, agreement, vote of stockholders . . . ." P argues that this subsection is a separate grant of indemnification power that is not limited by the good faith requirement of section 145(a).

♦   While no Delaware court has specifically decided the issue, related cases have supported D's contention that a corporation's grant of indemnification rights *must be consistent* with the substantive provisions of section 145. [*See* Hibbert v. Hollywood Park, Inc., 457 A.2d 339 (Del. 1983)] Our reading of the statute also supports this position. Section 145(a) gives a corporation the power to indemnify if the plaintiff acted in good faith and in a manner not opposed to the best interests of the corporation. This statutory limit must mean that there is no power to indemnify in the absence of good faith. To hold otherwise would render section 145(a) meaningless: a corporation could indemnify anyone in any manner it pleased regardless of good faith.

♦   P's interpretation would also render section 145(g) unnecessary. Section 145(g) explicitly allows a corporation to circumvent the good faith requirement by purchasing a directors' and officers' liability insurance policy to cover situations in which the corporation could not indemnify its officers and directors directly. This section would be completely unnecessary if a corporation could indemnify anyone in any situation.

♦   Thus, we find that D's article that would require indemnification of P in the absence of good faith is inconsistent with section 145(a) and thus exceeds the scope of a Delaware corporation's power to indemnify. We therefore affirm the lower court's decision on this issue.

♦   However, we find that, under section 145(c), D is required to indemnify P for the $1.2 million he expended from the private lawsuits. Section 145(c) requires corporations to indemnify officers and directors who are "successful" on the merits in defense of certain claims. P argued that he was successful in the private lawsuits because the suits were dismissed with prejudice and without any payment or assumption of liability by him. D argued that the claims against P were only dismissed because of D's $35 million in settlement payments, part of which was contributed on behalf of P, not because of P's innocence. The lower court agreed with D and held that section 145(c) mandates indemnification only when an officer or director is "vindicated," and here, P clearly was not.

♦   Courts have held that success or vindication under section 145(c) does not mean moral exoneration. [*See* Merritt-Chapman & Scott Corp. v. Wolfson, 321 A.2d 138 (Del. Super. Ct. 1974)] While P may not have been morally exonerated, he did escape liability. The reason for this outcome is irrelevant. Under *Merritt*, escape from an adverse judgment, for whatever reason, is determinative. Thus, D must indemnify P for his legal expenses in connection with the private lawsuits.

---

3.   **Right to Indemnification.** Section 145(c) of the Delaware General Corporation Code requires indemnification of expenses incurred in connection with the "defense of any action . . ." as to which the indemnification claimant is "successful on the merits or otherwise."

4.   **No Statutory Right to Indemnification for Attorney's Fees Incurred to Obtain Indemnification--**

Baker v. Health Management Systems, Inc., 98 N.Y.2d 80 (2002).

Facts. Several securities fraud class action suits brought against Health Management Systems, Inc. ("HMS") (D) and some of its executive officers named as a defendant D's Chief Financial Officer, Phillip Siegel (P). Unlike the other officers named in the suit, P had come to work for HMS after the alleged misconduct had occurred and had purchased rather than sold HMS stock. Because of these differences, P retained separate counsel to defend him against the securities fraud claims. All claims against P were dismissed. The other class action defendants settled for $4 million. P requested that HMS indemnify him for his attorney's fees and litigation costs, but HMS denied his request on the ground that separate counsel was not warranted. P moved that the district court order D to indemnify him not only for these fees and costs, but also for the fees and costs associated with securing indemnification. The district court granted the former, but denied the latter. P appeals.

Issue. Under the business corporation law, is a corporate officer entitled to indemnification for the attorney's fees and litigation costs incurred in attempting to secure indemnification for the fees and costs incurred in defending a securities fraud claim?

Held. No. Judgment affirmed.

- That section 722(a) of New York Business Corporation Law speaks only to expenses that are "actually and necessarily incurred as a result of such action or proceeding" means that there must be a reasonably substantial nexus between the expenditures and the underlying suit. P incurred the expenditures at issue here because HMS refused to indemnify P following his dismissal from the underlying litigation.

- Section 722(a) does use more expansive language in connection with indemnification related to non-derivative actions, but the legislative history shows that this language was "expressly intended to cover expenses incurred in settling claims even prior to the commencement of a suit."

- When the legislature amended these provisions in 1986 and 1987, in ways especially favorable to officers and directors, it considered incorporating provisions from several corporation acts which expressly authorize recovery of fees incurred to enforce indemnification rights, but did not add those provisions.

- Interpreting section 722(a) as granting officers the right to recover fees incurred to enforce indemnification rights would be inconsistent with the "American Rule" that each party must bear its own litigation expenses.

Dissent. Interpreting section 722(a) as not granting officers the right to recover fees incurred to enforce indemnification rights will significantly impair the legislative mandate for indemnification because defendant companies gain considerable leverage in keeping individual directors in the fold of a common defense, on pain of paying their own legal expenses if they seek to assert meritorious separate defenses. Neither the indeterminative legislative history nor the "American rule" require such an interpretation. The legislature's failure to amend the indemnification provisions in order to expressly permit the recovery of "fees for fees" reflects the fact that these provisions already permitted such recovery. And the "American Rule" is not controlling because the right to indemnification is provided by statute, not contract.

Comment. As the majority observes, its holding would not bar a corporation and an officer from contracting for "fees for fees." Of course, if the dissenter's interpretation had prevailed, a corporation and an officer could have contracted to bar "fees for fees." The real difference between the two interpretations of section 722(a) would be the size of the transaction costs that each would generate.

---

5. **Advance of Defense Costs Does Not Depend on Merit of Claim or Impact on Other Creditors--**

Ridder v. CityFed Financial Corp., 47 F.3d 85 (3d Cir. 1995).

Facts. Resolution Trust Corporation ("RTC"), as receiver for CityFed Financial Corporation (D), a Delaware corporation, sued Ridder and three other former employees of D's wholly owned subsidiaries (Ps), claiming that they had committed various frauds and breaches of their fiduciary duty to their employer. Upon being served with the complaint, Ps demanded that D advance funds for attorneys' fees that they would incur in defending the RTC litigation as provided in Article XI of D's bylaws. The bylaws require that D indemnify and hold harmless all employees sued or threatened to be sued by reason of their employment by D or any of its subsidiaries "to the fullest extent authorized by the Delaware Corporation Law;" they specify that the right to indemnity "shall include the right to be paid the expenses incurred in defending any such proceeding in advance of its final disposition; provided, however that, if the Delaware Corporation Law so requires [as it does] the payment of such expenses . . . shall be made only upon delivery to the corporation of an undertaking . . . to repay all amounts so advanced if it shall ultimately be determined that such employee is not entitled to be indemnified." D refused to advance the fees, so Ps sued to compel payment. They sought a preliminary injunction and summary judgment. At a hearing, Ps made a strong showing that, unless defense costs were advanced to them, their ability to defend the RTC action would be irreparably harmed. Nevertheless, the district court refused to issue the injunction, citing (i) the probability that RTC would prevail on the merits and (ii) the harm that D's other creditors would suffer if D advanced the fees. Ps appeal.

Issue. Under bylaws requiring a corporation to advance defense costs, is a covered employee entitled to such an advance even if he is likely to lose the case against him and the advance might harm other creditors of the corporation?

Held. Yes. Order reversed with instructions to issue an injunction requiring the advance of reasonable defense costs.

♦ Neither section 145(e) of the Delaware Corporation Code nor D's bylaws condition the advance of attorneys' fees on the likelihood that employees will prevail or on the potential harm that other creditors might suffer as a result. Both the statute and the bylaws contemplate that an employee who receives such an advance may lose since they both condition the obligation to advance defense costs upon an undertaking "to repay such amount if it shall ultimately be determined that [the officer] is not entitled to be indemnified by the corporation."

♦ Rarely, if ever, would directors breach a fiduciary duty by complying with the requirements of their corporation's bylaws, as expressly authorized by statute.

♦ The impact, if any, of advancing the fees was "purely speculative."

---

6. **Insurance.** Most director and officer ("D&O") insurance provides both officers and directors with coverage for certain unindemnified losses and the corporation with coverage for its indemnification. Many policies cover losses that the corporation could not indemnify. One might justify this coverage on the ground that the insurance company acts as an additional monitor to the benefit of the shareholders, but not all academics accept this argument.

IX. CORPORATE ACQUISITIONS, TAKEOVERS, AND CONTROL TRANSACTIONS

A. INTRODUCTION

Control transactions serve as a mechanism for outsider monitoring of management. Necessarily, then, these transactions pose a conflict of interest for management. Consider these illustrations:

(i)   An acquiring corporation's managers may favor a profit-reducing acquisition because expansion accompanied by a reduction in earnings volatility will reduce the risk that these managers will forfeit some of the value of their investment in their careers at the acquiring corporation and other "undiversified human capital" (which has no value to a public shareholder who can hold a diversified portfolio of investments);

(ii) A target corporation's managers may favor a profit-reducing transaction because of a promise of continued employment; or they may oppose it because they fear firing.

An individual, group, or corporation can obtain control of the productive assets of a "target corporation" by: (i) purchasing the target's assets, (ii) merging with it, or (iii) purchasing a controlling block of its voting shares. The first two transactions, however, require approval not only by the target's shareholders but by its board of directors as well. This explains why control block purchases serve as a vital mechanism for monitoring management. A potential control block purchaser will ordinarily prefer this transaction to a proxy fight, in part because if a proxy fight results in an increase share price, he would necessarily share this gain pro rata with other shareholders.

1.   **Control Transactions.** The casebook authors assert that "the goal of corporate law in the area of corporate acquisitions, takeovers, and control transactions is to specify a set of decision rules that provide reasonable assurance that good transactions—those that will increase shareholder value—will be approved and bad transactions rejected. On this view, some of the following issues arise: Once a target's board has declined an offer, what role should it adopt if the offeror seeks to purchase control directly from the shareholders, who generally possess less expertise than the directors about the target's business? Should the target's board or management bargain on behalf of the widely dispersed shareholders? If so, may the target's board or management take steps to prevent the offeror from bypassing the shareholders' agent? If the target's board or management may take such steps, should courts police their pursuit of self-interest? If so, how?

B. TENDER OFFERS AND THEIR REGULATION

A tender offerer makes a conditional public offer, open for a limited period, to buy the target's shares, usually at a price well above market. The conditions, which will include at least (i) a minimum tender and (ii) no material change for the worse in the business or financial structure of the target, appear in the offering documents. The bidder may offer to pay cash or to exchange a package of its securities for all or some of the share of the class sought. (In the case of a "partial bid," the bidder ordinarily reserves the right to accept more than the number of shares specified.) Acceptance requires depositing shares with a depository bank serving as the bidder's agent. If none of the contingencies entitling the bidder to cancel or reduce its offer occur or if the bidder waives its right to do so, this bank uses previously deposited funds to buy the tendered shares on behalf of the bidder.

Federal law, principally the 1968 Williams Act, which added sections 13 and 14 of the Securities Exchange Act of 1934, limit tender offers primarily by prescribing (i) the minimum period during which shareholders may tender, (ii) the disclosures that must be made in connection with a tender offer, and (iii) the withdrawal and "equal treatment" rights of tendering shareholders to their shares. State corporation law, particularly the law of fiduciary duties, serves as the principal limit on the conduct of target managements. Forty states have enacted anti-takeover statutes, some of which, such as Pennsylvania's, virtually prohibit hostile offers.

C. HOSTILE TRANSACTIONS

Because hostile transactions necessarily create a conflict of interest for the officers and directors of a target corporation, these transactions raise some difficult issues: Once a rejected suitor makes a hostile tender offer, what role, if any, should the target's officers and directors play? May they take actions to discourage the suitor from pursuing the tender offer? May they do so in order to induce the suitor to bargain with them rather than with dispersed, and thus perhaps less effective, share-holders? If the target's officers and directors may take such actions, under what standards should courts review them?

1. Early Doctrine--

Cheff v. Mathes, 41 Del. Ch. 494, 199 A.2d 548 (1964).

Facts. A derivative action by a minority shareholder, Mathes (P), seeking to set aside the purchase by the company (Holland) of its own securities from another corporation ("MP"). The company's sales and earnings had been declining; management had completed a reorganization, which it assumed would halt the decline. MP, owned by a man with a reputation for "raiding" other corporations, had purchased the interest in the company, then had inquired about a merger and sought representation on Holland's board. Holland's board consisted of the president and the legal counsel and others (Ds), all of whom owned stock in Holland. Ds voted to purchase the shares of Holland owned by MP at a price above the market price, based on the fact that: (i) if MP took over, it threatened to reorganize Holland's sales distribution system, and (ii) the threat of the takeover was causing poor employee morale and in some cases employees were quitting. P argued that the purchase was designed simply to perpetuate Ds in office.

Issue. Was the purchase of the corporation's shares undertaken for an improper purpose?

Held. No. Judgment for Ds.

♦ When directors face the threat of a corporation takeover and they purchase stock of the corporation, there is a conflict of interest (*i.e.,* the purchase may be to prevent a takeover and thus to perpetuate the directors or officers in office). When this occurs, the burden of proof is on the fiduciaries to show that they have acted in good faith in the interest of the corporation and its shareholders.

♦ Directors who have a pecuniary interest in the corporation (such as the president and the legal counsel, since they received salaries) are held to a higher standard of proof than other directors.

♦ In this case, the facts support a showing that Ds had a proper business motive for the stock purchases; thus, their actions were in good faith. They had reasonable grounds to believe that a threat existed to corporate policy that they believed was in the best interests of the corporation (maintenance of the sales system).

Comment. Because corporate tacticians could easily manufacture policy conflicts, *Cheff* practically immunized almost all defensive tactics.

---

2. **Defensive Tactics.**

   a. **Supermajority provisions.** A successful tender offeror typically eliminates a target's remaining shareholders through a "second step" merger requiring shareholder approval (unless the bidder has acquired nearly all the stock and can utilize a "short form" merger). A majority or a two-thirds vote ordinarily constitutes approval, but the articles may require more votes and perhaps an unusually large quorum, too. (The articles will also require this supermajority to amend this provision.) Such a provision discourages partial bids. Most corporation statutes permit a simple majority vote to adopt a supermajority provision, but the Revised Model Business Corporation Act ("RMBCA") and the American Law Institute's Corporate Governance Project would require the specified supermajority to adopt it.

   b. **"Fair price" provisions.** These provisions provide for the waiver of one or more takeover obstacles if the bidder pays a "fair price" in the second-step transaction. They usually define "fair price" as at least equal to the highest of: (i) the highest price paid by the bidder for any shares acquired during or immediately before the tender offer; (ii) the highest price at which the stock has traded during some period; (iii) a price that is in the same proportion of the share price at the time that the second-step transaction was announced as the tender offer price was to the share price at the time that the tender offer was announced; and (iv) the product of multiplying the target's average earnings per share by the bidder's average price-earnings ratio. The definition may yield a second-step price significantly higher than the tender offer price, which deters shareholders from tendering.

Some fair price provisions provide that if the bidder fails to propose a second-step merger at a "fair price," target shareholders may insist that the target purchase their stock at that price.

c. **Staggered board provisions.** A provision in the articles dividing the board into classes each elected in different years, may delay a bidder's acquisition of control—but only if the target's directors choose to remain on the board after a hostile bidder has acquired a majority of the stock.

d. **"Shark repellant" bylaws.** "Shark repellant" provisions typically (i) require that any person wishing to bring any matter before the shareholders' meeting or to nominate directors must give the board advance notice; (ii) grant the board, but not the shareholders, the power to fill newly created board positions; and (iii) constrain shareholder action through written consent.

e. **Poison pills.**

1) **A good illustration: the original pill.** The target board used the power bestowed on it by a "blank check" provision in the articles to create a new class of preferred stock possessing a critical conversion feature (the "poison in the pill") and distributed this stock as a dividend to its common stockholders. The critical conversion feature enabled a holder of the preferred stock to convert it into an acquirer's common stock in a ratio that effectively permitted the holder to purchase the common stock at a steep discount. This "flip-over" feature would become operative, however, only if an acquirer were to purchase more than a specified percentage of the target's stock and subsequently acquire the target in a business combination, such as a merger or an asset sale. A bidder trying to minimize the threat of dilution might offer to buy all or nearly all of the target's shares. A bidder might also negotiate with the board because the "flip-over" provision typically empowered the board to "call" or "redeem" the preferred stock at a low price for a short period after a triggering event occurred.

When poison pills are challenged in a lawsuit, courts often focus more on the board's failure to redeem (or its selective redemption) than on the board's decision to adopt the pill.

2) Adaptations.

    a) "Fair price" provision. The pill was made effective against bidders who declined to engage in a second-step transaction by adding a "fair price" provision to the redemption formula of the convertible preferred stock that entitled the holder to compel a buy-back from the target at a price equal to the highest paid by the bidder in acquiring target shares (the "flip-in"). Triggering events were expanded to include a bidder's substantial open-market purchases, intercorporate transactions between the two firms once the bidder acquired control, or the bidder's failure to propose a second-step merger within a specific period.

    b) "Share purchase rights plan." The target distributes a dividend of warrants or "rights" to its shareholders that conditionally entitles all but the bidder and its affiliates to purchase the target's stock for a specified period. The condition is typically the announcement of a tender offer or a major stock acquisition. If the target is taken over, the "rights" become exercisable against the acquiror ("flip-over").

    c) "Note purchase rights plan." Designed for use after a takeover campaign begins, this plan implements a "flip-in" pill. The rights holder may compel the target to exchange the holder's stock for a valuable package of securities if a triggering event occurs, and passing a specified level of share ownership is usually one of the events. The package of securities exchanged will customarily consist of senior debt securities subject to financial covenants designed to interfere with the bidder's financing.

f. "Greenmail." When a target's board purchases a potential bidder's stock for an above-market price, critics call the premium "greenmail." Claims that paying "greenmail" constitutes a breach of fiduciary duty, however, have met with little success. A well-counseled board usually creates a paper trail designed to show that continued shareholding by the bidder will likely disrupt operations, thereby endangering the value of the corporation. Most courts have deferred to the board's judgment under the business judgment rule.

g. Restructuring defenses. To compete with the bidder, target management may offer its shareholders a package of cash or securities whose value arguably exceeds that of the package offered by the bidder. It may finance this package by selling or spinning off assets just as the bidder had proposed to do. Restructuring often involves substantially increased use of debt borrowed by the target and paid out to shareholders in cash or debt securities. Leveraged buyouts ("LBOs") and recapitalizations are the most common forms.

1) In a typical LBO, the target's management and its allied investment bankers, operating through a newly organized corporation, offer to buy a target's stock with the proceeds of a loan for which the target's assets will serve as collateral. This offer often begins or prompts a bidding war. In this war, the management-led bidder may obtain some advantage from the target—such as a lock-up option on some prized asset or financial assistance—which almost inevitably yields a legal challenge and usually a judgment for the outside bidder.

2) In a typical *recapitalization*, the target's board offers public shareholders cash and debt securities while it offers management additional shares or options to purchase them. Management may prefer a recapitalization to an LBO because a recapitalization (i) leaves management with more equity without requiring them to borrow personally; (ii) does not require a shareholder vote; (iii) does not price the company (as an LBO tender offer does), which could start a bidding contest; and (iv) may also prompt the hostile bidder to back off if the new, more highly leveraged capital structure reduces the disparity between stock and liquidation values that originally attracted this bidder.

h. **Effect on shareholder wealth.** The casebook authors interpret the empirical evidence as showing that successful resistance by target management hurts shareholders, but that some particular defensive tactics seem to have no impact, while others may help.

3. **Proportionality Review--**

Unocal Corp. v. Mesa Petroleum Co., 493 A.2d 946 (Del. 1985).

Facts. Mesa (P) began a two-tier "front-loaded" cash tender offer for 64 million shares of Unocal Corp. (D) at $54 per share. The "back end" of the offer involved eliminating the remaining publicly held shares by an exchange of highly subordinated securities or "junk bonds." The board of directors of D met with their financial advisors to discuss the tender offer. In the opinion of the advisors, the offer was wholly inadequate. As a defense strategy, the advisors suggested a self-tender by D for its own stock at $70 to $75 per share. While D would incur substantial debt, D would remain a viable entity. D's directors adopted a resolution rejecting P's offer as grossly inadequate.

After another meeting, and on the advice of the investment bankers, D's directors adopted an exchange offer at $72 per share. The resolution provided that if P succeeded in acquiring 51% of the outstanding shares, D would buy the remaining 49% for an exchange of debt securities having an aggregate par value of $72 per share. The resolution excluded P from participating in the offer.

P brought suit challenging its exclusion from D's exchange offer. The trial court temporarily restrained D from proceeding with the offer unless P was included. The trial court recognized that directors could oppose a hostile takeover but that the directors had the burden of showing a valid corporate purpose and that the transaction was fair to all stockholders, including those excluded. After a hearing, the trial court granted P a preliminary injunction, finding that, while the directors' decision to oppose P's takeover was made in good faith, the business judgment rule does not apply to a selective exchange offer. The trial court certified this interlocutory appeal as a question of first impression.

Issue. Under the business judgment rule, may a corporation defend itself against a hostile tender offer by means of a self-tender for its own shares, which excludes from participation the stockholder making the hostile tender offer?

Held. Yes. Judgment reversed and preliminary injunction vacated.

♦   A board of directors has the power to oppose a tender offer. The power of the directors to act comes from its fundamental duty and obligation to protect the corporation, including the stockholders, from reasonably perceived harm irrespective of the source. In the acquisition of its own shares, a Delaware corporation may deal selectively with its stockholders, provided the directors have not acted solely to entrench themselves in office. If the directors are disinterested and have acted in good faith and with due care, their decision will be upheld as a proper exercise of business judgment.

♦   The business judgment rule, which presumes that directors making a business decision acted on an informed basis in good faith and in the honest belief that the action was in the best interests of the company, is applicable in the context of a takeover bid. However, because of the danger that the board may be acting in its own interests in such a situation, the directors must show that they had reasonable grounds for believing that a danger to corporate policy and effectiveness existed because of another person's stock ownership. This burden was met by the showing that the directors acted in good faith and upon a reasonable investigation of the facts pursuant to a clear duty to protect the corporation.

♦   To come within the business judgment rule, a defensive measure must be reasonable in relation to the threat posed. Concerns may include the inadequacy of the price offered, the nature and timing of the offer, questions of illegality and the impact of the sale on stockholders and others, such as creditors, customers, employees, and the community.

♦   While the exchange offer is a form of selective treatment, it is lawful and is reasonably related to the threats posed. D's directors concluded that the value of D's shares was substantially above $54 per share. D also determined that the "junk bonds" were worth much less than $54. The directors' objective was either to defeat P's inadequate tender offer or, if P succeeded, to provide $72 worth of superior debt to the remaining stockholders, who would otherwise be forced to accept the "junk bonds."

♦ P's participation in D's offer would have thwarted the purpose of the offer, as D would be subsidizing P's effort to purchase stock at $54 per share. Also, P is not within the class of stockholders D is seeking to protect. That some of the directors are stockholders does not alone create a disqualifying "personal pecuniary interest" to defeat the operation of the business judgment rule. The directors are receiving a benefit shared generally by all stockholders except P. If P is dissatisfied, P may use its voting powers to vote the directors out.

Comment. S.E.C. Rule 13e-4 now forbids reporting companies from employing a selective self-tender. But the decision may have significant implications for use of the "flip-in" pill, which grants all shareholders except the bidder valuable rights to purchase the target's stock at a discount (or to redeem their shares at a premium). Apparently, the discrimination inherent in such a pill may pass judicial scrutiny if the pill is "reasonable in relation to the threat posed"—although just what would be considered reasonable is difficult to predict.

---

4. **Proportionality and the Pill.** Invoking *Unocal*, the Delaware Supreme Court upheld the validity of a poison pill in *Moran v. Household International, Inc.*, 500 A.2d 1346 (Del. 1985). Household's "flip-over" pill was triggered by the acquisition of 20% or more of its stock or by the announcement of a tender offer for at least 30%. According to the court, the pill provided reasonable protection against a coercive two-tier offer without deterring tender offers generally. In its opinion the court noted that the board had adopted the pill before any identifiable bidder had materialized, saying that it favored "pre-planning for the contingency of a hostile takeover [because it] might reduce the risk that, under the pressure of a takeover bid, management will fail to exercise reasonable judgment." The court seemingly attached considerable importance to the fact that the board had retained the power to redeem the pill in the face of an attractive takeover bid. "They [the directors] will be held to the same fiduciary standards any other board of directors would be held to in deciding to adopt a defensive mechanism [citing *Unocal*]."

5. **Defensive Stock Repurchases.** In *AC Acquisitions Corp. v. Anderson, Clayton & Co.*, 519 A.2d 103 (Del. Ch. 1986), the chancery court invoked *Unocal* when it enjoined a coercive defensive stock repurchase plan that management claimed was designed to protect shareholders from an inadequate coercive tender offer. Management had to permit shareholders to make a free choice between the two. This decision could imply that the only response "reasonably related" to the "threat" of a 100% offer is a higher bid.

6. **Redeeming a Poison Pill.** In *City Capital Associates v. Interco., Inc.*, 551 A.2d 787 (Del. 1988), the Delaware Chancery Court opined that when confronted with a hostile offer, a board may leave a poison pill in place while the board "take such steps as it deems appropriate to protect and advance shareholder interests," but once the board has taken these steps, "and it is apparent that the board does not intend to institute [an] auction, or to negotiate for an increase in the unwanted offer, and that it has taken such time as it required in good faith to arrange an alternative value-maximizing transaction, then, in most instances, the legitimate role of the poison pill in the context of a noncoercive offer will have been fully satisfied." The decision may reflect the idea that, in comparison to a judge, shareholders and the market enjoy a comparative advantage in valuing a business.

7. **Restructuring an Acquisition Threatened by a Competing Bid to Pursue a "Strategic Plan"--**

Paramount Communications, Inc. v. Time Inc., Fed. Sec. L. Rep. (CCH) ¶ 94,514 (Del. Ch. 1989).

Facts. On July 21, 1988, the board of Time Inc. (D) authorized management to negotiate a merger agreement with Warner Communications Inc. as long as the agreement provided that D's senior management would "ultimately come to control the combined entity." Such a merger would have advanced D's "long-term strategic plan." This plan called for D (i) to "create for itself . . . the video or film products that it delivers through its cable network (HBO) and cable franchises" and (ii) to expand internationally while (iii) preserving D as an independent enterprise with a "distinctive . . . 'Time culture,'" which embraced "a managerial philosophy and distinctive structure [Time's editor-in-chief reports directly to a special committee of the board] . . . intended to protect journalistic integrity from pressures from the business side of the enterprise."

On March 3, 1989, after months of sometimes rocky negotiations, the boards of D and Warner entered into a merger agreement providing for the exchange of .465 share of D for each share of Warner. At then-prevailing prices, this agreement would have provided Warner holders with a 12% premium over market. Collectively, they would have owned 62% of D's shares.

Because of the number of shares that D would have had to issue, NYSE rules required shareholder approval. Seeking this approval significantly increased the odds that one or more third parties would propose a competing transaction. But a third party would have to surmount D's "full armory of [takeover] defenses," including a poison pill preferred stock rights plan triggered by a 15% acquisition and a requirement of supermajority approval for a second-stage merger.

For the "principal purpose" of "discourag[ing] any effort to upset [this] transaction:"

(i) The two boards entered into a "Share Exchange Agreement" giving each an option to trigger a mutual share transfer: 11.1% of D's shares to Warner, 9.4% of Warner's shares to D;

(ii) D's board paid "dry up" fees to various banks for commitments to refuse financing for a takeover of D, a "dubious, futile innovation . . . when the global economy seems awash in cash available to finance takeovers."

Probably for the same purpose, D promised, as part of the merger agreement, that it would not "solicit or encourage or take any other action to facilitate any inquiries on the making of any proposal which constitutes or may . . . lead to, any takeover proposal" except in two circumstances. In the event of a hostile tender offer for at least 25% of its stock or a purchase of 10%, D could communicate with the offeror or purchaser but still had to perform under the agreement; Warner, however, could opt out.

On June 7, Paramount Communications, Inc. (P) offered to purchase all of the outstanding common stock of D for $175 cash per share, subject to the following, among other, conditions:

(i) Termination of the Time-Warner merger agreement;

(ii) Termination or invalidation of the Share Exchange Agreement without liability to D;

(iii) All material approvals, consents, and franchise transfers relating to D's programming and cable television business obtained on terms satisfactory to Paramount (in its sole discretion);

(iv) Removal of several obstacles created or controlled by D, such as D's poison pill and its requirement of supermajority approval for a second-stage merger; and

(v) Financing and tender of at least a majority of D's shares.

At a June 16 board meeting, after receiving "what would appear competent advice" from D's investment bankers at Wasserstein, Perella ("WP"), the board rejected P's offer for three reasons ("the record contains no evidence to support a supposition that [good faith] does not [exist]"). First, the conditions of P's offer, in particular condition "(iii)" relating to regulatory approvals for the transfer of D's cable franchises, would delay the acquisition, "at a minimum, some months or as much as a year," and thus effectively give P an option to purchase D while it sought these approvals (especially because of the language, "on terms satisfactory to Paramount (in its sole discretion)"). Second, and more importantly, the board believed that $175 per share was inadequate because, according to WP, the board could get more for shareholders via a recapitalization, a leveraged buyout, or a sale to a third party. (WP advised that an acquiror not contemplating a "bust-up" of D would probably pay more than $250 per share.) Third, and perhaps most importantly, the board believed that, even though Time-Warner stock would likely trade at a price "materially lower" than $175 per share when the merger closed, this price would rise much higher than $175 in subsequent years. WP reported that an analysis of both cash flow and earnings per share suggested that, when the merger closed, Time-Warner stock would trade in the $106 to $188 per share range, most probably at around $150 per share, but that it would trade in the $159 to $247 range in 1991, $230 to $332 range in 1992, and still higher in subsequent years.

D's board realized that D's largely institutional shareholders would probably favor accepting P's offer, so the board decided to restructure the Warner transaction so that it would not require shareholder approval and to trigger the Share Exchange Agreement. D proposed to buy 51% of Warner's outstanding common stock for $70 cash per share and then to merge with it. This price represented a 56% premium over the price of Warner stock prior to the announcement of the merger, and WP opined that $70 per share was "fair." On June 22, P raised its offer to $200 per share, but D's board rejected it for the same reasons that the board had rejected the $175 offer. P and several D shareholders filed several suits and sought a preliminary injunction against D's purchase of Warner stock.

Issues.

(i)   Must D's restructured acquisition of D pass muster under the business judgment rule or under the *Unocal* standard for defensive measures?

(ii)   Did P's offer threaten an interest that D's board may protect under *Unocal*?

(iii)   If P's offer does threaten such an interest, does D's restructured acquisition constitute a reasonable defensive measure?

Held. (i) Yes. (ii) Yes. (iii) Yes. D's restructured acquisition passes muster under *Unocal*. Preliminary injunction denied.

♦   Because D's board restructured the Warner acquisition in reaction to the emergence of P's offer and its likely effect on the proposed transaction, *Unocal* applies—even though the acquisition itself appears at this stage to have been chiefly motivated by strategic business concerns.

♦   The record did not establish a reasonable likelihood that D's board pursued Warner primarily to preserve its control. The restructured acquisition did not amount to the functional equivalent of P's offer in the same way as did the challenged transactions in *AC Acquisitions*, *Bass*, or *Interco*. Because the board has continued to manage the corporation for long-term profit pursuant to a preexisting business plan that itself is not primarily a control device or scheme, the corporation has a legally cognizable interest in achieving that plan. No persuasive evidence suggests that D's board had a corrupt or venal motivation in electing to continue with its plan.

♦   The "great importance" of pursuing D's major strategic business plan could justify strong defensive measures under *Unocal*, but D's board did only what was necessary to carry forward a preexisting transaction in an altered form. The restructured acquisition did not legally preclude a hostile tender offer. While the restructured acquisition reduced the chances that such an offer would succeed, the record as well as other contemporaneous takeover battles suggest that it did not foreclose such an offer.

- That many, presumably most, shareholders would prefer the board to do otherwise than it has done does not, in the circumstances of a challenge to this type of transaction, afford a basis to interfere with the effectuation of the board's business judgment.

Comment. In footnote 22, the chancellor states that a "decision not to redeem a poison pill, which by definition is a control mechanism and not a device with independent business purposes, may present distinctive considerations than those presented in this case." This statement may suggest that a paper record evidencing a long-term strategic plan might not thwart challenges to all defensive measures.

---

8. Appeal--

Paramount Communications, Inc. v. Time Inc., 571 A.2d 1140 (Del. 1990).

Facts. *See* previous case.

Issues.

(i) Did Paramount's cash offer for all shares of D pose a "threat" justifying defensive action by D's board?

(ii) If so, were the actions taken by D's board reasonably related and proportionate to this threat?

Held. (i) Yes. (ii) Yes. Judgment affirmed.

- "Coercion" from a two-tiered hostile tender offer and inadequate price are not the only "threats" justifying defensive action by a target board under *Unocal*. Paramount's cash offer for all of D's shares that had "values reasonably in the range of acceptable price" might have led D's shareholders to tender "in ignorance or a mistaken belief of the strategic benefit which a business combination with Warner might produce"—especially because of (i) the uncertainty resulting from the conditions attached to the offer and (ii) the fact that P made its offer after D's board mailed its proxy notice. The evidence does not show that when D's board concluded that "Paramount's offer posed a threat to corporate policy and effectiveness," the board lacked good faith or was "dominated by motives of either entrenchment or self-interest."

♦ Directors need not abandon a carefully conceived corporate plan for short-term shareholder profit unless there is clearly no basis to sustain the corporate strategy. Because the action taken by D in response to Paramount's offer had as its goal the carrying forward of a preexisting transaction in altered form, it was reasonably related to the threat. Because it did not preclude Paramount from making an offer for the combined Time-Warner company or from changing the conditions of its offer so as not to make the offer dependent upon the nullification of the Time-Warner agreement, it was proportionate.

---

9. **To Which "Threats" May a Board Lawfully Respond?** In *Paramount Communications, Inc. v. Time Inc.*, *supra*, the Delaware Supreme Court held that the "inadequate value" of an all, cash for all, shares offer is a "legally cognizable threat." More generally, commentators have identified three kinds of threats: (i) lost opportunity—perhaps a hostile offer could deprive target shareholders of the opportunity to accept a superior alternative offered by a rival bidder or by target management; (ii) "structural coercion"—perhaps a hostile offer that treats tendering and nontendering shareholders differently would distort shareholders' tender decisions; and (iii) "substantive coercion"—perhaps shareholders will accept a hostile offer because they mistakenly disbelieve management's representations of intrinsic value.

10. **Target's Open Market Purchases of Its Own Shares May Pass *Unocal* Proportionality Test Even If More than "Necessary" to Defeat "Inadequate" Hostile Offer--**

Unitrin, Inc. v. American General Corp., 651 A.2d 1361 (Del. 1995).

Facts. American General (P) proposed to merge with Unitrin (D) for $50 per share ($2.6 billion), a 30% premium over the market price of D's shares. The proposal stated that P "would consider offering a higher price" if D "could demonstrate additional value." P also offered to consider tax-free "[a]lternatives to an all cash transaction."

When the offer was made, D's articles required approval of a business combination with a more-than-15% stockholder by a majority of continuing directors or a 75% stockholder vote. D's board consisted of two insiders, CEO Vie and board chairman Jerome, and five outsiders, each of whom received $30,000 per year. The directors owned 23% of D's stock. (The outsiders owned stock whose value exceeded $450 million at P's offering price.) Twenty institutions owned 33% of D's shares; other institutional investors owned 9% of D's shares.

The board considered P's offer during two July meetings. CEO Vie reviewed D's financial condition and its ongoing business strategies. The board's investment advisor, Morgan Stanley & Co., made a presentation expressing the opinion that the offer was financially inadequate. Legal counsel expressed concern that the combination of D and P would raise antitrust complications due to the resultant decrease in competition in the home service insurance markets. The board unanimously concluded that P's merger proposal was not in the best interests of D's shareholders and voted to reject the offer. The board's advisors suggested that the board consider adopting a shareholder rights plan ("poison pill") and an advance notice provision for shareholder proposals because the articles and bylaws might not effectively deter all types of takeover strategies. The board declined to do so apparently because the director believed that P planned to keep its offer private.

In early August, P publicly announced its offer, noting that D's board had rejected P's offer. The price of D's stock rose to a level slightly below the price in P's offer and trading volume increased. At its regularly scheduled mid-August meeting, the board concluded that P's announcement constituted a hostile act designed to coerce the sale of D at an inadequate price. Identifying inadequate price and the possibility that antitrust laws and state insurance regulations might prevent consummation of the merger as the dangers posed by P's offer, the board unanimously approved the poison pill and the proposed advance notice bylaw that it had considered previously.

The board also approved the purchase of D's own stock as a vehicle for permitting the realization of immediate gains by stockholders who wished to do so, while providing enhanced value to stockholders who wished to maintain a long-term investment. Morgan Stanley explained alternatives for making the purchase and recommended open market transactions. The board adopted this recommendation and authorized the purchase of as many as 10 million shares. The announcement of this "Repurchase Program" stated that the director stockholders would not participate and that the repurchases "would increase the percentage ownership of those stockholders who choose not to sell," noting that the directors then owned 23% of D's stock and also noting the supermajority voting provision in D's articles.

P sued to enjoin the "Repurchase Program," and some of D's shareholders sued to compel sale of the company. After a hearing, the court of chancery found that D's board had invoked regulatory complications as a "makeweight excuse" for its defensive measures, but that D's board reasonably believed that P's offer was inadequate and posed a threat to D's uninformed stockholders. While noting that this threat was "mild" because the offer was negotiable both in price and structure, the court held that the board properly employed a poison pill and advance notice bylaws as proportionate defensive responses. The court also held, however, that, given the poison pill and advance notice bylaw, the "Repurchase Program" exceeded what was "necessary" to protect D's stockholders from a "low ball" negotiating strategy and was designed to keep the decision to combine with P within the control of the members of D's board, as stockholders, under virtually all circumstances.

The latter holding reflected the court's finding that the board expected the Repurchase Program, along with the directors' nonparticipation, "to create a 28% voting block to support the board's decision to reject [a future] offer by P." According to the court, when the directors cast their votes as stockholders in a proxy contest, they would be "subconsciously" motivated to vote against otherwise excellent offers that did not include a "price parameter" to compensate them for the loss of the "prestige and perquisites" of their directorships. The court made this finding despite the admission of P's chairman that the

Repurchase Program was not a "show stopper" because D's directors would sell their stock if the offer price were high enough. Invoking *Unocal,* the court preliminarily enjoined D from continuing the Repurchase Program.

Issue. If a target's open market purchases of its own shares is more than "necessary" to defeat an "inadequate" hostile offer, do the purchases necessarily constitute disproportionate responses under *Unocal?*

Held. No. Judgment reversed and remanded.

♦ The record did not support the chancellor's analysis of the likely impact of the Repurchase Program.

♦ The chancellor improperly "presumed" that, as stockholders, D's directors would be "subconsciously" motivated in a proxy contest to vote against "excellent offers" unless compensated for giving up the "prestige and perquisites" of their directorships.

♦ The directors did not need the Repurchase Program to give them the 25% voting power in a proxy contest to block a combination with a more-than-15% holder since they already owned 23% of D's stock and would already constitute actual voting power greater than 25% in a proxy contest and normal shareholder participation in such a contest is below 100%.

♦ Only a proposed combination with a more-than-15% holder would trigger the supermajority vote provision in D's articles, so an offeror such as P would not acquire more than 15% of D's stock before initiating a proxy contest. In such a context, the offeror could readily appeal to the institutional investors who owned 42% of D's stock, since such investors are "more likely than other shareholders to vote at all, more likely to vote against manager proposals, and more likely to vote for proposals by other shareholders."

♦ The chancellor erred in applying *Unocal's* "proportionality" by focusing on the "necessity" of the Repurchase Program rather than on whether it was preclusive or coercive and thus "draconian," and if not "draconian," whether it fell within a range of reasonable responses to the threat posed by P's offer.

♦ The "range of reasonableness" standard gives a board latitude in discharging its fiduciary duties to the corporation and its shareholders when defending against perceived threats.

♦ Under *Unocal,* a court should decide "whether the directors made a reasonable decision, not a perfect decision. If a board selected one of several reasonable alternatives, a court should not second guess that choice even though it might have decided otherwise or subsequent events may have cast doubt on the board's determination." The chancellor substituted his "business judgment for that of the board, contrary to . . . the 'range of reasonableness'" holding in *Paramount Communications, Inc v. QVC Network, Inc.*, 637 A.2d 34 (Del. 1994).

- A limited nondiscriminatory self-tender, like some other defensive measures, may thwart a current hostile bid, but is not inherently coercive. Moreover, it does not necessarily preclude future bids or proxy contests by stockholders who decline to participate in the repurchase. Even in combination with D's supermajority vote provision the Repurchase Program would not appear to have a preclusive effect upon P's ability to win a proxy contest.

- Proper and proportionate defensive responses are intended and permitted to thwart perceived threats. When a corporation is not for sale, the board of directors is the defender of the metaphorical medieval corporate bastion and protector of the corporation's shareholders. The fact that a defensive action must not be coercive or preclusive does not prevent a board from responding defensively before a bidder is at the corporate bastion's gate.

- The chancellor did not decide whether the Repurchase Program fell within a "range of reasonableness." The record suggests, however, that the Repurchase Program responded to the perceived inadequacy of the price offered, the nature and timing of P's offer, and the basic stockholder interests at stake, including those of short-term speculators whose actions may have fueled the coercive aspect of the offer at the expense of the long-term investor—all legitimate concerns under *Unocal*. On remand, the chancellor would have to determine whether the Repurchase Program was preclusive because it would render P's success mathematically impossible or realistically unattainable. If not preclusive, the chancellor would have to determine whether the Repurchase Program fell within the range of reasonableness, taking into account whether the Repurchase Program (i) was a "statutorily authorized form of business decision which a board of directors may routinely make in a non-takeover context;" (ii) was "limited and corresponded in degree or magnitude to the degree or magnitude of the threat [posed by P's Offer] (*i.e.,* assuming the threat was relatively 'mild,' was the response relatively 'mild?')"; and (iii) reflected the board's legitimate recognition that all shareholders are not alike, and provided immediate liquidity to those shareholders who wanted it.

Comment. The court noted, but did not seem to make much of the fact that, prior to the meeting, D's outside counsel sent D a draft press release and script for the meeting contemplating the adoption of the poison pill, advance notice provision, and the Repurchase Program. Such documents fueled P's argument that the meeting was window dressing for the board's decision to adopt these defensive actions; D explained the documents as contingency planning.

D. FRIENDLY TRANSACTIONS

Recall that friendly transactions, like hostile ones, can pose a conflict of interest for the officers and directors of a target corporation. For example, they may favor the transaction at least in part because of post-transaction employment prospects. To some extent, shareholders can use self-help to protect themselves by withholding their approval of a proposed merger or asset sale or by declining to tender their shares to a tender offeror. The target's officers and directors, however, may take steps that reduce the effectiveness of this self-help. For example, they may refrain from "shopping" for a more lucrative transaction, perhaps even contractually committing to such passivity. The courts have not provided easy-to-use guidelines for ascertaining whether, or under what circumstances, officers and directors can take such action.

1.   Defensive Measures Constituting Breach of Directors' Duty--

Revlon, Inc. v. MacAndrews & Forbes Holdings, Inc., 506 A.2d 173 (Del. 1986).

Facts. Pantry Pride (P) expressed interest in acquiring Revlon (D). D rebuffed all of P's subsequent attempts to discuss a friendly takeover. D's board of directors met to discuss the threat of a hostile bid by P. D's investment banker advised the board that P's proposed hostile tender offer at $45 per share was grossly inadequate. As a defensive measure, D's board adopted a proposal to buy five million of its 30 million outstanding shares. It also adopted a Note Purchase Rights Plan under which each of D's shareholders would receive as a dividend one Note Purchase Right ("the Rights") for each share of common stock owned, with the Rights entitling the holder to exchange one common share for a $65 principal note at 12% interest with one year maturity. The Rights would become effective whenever anyone acquired ownership of 20% or more of D's stock for cash at $65 per share. The Rights would not be available to such acquiror and, prior to the 20% triggering event, D could redeem the rights for 10¢ each. P made its first hostile offer at $47.50 per common share, subject to P's obtaining financing and the Rights being redeemed, rescinded, or voided. D's board advised stockholders to reject P's offer. D began a new offer for up to 10 million of its own shares, exchanging each share of common stock tendered for one Senior Subordinated Note ("the Notes") of $47.50 principal at 11.75% interest and one-tenth of a share of $9 cumulative convertible exchangeable preferred stock valued at $100 per share.

In view of D's exchange offer, P made a new tender offer of $42 per share, then raised it to $50 and then $53 per share. D agreed to a leveraged buyout by Forstmann. Under the terms of the agreement, each of D's stockholders would get $56 per share, D's management would purchase stock in the new company by exercising "golden parachutes," Forstmann would assume D's debt resulting from the issuance of the Notes, and D would redeem the Rights and waive the Notes covenant for Forstmann. Because of this agreement and the waiver of the Notes covenant, the market value of the Notes began to fall. D's directors received many complaints from noteholders and there were threats of litigation.

P made a new offer of $56.25 per share subject to nullification of the Rights, a waiver of the Notes covenant, and the election of three of P's directors to D's board. P met with D and Forstmann and announced that it would top any bid made by Forstmann.

Forstmann proposed a new offer of $57.25 based on several conditions. Forstmann demanded a lock-up option to purchase two of D's divisions at a price below actual value if another acquiror got 40% of D's shares. D was also required to accept a "no-shop" provision requiring D to deal only with Forstmann. Forstmann demanded removal of the Rights and Notes covenants and a $25 million cancellation fee to be placed in escrow and released to Forstmann if the new agreement terminated or another party acquired more than 19.9% of D's stock. There was to be no participation by D's management in the merger. In exchange, Forstmann agreed to support the par value of the Notes. Forstmann required immediate approval of the proposal or it would be withdrawn. D's board unanimously approved the proposal because it was for a higher price than P's offer, it protected the noteholders, and Forstmann's financing was in place. The covenants were waived.

P, which had originally sought injunctive relief from the Rights plan, filed an amended complaint challenging the lock-up, the cancellation fee, and the exercise of the Rights and Notes covenants. P also sought a TRO to prevent D from placing assets in escrow or transferring them to Forstmann. The trial court prohibited the transfer of assets and enjoined the lock-up, no-shop, and cancellation fee provisions of the agreement. The trial court found that D's directors had breached their duty of loyalty by making concessions to Forstmann out of concern for their liability to the noteholders. D appeals.

Issue. Were the defensive measures taken to avoid a hostile takeover consistent with the directors' duties to the shareholders?

Held. No. Judgment affirmed.

♦ The directors of a corporation owe fiduciary duties of care and loyalty to the corporation and its shareholders. When a board implements anti-takeover measures, there is a possibility that the board is acting primarily in its own interests. The directors must prove that they had reasonable grounds for believing there was a danger to corporate policy and effectiveness by showing good faith and reasonable investigation.

♦ In adopting the Rights plan, which gave shareholders the right to be bought out by the corporation at a premium whenever anyone acquired beneficial ownership of 20% or more of D's shares, D was protecting the shareholders from a hostile takeover at a price below the corporation's intrinsic value. The Rights plan was not unreasonable considering the threat posed. Thus, D's directors acted in good faith upon reasonable investigation. However, the usefulness of the plan was rendered moot by D's actions in redeeming the Rights conditioned upon consummation of a merger with Forstmann or to facilitate any more favorable offer.

♦ D's exchange offer for 10 million of its own shares was proper. The directors concluded that P's offer of $47.50 per share was grossly inadequate. The board acted in good faith on an informed basis and with reasonable grounds to believe there existed a threat to the corporation. However, when P increased its offer to $50 and then to $53 per share, it became obvious that the break-up of the company was inevitable. The duty of the directors changed from preserving the corporate entity to maximizing the sale value for the shareholders' benefit.

- The lock-up agreement with its emphasis on shoring up the value of the Notes was inconsistent with the directors' responsibility. Obtaining the highest price for the benefit of the shareholders should have been the directors' goal. By preferring the noteholders, the directors breached their primary duty of loyalty. Concern for nonshareholder interests is inappropriate when the object is no longer to protect the corporation but to sell it to the highest bidder.

- A lock-up provision is not per se illegal. Those lock-ups that draw bidders into the battle benefit shareholders, but similar measures that end an active auction and foreclose further bidding operate to the shareholders' detriment. D's lock-up agreement ended the auction in return for very little actual improvement in the final bid. The principal benefit went to D's directors, who avoided personal liability to a class of creditors to whom the board owed no further duty. When a board ends an intense bidding contest on an insubstantial basis and a significant result of the action is to protect the directors, the action cannot withstand the enhanced scrutiny that *Unocal* requires of director conduct.

- The no-shop agreement is also impermissible because the board's duty was to sell the corporation to the highest bidder. The agreement to negotiate with only one buyer ended rather than intensified the bidding contest.

- P showed irreparable harm by establishing that, unless the lock-up and other aspects of the agreement are enjoined, P's opportunity to bid for D will be lost.

---

2. **Under What Circumstances Does *Revlon* Require the Board to Auction the Company?** Because *Unocal*'s proportionality test is far more permissive of defensive tactics than *Revlon*'s value-maximization test, target management will almost never admit that sale of the corporation has become inevitable. *Ivanhoe Partners v. Newmont Mining Corp.*, 535 A.2d 1344 (Del. 1987), arose out of a hostile bid by Ivanhoe partnership (led by Boone Pickens, who had been characterized in *Unocal* as a "greenmailer") for Newmont. Newmont responded by declaring an enormous dividend ($33 per share), which enabled its largest shareholder (Consolidated Gold Fields, PLC) to purchase sufficient shares from arbitrageurs to raise its share holdings from 26% to 49.7%. In conjunction with this dividend declaration, Gold Fields and Newmont entered into a "standstill agreement" limiting Gold Fields's representation on the board to 40%. Upholding these defensive maneuvers, the Delaware Supreme Court rejected the claim that they had transferred control of Newmont to management, much like a recapitalization might. *Note*: Perhaps the court perceived Newmont's board as trying to help shareholders deal with two pressure-filled partial bids: one from Ivanhoe, which had not specified when it would merge out the remaining shares or what it would pay, and the other from Gold Fields in the form of a "street sweep."

In any event, in *Black & Decker Corp. v. American Standard, Inc.,* 682 F. Supp. 772 (D. Del. 1988), the court declined to interpret *Ivanhoe Partners* broadly. This case arose out of the decision of a target's board to declare an extraordinary dividend payable to public shareholders in cash, to management in stock. The dividend would have given management effective control over 54.5% of the target's stock: 23.9% (up from 4.8%) owned outright and the remainder owned by a newly created ESOP. The court interpreted *Revlon* as requiring an auction, at least in the context of a control contest, when a board-initiated transaction would result in a transfer of control.

3. ***Revlon* vs. The Business Judgment Rule.** The boundary between *Revlon* and the business judgment rule becomes critical when management attempts to protect a friendly transaction, say by agreeing to a "lock-up" that will deter potential competing bidders.

4. ***Revlon's* Substantive Obligations.** To obtain the highest price, the target board must possess sufficient information to properly assess the company's value, and structure the sale process so that the price obtained approximates this value.

   a. **Information.** To assess a company's value, its board might (i) rely on the information that the directors possess by virtue of their service on the board as augmented in the negotiation process, (ii) seek an opinion from its investment banker, (iii) retain an investment banker to seek bids ("shop" the company); or (iv) conduct a formal auction. According to the Delaware Supreme Court in *Barkan v. Amsted Industries,* 567 A.2d 1279 (Del. 1989), *Revlon* does not necessarily require a formal auction. Indeed, its opinion seems to suggest that the court will customarily defer to the board's decision.

      The court observed that "[w]hen the board is considering a single offer and has no reliable grounds upon which to judge its adequacy, [it must] . . . canvas . . . the market to determine if higher bids may be elicited. When, however, the directors possess a body of reliable evidence with which to evaluate the fairness of a transaction, they may approve that transaction without conducting an active survey of the market. . . . [T]he circumstances in which this passive approach is acceptable are limited. . . . Here the Chancellor found that the advice of the Special Committee's investment bankers, when coupled with the special circumstances surrounding the negotiation and consummation of the management-sponsored leveraged buyout ("MBO"), supported a finding that Amsted's directors had acted in good faith to arrange the best possible transaction for shareholders."

      The court revisited this matter in *Paramount Communications, Inc. v. QVC Network, Inc. (infra).*

   b. **Structuring the transaction.** It remains to be seen whether courts can meaningfully review favoritism so as to distinguish the kind that yields a higher price for shareholders from the kind that yields a better deal for management.

c.   **Standard of review--**

Mills Acquisition Co. v. Macmillan, Inc., 559 A.2d 1261 (Del. 1989).

Facts. To deter an unsolicited takeover bid for Macmillan (D), its CEO and its president pursued a restructuring plan that would have permitted senior management to obtain control without investing additional capital. The plan would have paid shareholders $64.15 per share, an amount deemed "fair" by management's investment advisors at Wasserstein, Perella ("WP"). In mid-July 1988, Chancery enjoined the plan in the face of a "clearly superior" $73 per share cash offer from Bass Group. Management then began discussions with investment bankers at Kohlberg Kravis Roberts ("KKR") about defensive measures to thwart the Bass offer. Six days later, Maxwell (P) proposed to acquire D in a merger for $80 cash per share.

Management did not respond to this proposal except to intensify discussions with KKR about a leveraged buyout, providing KKR with confidential financial information. In mid-August, having heard nothing from D, P made an $80 cash tender offer for all D shares, conditioned solely upon receiving the same information provided to KKR. P then opined that $80 was inadequate, even though WP had opined some months earlier that D had a maximum value of $80 per share.

At an August 30 meeting with D's CEO, P received some of the requested information, but the CEO stated that he would do everything within his power to prevent P from acquiring D (the CEO did hold out the possibility of selling $1 billion worth of D's assets to P). P "indicated his intent and ability to prevail in an auction for the company, as 'nobody could afford' to top a [P] bid due to the operational economies and synergies available through a merger of [P's] companies with [D]."

On September 6, representatives of D and KKR negotiated about a leveraged buyout that would permit D's senior management to own as much as 20% of the new company. The negotiations did not establish the price that KKR would pay for D's shares, yet D's CEO and "his senior managers suggested that they would endorse the concept and structure of the buyout to the board of directors." When KKR announced the leveraged buyout offer, D's board recommended it to D's shareholders, but later withdrew this recommendation in the face of higher offers from P. On September 11, the board formally concluded that selling D would advance the best interests of the stockholders. The board retained Lazard as the independent directors' financial advisor, but "throughout, [Lazard] acquiesced in Wasserstein's predominant role." WP proceeded to solicit bids.

By the September 26 "deadline," P had offered to pay $89 in cash for each of D's share. KKR had offered $82 in cash and subordinated securities valued by KKR at $7.50. KKR made its "'blended' front-loaded" offer subject to three conditions that were "designed to end the auction:" (i) D could not shop the KKR offer, which meant, according to KKR, that D could not disclose any portion of it; (ii) D would grant KKR a "lock-up" option to purchase eight of D's subsidiaries for $950 million; and (iii) D would execute a definitive merger agreement by noon the next day.

D's financial analysts deemed the bids too close to favor one over the other so they recommended that the auction continue. Unidentified financial advisors of D then disclosed to its CEO and president the price and the structure of each bid. In the president's presence, the CEO then telephoned a KKR representative to tip him that P had offered "$89, all cash."

Apparently ignorant of the CEO's "tip," Wasserstein read a prepared text to representatives of both bidders: "We are not in a position at this time to recommend any bid. If you would like to increase your bid price, let us know by 10 p.m." Allegedly in response to questions from KKR, Wasserstein impressed upon KKR "the need to go as high as [KKR] could go" in terms of price. Wasserstein also told KKR: "Focus on price but be advised that we do not want to give a lock-up. If we granted a lock-up, we would need: (i) a significant gap in your bid over the competing bid; (ii) a smaller group of assets to be bought; and (iii) a higher price for the assets to be bought."

At about 10 p.m., Pirie telephoned Wasserstein to ask whether anyone had offered more than P. Pirie explained that, if the answer was "no," P would not raise his price, but that P might do so if the answer was "yes," and would promptly notify D of P's decision. Wasserstein testified that he had believed that providing this information might run afoul of KKR's "no-shop" condition. He refused to answer Pirie's question and announced that, if WP were to receive a higher bid, WP would not alert P. Pirie and P "reasonably . . . concluded that P had made the highest bid," and Wasserstein knew that they had so concluded. Wasserstein did not correct this belief even after KKR submitted a higher bid 10 minutes before the deadline. D's advisors never suggested that P raise its bid even though they negotiated with P's representatives for several hours about some unresolved terms of P's offer.

In their negotiations with KKR, on the other hand, these advisors pressed it to raise its revised bid, and KKR agreed to raise the face value from $90 to $90.05 per share. KKR had made its revised bid subject to the same conditions as its earlier bid except for changes in the "lock-up" option. In its revised bid, the option covered four, not eight, subsidiaries and called for KKR to pay $775 million, not $950 million. In the negotiations with D's representatives, KKR agreed to extend the option to cover three more divisions and to pay an additional $90 million. KKR also agreed to structure the purchase of these assets on a "cash basis," which meant that, upon the exercise of the option, D would bear a $250 million tax liability. D could have avoided this liability had it structured the purchase on an "installment basis." KKR and D knew that this potential tax liability would serve as a de facto financial "poison pill" that would effectively end the auction process.

D's board met on the morning of September 27 to consider the competing bids. "Wasserstein falsely claimed that [he] had conducted 'a level playing field auction where both parties had equal opportunity to participate.'" He "mistakenly assured the board that he had been the 'only conduit of information' during the process and, falsely, that both parties had received *identical* information during the auction." Neither the CEO, who chaired the meeting, nor the president, who attended, corrected these statements even though each knew them to be untrue. Wasserstein opined that KKR's bid was higher than P's, and the Lazard representative concurred. The board discussed inviting P to top KKR's bid but did not to do so because of fear that KKR would invoke the "no-shop" condition to withdraw its bid. The board accepted KKR's offer, granting it the lock-up option that it had sought, break-up fees, and expenses.

The next day, P sought a preliminary injunction against these moves, adding KKR as a defendant in its suit against D. Two days later, P raised its offer from $89 to $90.25 per share.

P made its offer conditional on the invalidation of the lock-up option granted to KKR. P also announced that he was prepared to pay $900 million for the four subsidiaries originally covered by KKR's revised bid ($125 million more than KKR had offered and $35 million more than KKR had promised to pay for these subsidiaries and three divisions to boot). On October 4, D's board rejected P's offer, citing the requirement that the lock-up option be invalidated.

After a hearing, the court of chancery found that, while D's board and management had favored KKR, they had neither prevented P from submitting a higher bid for D nor tricked P into refraining from doing so. Accordingly, the court denied P's motion for a preliminary injunction, and P appealed. The court held that D's shareholders should have the opportunity to consider P's offer, and so enjoined the application of D's "poison pill" shareholder rights plan to P's offer.

Issues.

(i) Was the decision to grant the lock-up option and agree to the no-shop provision entitled to the protection of the business judgment rule?

(ii) If not, was the decision "fair?"

Held. (i) No. (ii) No. Judgment denying P's motion for preliminary injunction reversed.

♦ In a matter as significant as the sale of corporate control, a board cannot simply rely upon corporate officers as provided by section 141(e) of the Delaware General Corporation Law, particularly where insiders are among the bidders. Because D's board's lack of oversight in structuring and directing the auction (which the court characterized in dicta as a breach of fundamental duties of loyalty and care) afforded D's management the opportunity to indulge in misconduct designed to favor the KKR bid in which they were participating, D must show that the challenged transaction was "fair."

♦ D could not justify, among other things, (i) subjecting P to a series of short bid deadlines in a seeming effort to prevent the submission of a meaningful bid; (ii) the tone and substance of the CEO's communication with P; (iii) giving more information to KKR; (iv) the CEO's tip of the two principal strategic components of P's bid; and (v) the misleading and deceptive silence of the CEO, the president, and Wasserstein, which constituted a fraud upon the board. Indeed, this conduct constituted a breach of the *Revlon* duty to seek the "highest price reasonably available for the company," at least insofar as the conduct occurred after the board decided to sell D.

♦ When the decision of the directors, granting the lock-up option, was not informed or was induced by breaches of fiduciary duties, such as those here, it cannot survive.

♦ The lock-up granted to KKR effectively ended the auction as it was designed to do. To withstand challenge, an auction-ending provision must confer a substantial benefit upon the stockholders, especially a lock-up such as this one that covered some of D's most valuable assets, its "crown jewels." This lock-up was not necessary to draw any of the bidders into the contest. This lock-up did not result in a final bid that materially enhanced general stockholder interests. When one compares what KKR received for the lock-up to its inconsiderable bid, the invalidity of the agreement becomes patent. When the intended effect is to end an active auction, at the very least the independent members of the board must attempt to negotiate alternative bids before granting such a significant concession. They failed to do so even when P announced that he was prepared to pay $900 million for the four subsidiaries originally covered by KKR's revised bid, which was $125 million more than KKR had offered.

♦ *Revlon* teaches that the use of a no-shop clause is even more limited than a lock-up agreement.

---

5. **Restructuring an Acquisition Threatened by a Competing Bid in Order to Pursue a "Strategic Plan"--**

Paramount Communications, Inc. v. Time Inc., Fed. Sec. L. Rep. (CCH) ¶ 94,514 (Del. Ch. 1989).

Facts. [The facts are set forth in the brief of this case that appears earlier in this chapter.]

Issue. Did the decision of D's board to consider the original merger agreement trigger *Revlon* duties?

Held. No.

♦ Because consummation of the original merger agreement would have left control in a "large, fluid, changeable and changing market" and would not have exposed D's shareholders to the "risks and consequences of holders of minority shares," consideration of the original merger agreement did not trigger *Revlon* duties.

- *Revlon* duties were not triggered simply because consummation might have reduced the chances, perhaps dramatically, of D's shareholders realizing a control premium in the foreseeable future.

---

6. **Appeal--**

Paramount Communications, Inc. v. Time Inc., 571 A.2d 1140 (Del. 1990).

Facts. *See supra.*

Issue. Did the decision of D's board to consider the original merger agreement trigger *Revlon* duties?

Held. No. Judgment affirmed.

- The chancellor's findings of fact and his conclusion are correct as a matter of law, but we invoke broader grounds: consideration of the original merger agreement did not trigger *Revlon* duties because of the absence of substantial evidence to conclude that Time's board, in negotiating with Warner, made the dissolution or breakup of the corporate entity inevitable, as was the case in *Revlon*. *Revlon* duties were not triggered simply because the agreement may have put Time "in play" or simply because Time's board adopted "structural safety devices" (a lock-up, a no-shop agreement, and the payment of "dry up" fees to various banks for commitments to refuse financing for a takeover of D).

---

7. **Acquisition by a Controlling Shareholder/Defensive Measures Deterring a Competing Offer--**

Paramount Communications, Inc. v. QVC Network, Inc., 637 A.2d 34 (Del. 1994).

Facts. On September 12, 1993, Paramount's (D's), board approved a merger with Viacom. Viacom's chairman and CEO, Sumner Redstone, owned more than 91% of National Amusements, Inc., which owned more than 85% of Viacom's Class A voting stock and almost 70% of its nonvoting Class B stock. As part of this "Original Merger Agreement," D promised to amend its poison pill to exempt the proposed merger. The agreement provided that for each share of D, a holder would receive .1 shares of Viacom Class A voting stock, .9 shares of Viacom Class B nonvoting stock, and $9.10. This consideration would have provided a "modest change of control premium."

In the "No-Shop Provision" of the Original Merger Agreement, D promised to refrain from even discussing or encouraging any competing transactions (absent "an unsolicited written, bona fide proposal . . . not subject to any material [financing] contingencies"). D also promised that, if its board recommended a competing transaction or terminated the agreement because of one, or if its shareholders failed to approve the merger, D would pay Viacom $100 million ("Termination Fee") and either (i) sell to Viacom as much as 19.9% of D's outstanding stock for $69.14 per share—for which Viacom could pay with senior subordinated notes of "questionable marketability" (the "Note Feature")—or, if Viacom preferred, pay it, in cash, the difference between $69.14 and the market price of D's stock, no matter how high (the "Put Feature"). This "Stock Option Agreement" as well as the "No-Shop Provision," and "Termination Fee," were "designed to make it more difficult for a competing bid to succeed."

Viacom's Redstone attempted to discourage QVC from making a competing bid, but failed. On October 21, 1993, QVC announced an $80 cash tender offer for 51% of D's outstanding shares, upon the successful completion of which, remaining D holders would receive 1.4+ shares of QVC common stock for each share of D in a second-step merger. QVC made its offer conditional on, among other things, invalidation of the Stock Option Agreement. On the same day, QVC filed suit and requested a preliminary injunction against enforcement of the "No-Shop Provision," "Termination Fee," "Stock Option Agreement," and other defensive measures.

Because QVC's offer had a face value $10 per share greater than Viacom's, Viacom recognized that it would have to renegotiate the terms of its proposed merger in favor of D's holders. The "Amended Merger Agreement" called for Viacom to make an $80 cash tender offer for 51% of D's outstanding shares, upon the successful completion of which, remaining D shareholders would receive a package of Viacom securities for each share of D: .2+ shares of Class A voting stock, almost one share of Class B nonvoting stock, and .2+ shares of convertible preferred stock. This agreement gave D (i) the right to refuse to exempt Viacom's offer from D's poison pill if, because of a better offer, D's board concluded that its fiduciary duties required a refusal and (ii) the power to terminate the agreement if D's board withdrew its recommendation of the Viacom transaction or recommended a competing transaction. Except for these provisions, the Amended Merger Agreement was "essentially the same" as the Original Merger Agreement. Although QVC's bid gave Paramount "considerable leverage with Viacom," Paramount did not attempt to eliminate or modify the "No-Shop Provision," "Termination Fee," or "Stock Option Agreement."

On November 6, Viacom raised its cash tender offer to $85 and made a comparable increase in the amount of Viacom securities that holders of D shares would receive in a subsequent second-step merger. Later that day, D's board agreed to recommend this bid to its holders. On November 12, QVC raised its cash tender offer to $90 per share and made a comparable increase in the amount of QVC securities that holders of D shares would receive in a subsequent second-step merger. The face value of this bid exceeded that of Viacom's by more than $1 billion.

D's board met three days later to consider QVC's bid. D's executive vice president, a board member, had distributed to his colleagues a summary of "conditions and uncertainties" attendant to the offer, a summary that, according to one director's testimony, gave a "very negative impression of the QVC bid." Management also distributed an analysis of the dollar value of the securities that shareholders would receive pursuant to each bid, but the analysis did not reflect an estimate of the price that the securities would have when the shareholders received them. Instead, it reflected then-current prices, "which fluctuated depending upon which company was perceived to be the more likely to acquire Paramount." At the meeting, D's board concluded that QVC's November 12 bid would not serve the best interests of the stockholders, purportedly because the bid was "excessively conditional." (Several directors testified that they believed that a merger with Viacom would prove more advantageous to D's future business prospects.) D's board did not communicate with QVC about the conditions attached to the offer because the directors believed that the No-Shop Provision barred such communication until QVC obtained firm financing.

On November 16, the chancery court held a hearing in connection with QVC's request for a preliminary injunction. At that time, the potential payment due Viacom under the Put Feature of the Stock Option Agreement neared $500 million, an "unreasonable level." Three days later, QVC's CEO advised D's board in writing that QVC had obtained financing commitments and that antitrust law posed no obstacle to its tender offer. The chancellor granted the preliminary injunction, and D appeals.

Issues.

(i)   Did the Original Merger Agreement obligate D's board to "seek the transaction offering the best value reasonably available to the stockholders" and subject the board's related conduct to "enhanced judicial scrutiny"?

(ii)   Did the No-Shop Provision, Termination Fee, and Stock Option Agreement help realize the "best value reasonably available to [D's] stockholders" or did D's board have reason to believe that these defensive measures would do so?

(iii)   If D's board cannot abide by the Amended Merger Agreement because of the directors' fiduciary duties, may Viacom obtain compensation from D as provided in the No-Shop Provision and the Stock Option Agreement?

Held. (i) Yes. (ii) No. (iii) No. Judgment affirmed.

♦   The Original Merger Agreement, if consummated, would have shifted control of D from a "fluid aggregation of unaffiliated stockholders" to a majority holder, one who could unilaterally change D's board's vision of a strategic alliance with Viacom.

♦   A shift in control would have deprived D's shareholders of the leverage to obtain another control premium. Therefore, since D's board initiated this potential shift, albeit unintentionally, D's shareholders became "entitled to . . . a control premium and/or protective devices of significant value"—even though D's board did not envision a breakup of D. Neither the Original Merger Agreement nor the Amended Merger Agreement included any "protective devices," so D's board became obligated to "seek the transaction offering the best value reasonably available to stockholders."

♦ D's board also became obligated to discharge its fiduciary duties to this end regardless of the provisions in the merger agreements, including the No-Shop Provision. Because D's board agreed to a potential control shift for a modest premium, and to the No-Shop Provision, Termination Fee, and Stock Option Agreement, and because the board treated competing bidders QVC and Viacom unequally, *Macmillan* requires enhanced judicial scrutiny. The board bears the burden of showing that it discharged its fiduciary duties.

♦ The board did not meet its burden with respect to process or result. The board clearly gave insufficient attention to the potential consequences of the defensive measures demanded by Viacom, particularly the unusual and potentially "draconian" provisions of the Stock Option Agreement, such as the Note Feature and the Put Feature. By the time QVC made its tender offer, the board should have realized that this agreement, coupled with the Termination Fee and the No-Shop Provision, were impeding the realization of the best value reasonably available to D's stockholders. Yet the board made no effort to "modify the improper defensive measures" despite Viacom's willingness to renegotiate in light of the QVC bid. Nor did the board seek more information from QVC or negotiate with it, apparently believing, based on advice from D's management, that the No-Shop Provision barred such conduct and that the QVC offer was too conditional. Even when QVC revised its offer so that on its face it exceeded Viacom's by more than $1 billion, D's board declined to negotiate with QVC, "paralyzed by this uninformed belief that the QVC offer was 'illusory.'" In light of this difference between the two offers, D's board could not justify its conduct on the basis of its vision of a strategic alliance with Viacom because (i) the merger would have deprived the board of the power to implement its vision, and (ii) its uninformed process had deprived this vision of much of its credibility. (When assessing the value of non-cash consideration, a board should focus on its value as of the date it will be received by the stockholders.)

♦ Because D's board breached its fiduciary duties when it agreed to the No-Shop Provision and the Stock Option Agreement containing "draconian" features, neither vested any rights in Viacom, a sophisticated party with experienced legal and financial advisors who knew of (and demanded) the unreasonable features.

---

8. **Change in Control After *QVC*?** *QVC* may raise more questions about what constitutes a "change in control" for the purposes of triggering *Revlon* obligations than it provides answers. A friendly merger that resulted in target share-

holders becoming minority shareholders in the widely held acquiring company did not constitute a "change in control," according to the Delaware Supreme Court in *Arnold v. Society for Savings*, 650 A.2d 1270 (Del. 1994). Nor did the negotiation of the merger amount to putting the company up for sale. "To fall within that category," the court reasoned, "the target must have initiated an active bidding process." Of course, an active bidding process might ensue even if the target does not initiate it; indeed, this is what happened in the *QVC* scenario. It is not at all clear whether this scenario would have changed the outcome in *Arnold*.

9. "No-Talk" Clauses--

Ace Limited v. Capital Re Corp., 747 A.2d 95 (Del. Ch. 2000).

Facts. ACE Limited ("ACE") (P) entered into a merger agreement with Capital Re Corporation (D), section 6.3 of which limited discussions about competing transactions. Section 6.3 provided that if D decided to engage in such discussions, its decision had to be based on the written advice of outside counsel that the fiduciary duties of D's board required the discussions. Without receiving such advice, D entered into negotiations with XL Capital, which had proposed a more valuable deal. P sought a TRO against what it claimed was a breach of section 6.3.

Issue. If a provision in a merger agreement provides that a board's discussions with a competitive bidder must be based on outside counsel's written advice that the board's fiduciary duties require such discussions, is the board prohibited from engaging in these discussions in the absence of outside counsel's written advice, even if the board knows that, without the discussions, the stockholders will be forced into a less favorable deal?

Held. No. TRO denied.

♦   The language of section 6.3 does not expressly bar the board from concluding, even if its outside counsel equivocates, that its fiduciary duties required discussions about a competing transaction. If the language were interpreted otherwise, it would probably be unenforceable for at least two reasons:

   It might preclude other transactions in a manner that raises eyebrows under *Unocal*, especially where a competing transaction appeared to be appreciably more valuable. In this "non-change of control context," the board's approval of the Merger Agreement is as formidable a barrier to another offer as a non-redeemable poison pill. It might well constitute an unreasonable preclusive and coercive defensive obstacle within the meaning of *Unocal*.

   It might prevent the board from discharging its duty of care, say by becoming informed about the competing offer.

10. Need for a "Fiduciary Out" Clause--

Omnicare, Inc. v. NCS Healthcare, Inc., 818 A.2d 914 (Del. 2003).

Facts. In the summer of 2001, NCS Healthcare, Inc. (D), an insolvent publicly traded Delaware corporation, invited Omnicare, Inc. (P) to discuss acquiring D. P proposed to acquire D's assets in a bankruptcy sale at a price that would have provided a small recovery for D's note holders and no recovery for its stockholders. D represented that it was not interested in any other kind of transaction other than an asset sale in bankruptcy.

In January 2002, a committee representing D's note holders solicited the interest of Genesis in acquiring D. Genesis made it clear that if it were going to engage in any negotiations with D, it would not do so as a "stalking horse." When Genesis displayed serious interest, D's four-member board, which included its two top executives who together as shareholders held voting control (65%) of D, appointed the two outside directors as a special committee to negotiate the terms of an acquisition. The entire board, however, retained authority to approve any transaction. The committee employed the board's legal counsel and financial advisors.

In June 2002, Genesis proposed a merger, which would take place outside the bankruptcy context, and as negotiations continued, the terms improved along with D's financial situation. Before Genesis would submit a formal offer, however, it insisted that D promise to refrain from engaging or particpating in any discussions or negotiations with respect to a competing transaction or a proposal for one, and D did so. Genesis's insistence on this exclusivity agreement reflected its previous loss to P in a bidding war. This experience also led Genesis to condition the proposed merger on:

(i) an agreement by D's board to submit the proposed merger to D's stockholders regardless of whether the board recommended the transaction;

(ii) an agreement by the two controlling shareholders to vote for the merger; and

(iii) an agreement by D's board to refrain from discussing competing transactions or providing non-public information to potential acquirers unless (i) the potential acquirer provided an unsolicited, *bona fide* written proposal documenting the terms of the acquisition and (ii) D's board believed in good faith that the proposal was or was likely to result in an acquisition on superior terms.

D's board and the two controlling shareholders so agreed.

On July 26, 2002, P proposed to acquire D in a transaction that would retire D's debt at par plus accrued interest and pay D's stockholders $3 cash for their shares—conditional on negotiating a merger agreement, obtaining certain third-party consents, and completing its due diligence. The special committee considered P's proposal even though it constituted a "competing transaction" within the meaning of the exclusivity agreement. The committee concluded that discussing the proposal with P would create an unacceptable risk that Genesis would abandon merger discussions. Nevertheless, the committee did instruct its advisors to use P's proposal to negotiate for improved terms with Genesis. Genesis did offer substantially improved terms, but made them conditional on board approval of the transaction by midnight the next day, July 28. Genesis represented that absent such approval it would withdraw its offer and terminate discussions. D's board approved.

In early August 2002, P began a tender offer for D's shares at a price of $3.50 per share. P also expressed a desire to discuss the terms of its offer, but it made any proposal conditional on satisfactory completion of a due diligence investigation of D. Because of this condition, the board did not conclude that P's expressions of interest were likely to lead to a "superior proposal" within the meaning of the merger agreement with Genesis. In early October, P dropped the condition and proposed to acquire all of D's outstanding shares for $3.50 per share in cash. D's board then withdrew its recommendation that the stockholders vote in favor of the merger with Genesis.

P sued to enjoin enforcement of the board's agreement to submit the proposed Genesis merger transaction to the stockholders regardless of the board's recommendation. The lower court evaluated this agreement under the *Unocal* standard because this agreement and the agreement by the controlling shareholders to vote in favor of the transaction both constituted "deal protection devices" which require "enhanced judicial scrutiny." The lower court held that these measures were reasonable in proportion to the threat posed to the corporation, and P appeals.

Issue. Is a board's agreement to submit a proposed merger transaction to the stockholders regardless of the board's recommendation enforceable when coupled with an agreement by the controlling shareholders to vote for the transaction?

Held. No. Judgment reversed.

♦ In applying enhanced judicial scrutiny to deal protection devices, a court must determine whether those measures are not preclusive or coercive before evaluating their "reasonableness."

♦ The agreement by the board to submit the Genesis merger to a shareholder vote regardless of the board's recommendation must be evaluated in light of the agreement by the controlling shareholders to vote in favor of the merger, even though stockholders are entitled to vote in their own interest.

♦ Together, these deal protection devices made it mathematically impossible for any other proposal to succeed no matter how superior it was. These devices "accomplished *a fait accompli*" which made them preclusive and coercive.

♦ These devices are also unenforceable because they completely prevented the board from discharging its fiduciary responsibilities to the minority stockholders at a time when the board's own judgment is most important.

♦ The marked improvements in D's financial situation during the negotiations with Genesis strongly suggests that D's board should have been alert to the prospect of competing offers or, as eventually occurred, a bidding contest. D's board was required to contract for an effective fiduciary out clause to exercise its continuing fiduciary responsibilities to the minority stockholders. The issues in this appeal do not involve the general validity of either stockholder voting agreements or the authority of directors to insert a Section 251(c) provision in a merger agreement. In this case, the NCS board combined those two otherwise valid actions and caused them to operate in concert as an absolute lock up, in the absence of an effective fiduciary out clause in the Genesis merger agreement.

Dissent. *Unitrin* polices the effect of board action on existing tender offers and proxy contests to ensure that the board cannot permanently impose its will on the stockholders, leaving the stockholders no recourse to their voting rights. D's board did not unilaterally adopt the challenged deal protection measures to fend off an existing hostile offer, but rather because, if they had not, "the only value-enhancing transaction available would have disappeared." The challenged deal protection measures should be evaluated under the business judgment rule.

In any event, the board's actions did not cause the stockholders to vote in favor of the proposed transaction for some reason other than the merits of that transaction. D's controlling stockholders' decision to commit their voting power to the merger was fully informed, so they were not "coerced." The other shareholders knew, or should be treated as knowing, that controlling stockholders with 65% of the vote can approve a merger over the objection of the minority holders, so if they felt coerced, the coercion was meaningless. That minority stockholders must rely for protection on the fiduciary duties owed to them by directors does not create a special duty to protect the minority stockholders from the consequences of a controlling stockholder's ultimate decision unless the controlling stockholder stands on both sides of the transaction, which is certainly not the case here. A board's *QVC* responsibilities when asked to lock up a deal when confronted with a superior transaction do not bar a board from committing itself to the only value-enhancing transaction available.

The Vice Chancellor correctly found that the board reasonably perceived that, when Genesis threatened to walk away, D had not received a viable offer from Omnicare—or anyone else—to pay off its creditors, cure its insolvency, and provide some payment to stockholders. The board's decision to treat that threat as real was indisputably a reasoned one. And the creditors could have forced D into bankruptcy at any time. So the board's actions were reasonable in relation to the threat posed to D.

Dissent. We should not encourage proscriptive rules that invalidate or render unenforceable precommitment strategies negotiated between two parties to a contract who will presumably, in the absence of conflicted interest, bargain intensely over every meaningful provision of a contract after a careful cost benefit analysis.

E. SALE OF CONTROL AT A PREMIUM

1. Three Arguments for Compulsory Sharing of the Premium.

a. "Control belongs to the corporation."

b. "The seller of control is essentially usurping a corporate opportunity to which all the shareholders are equally entitled."

c. "Any control premium . . . must have been paid to loot the corporation or injure the remaining shareholders."

2. Sale of a Corporate Asset--

Perlman v. Feldmann, 219 F.2d 173 (2d Cir. 1955).

Facts. Derivative shareholder action by minority shareholders (Ps) against the president, chairman of the board, and owner of 37% of the common stock of the company (D) for selling his shares at $20 per share to a syndicate of the company's customers who manufactured steel products (who thereby gained control of the company's steel output in a Korean War shortage market). After the sale, the directors of the company (who were the appointees of D) resigned, and the new purchasers were appointed as the board. The market price of the stock at the time of sale was $12 per share; the book value was $17. Ps claimed that the compensation received by D included compensation for the sale of a "corporate asset" held in trust by D as fiduciary for all the shareholders (the asset being the power to control allocation of the company's steel output in a tight market). The trial court found the price paid was "fair" (although it did not indicate what the price would have been if the power to control steel distribution had not been included; Ps had the burden of proof to show that the value of the stock was lower than what was paid). It was alleged by Ps that, due to the shortage, the company might have been able to use its supplies to get interest-free advances from customers to build new plant facilities, as well as to build up patronage in the area where it then could have competed successfully in normal markets. The trial court found that it had not been proven that these advantages existed. Ps appeal the judgment of the lower court.

Issue. Has there been a breach of fiduciary duty by D in selling majority control in these factual circumstances?

Held. Yes. Judgment for Ps. Case remanded to the lower court for a finding of the value of the premium received for the stock of D. Premium to be distributed among all of the remaining shareholders.

♦ The director, officer, and majority shareholders all have a fiduciary duty to the corporation and to the minority shareholders.

- Normally, a majority shareholder may sell his stock, even to his customers. But here, there was an element of corporate goodwill that belonged to all shareholders. As a fiduciary, D may not take this profit for himself in the form of a premium price for his stock.

- The goodwill consisted of the opportunity to get interest-free money from customers, etc., which was created by a wartime shortage market. D had the burden to show that these advantages did not exist.

Dissent. What duty is owed as a director, and how was it breached? What duty is owed as a majority shareholder? The evidence shows that the buyer bought from the corporation at the same prices that other customers paid; so no detriment was suffered on this basis. The trial court found that the shares were worth a fair value of $20 per share; D therefore did not sell the director positions. One cannot separate control value from a control block of stock. And there is nothing wrong with selling it, unless some type of fraud or looting occurs to the minority as a result. Also, if a "corporate asset" was sold, then recovery should go to the corporation and not to the individual minority shareholders.

---

3. Freeze Out Mergers and *Revlon*--

Mendel v. Carroll, 651 A.2d 297 (Del. Ch. 1994).

Facts. Wallace Carroll, Sr. (who died in 1990) or his children have always exercised control over Katy Industries, the company that he founded, even after its shares began trading on the New York Stock Exchange. In June 1992—when Katy stock was trading for about $16 per share—the Carroll family announced that it was reviewing its options in connection with its 52.6% interest in Katy. On September 1, family members formally agreed to act in concert to acquire Katy's publicly held shares, which were then trading at about $24 per share. Their "Participation Agreement generally provide[d] that . . . [they would] . . . (i) transfer shares only to a newly formed acquisition entity or to other family members; (ii) . . . vote in favor of a Carroll Merger . . .; and (iii) not solicit or vote in favor of any third party proposal."

The family offered to buy Katy's publicly held shares for $22 each. A "Special Committee comprised of directors who were apparently disinterested in the proposal" demanded $26. On the advice of Goldman, Sachs, the committee's investment bank advisor, the committee declined an offer of $24 per share, and the family withdrew its offer. In contemplation of a new offer, members of the family owning 48% of Katy's stock ("the Carroll Group") agreed to amend the Participation Agreement to enable Barry Carroll and his affiliates to sell their 4.6% holding. In March 1993, the Carroll Group made a new offer of $25.75 per share. Goldman, Sachs opined that this price was "fair," and so the Special Committee recommended acceptance. Accordingly, the board authorized Katy's officers to enter into a merger agreement with a family-controlled entity.

Before the merger closed, however, Pensler Capital Corp. and its partner, Rosecliff, Inc., proposed a "friendly" transaction in which their partnership would purchase all Katy shares for at least $29 each—subject to completing their "due diligence" investigation, obtaining financing, and securing required government approvals. Goldman, Sachs then withdrew its fairness opinion, pending clarification and evaluation of this offer, and in turn, the special committee withdrew its recommendation. Subsequently, Pensler and a new partner, Steinhardt Enterprises, offered $28 per share for all of Katy's stock, subject only to securing required government approvals. Barry Carroll decided to sell his shares. (A Stock Purchase Agreement required that he give the right of first refusal to the other members of the Carroll family.)

On December 1, 1993, the family exercised its right to terminate the merger agreement. It also filed with the S.E.C. a required disclosure form announcing that family members would make open market purchases of Katy stock "to establish the . . . [Carroll Group] as the holders . . . of a majority of the outstanding Shares and thereby to assure the control of the Company by the members of the . . . Family regardless of the level of shareholding of Mr. Barry Carroll." Purchases on the next two days brought the Carroll Group's holdings to 50.6%.

On December 5, Steinhardt Pensler proposed a merger that called for the partnership to pay $28 cash per share and for Katy's board to grant the partnership an option to purchase up to 1.8 million shares of authorized but unissued shares at the same price as they traded pursuant to the merger (and an option to put these shares to Katy if the shareholders failed to approve the merger). The Special Committee asked its Delaware counsel whether granting this option would violate a fiduciary duty owed by the board to the Carroll Group. The committee's Delaware counsel concluded in a formal opinion that this issue was "unclear." In light of this opinion, the Special Committee recommended that it discontinue negotiations with Steinhardt Pensler.

The committee also recommended that the board create a new committee to consider other methods of increasing the value of Katy shares, including: (i) a self-tender by Katy; (ii) a Dutch auction of Katy; or (iii) a dividend in excess of $10 per share. The new committee recommended a special cash dividend of $14 per share. The board endorsed this recommendation but did not declare the dividend because Katy shareholders sued and sought a preliminary injunction directing the board to grant the option requested by Steinhardt Pensler and prohibiting the board from distributing the special dividend (and prohibiting members of the Carroll Group from voting the shares acquired in open market purchases).

Issue. Was the Katy board obliged to grant the requested option and otherwise facilitate the Steinhardt Pensler offer?

Held. No. Preliminary injunction denied.

◆   No such obligation arose simply because the proposed Steinhardt Pensler merger would have permitted the minority shareholders to realize more cash than the proposed Carroll Group merger. They would have realized more cash because the price offered by Steinhardt Pensler necessarily included a control block premium.

One would not expect the price offered by the owners of the control block, the Carroll Group, to include such a premium, and there is nothing in the record that suggests that this price was inadequate or "unfair."

♦ Had a transaction of the kind proposed by Steinhardt Pensler occurred, the board would have been obliged to insure that the minority shareholders received a "fair" price. But the board was obliged to respect the rights of the Carroll family, and the family had no duty to sell its shares and never offered to do so. The board would have breached its fiduciary duty had it issued the requested option.

♦ The board may declare the proposed special dividend, despite its likely impact on the Steinhardt Pensler merger, because the board had no *Revlon* duty to facilitate this merger.

---

4. **Equal Opportunity in the Courts.** Many opinions have rejected the rule that controlling shareholders must provide an equal opportunity to share in the control premium. The strongest argument against it is that it will deter some wealth-creating control transactions. Indeed, from the perspective of foresight rather than hindsight, investors might well prefer a rule of unequal opportunity because this rule would permit the creation of a bigger pie, and an investor could partake as a shareholder in the target or the bidder.

5. **Sale of Office.** In theory, some sales of control at a premium might be attacked as the sale of a corporate office, which is prohibited. Consider, for example, a sale in which the purchaser obtains a board majority through seriatim resignations followed by vacancy-filling elections. The courts have not dealt uniformly with such sales. If the control transaction falls within the Williams Act, section 14(f) requires disclosure substantially equivalent to that required by the federal proxy rules. The continuing vitality of the sale-of-an-office theory is uncertain.

6. **S.E.C. Regulation.** Rule 14d-10, purportedly adopted pursuant to the Williams Act, requires that tender offerors accept securities from all holders of the class and pay the same price.

7. **Directors of Parent Who Sit on Board of Subsidiary Must Demonstrate Fairness of Transaction to Minority Holders of Subsidiary--**

In re **Digex Shareholders Litigation**, 789 A.2d 1176 (Del. Ch. 2000).

Facts. WorldCom sought to acquire Digex, Inc., a controlled subsidiary of Intermedia Communications, Inc. ("Intermedia"), by acquiring Intermedia. The Digex board had created a special committee "to evaluate the fairness to the Digex public shareholders of any transaction which involved the sale of [Intermedia's] Digex stock and to participate in any such transaction" because four of the seven members of the board represented Intermedia, which stood to share in the control premium as a result of such a transaction.

The acquisition of Intermedia did not require the approval of the Digex board, but WorldCom requested that the Digex board grant it a waiver from Delaware General Corporation Law section 203, the business combination statute. Section 203 provides that an acquirer of more than 15% of a target's shares may not engage in a range of interested transactions with the target for a period of years, except in a number of situations, one of which is where the target has granted a waiver. The request came during the hectic negotiating period from the evening of August 30 to the morning of September 1, less than 12 hours before the Digex board was scheduled to vote on the proposed transaction. The special committee did not participate in these negotiations. The Intermedia directors agreed to the waiver, in part, in exchange for an amendment to the Digex certificate of incorporation that would require the approval of independent directors of any material transaction between WorldCom and Digex after the merger. The record is silent as to exploration by the interested parties of any other options available to Digex.

At the Digex board meeting, one of the independent directors moved to postpone the vote on the WorldCom transaction for three days to allow Intermedia's financial advisors to solicit final offers from WorldCom and its competitors Exodus and Global Crossing. The four Intermedia directors defeated the motion. The board then discussed who should be allowed to vote the requested waiver, with the special committee's lawyer opining that the interested directors should not be allowed to vote and the interested directors' lawyer disagreeing. The four Intermedia directors decided to vote, and without any debate on the merits of granting the waiver, the board voted to grant it, with the four interested directors voting in favor and the three independent directors against.

Digex shareholders (Ps) sued to enjoin the waiver.

Issue. Did the four Intermedia directors breach their fiduciary duties by approving the waiver?

Held. Yes. Judgment for Ps.

♦   Because Intermedia stood to share in a control premium if WorldCom acquired it by acquiring Intermedia, its representatives on the Digex board were "interested." So, absent an independent negotiating structure, or the directors' total abstention from any participation in the matter, these directors bear the burden of demonstrating that the transaction, including the waiver, was "entirely fair" to Digex shareholders.

♦   It is not reasonably likely that the interested directors will be able to demonstrate "fair dealing," one of the components of "entire fairness." They learned of WorldCom's request for the waiver only hours before voting on it, but because they were also directors of Intermedia, they could not even devote the little time they had before the board vote to considering their options as Digex directors and negotiating solely in the interests of Digex. Rather, they had to spend much, if not most, of their time considering and negotiating the terms of the merger from the perspective of Intermedia, the actual participant in the deal with WorldCom. And these interested directors controlled the flow of all information from WorldCom to the independent directors. The lack of information coupled with the lack of discussion at the board meeting indicates that the waiver vote might not even pass muster under the business judgment rule.

- ♦ It was not in Digex's interest to make a quick decision. Because of Intermedia's poor financial condition, the independent directors reasonably believed that, to remain solvent, Intermedia would have to sell at least some of its stake in Digex.

- ♦ Because of the manner in which the negotiating process was handled, it is impossible to determine if a fair price was received.

F. REGULATION OF THE BIDDER

1. **Basic Structure of the Williams Act.** This Act not only requires disclosure and prohibits fraud, as do the other federal securities laws, it also contains substantive rules.

   a. **Alerting the market.** Section 13(d) requires disclosure by any person who becomes (directly or indirectly) the beneficial owner of more than 5% of a class of securities registered under section 12 of the 1934 Act. The disclosure takes the form of a Schedule 13D, and it must be filed with the S.E.C. and sent to the target and the relevant exchanges within 10 days of the transaction crossing the 5% threshold.

   b. **The offer.** Section 14(d) dictates some of the terms of a tender offer as well as requiring disclosure in the form of Schedule 14D-1.

   c. **No "fraud."** Section 14(e) prohibits "fraud" in connection with a tender offer in a manner that may be even broader than Rule 10b-5. Unlike sections 13(d) and 14(d), section 14(e) applies to tender offers regardless of the amount of shares sought or the status of the target as a reporting company.

2. **S.E.C. Rules.** The rules purportedly promulgated under the Williams Act impose requirements on tender offers that are far more draconian than the requirements contained in the Act itself. The rules make it far easier for a shareholder given a tender offer to shop around for alternative transactions. Whether the S.E.C. has the authority to promulgate these rules remains an open question.

3. **What Is a Tender Offer?**

   a. **"Tender offer" broadly defined.** In *Wellman v. Dickinson*, 475 F. Supp. 783 (S.D.N.Y 1979), Sun Company wished to acquire a controlling stake in Becton, Dickinson & Company *without* complying with the Williams Act. Sun telephoned 39 large holders and offered to buy their Sun stock at a large premium, with each holder given a short time to respond. The court held that Sun's solicitation of stock sales from various individual and institutional stockholders and subsequent purchases constituted a tender offer subject to the pre-acquisition disclosure provisions of the Williams Act. The court concluded that there had been a public solicitation after focusing on eight characteristics of a tender offer that the S.E.C. had suggested in other cases: (i) active and widespread solicitation of public shareholders for the shares of an issuer; (ii) solicitation made for a substantial percentage of the issuer's stock; (iii) terms of the offer are firm rather than negotiable; (iv) offer open only for a limited period of time; (v) offeree subjected to pressure to sell his stock; (vi) public announcements of a purchasing program concerning the target company preceding or accompanying rapid accumulation of large amounts of the target company's securities; (vii) the offer of a premium price; and (viii) conditioning the offer on the acquisition of a specified number of shares.

b. **Large open market purchases distinguished.** In *Brascan Ltd. v. Edper Equities Ltd.*, 477 F. Supp. 773 (S.D.N.Y. 1979), Edper quickly acquired 3.1 million shares of Brascan shares by contacting investors who held large blocks of Brascan and advising them that if they offered their shares on the American Stock Exchange at a price above the then trading price, Edper might be willing to purchase them. The court considered the same factors as did the *Wellman* court, *supra*, but held that because only one of the eight criteria was met—that the offer was for a substantial percentage of the target's stock—the stock exchange-mediated alternative to a tender offer fell outside the Williams Act.

4. **Market Sweeps.** The announcement of a tender offer prompts risk arbitrageurs to assemble huge blocks of the target's securities by "sweeping" the market. Because the arbs engage in this unsolicited activity, a bidder could cancel its tender offer and then acquire a control block on the open market from the arbs. The S.E.C. has proposed Rule 14d-11, which would bar open market purchases by a bidder for 30 days after a canceled tender offer. The second circuit has held that a bidder who cancels in bad faith must still comply with Rule 14(d)(7)'s "best price" provision.

5. **Disclosure.**

a. **The bidder's dual disclosure obligation.** When a bidder crosses the 5% threshold specified by section 13(d), it must file Schedule 13D. When it actually commences a tender offer, it must file a Schedule 14D-1 and provide investors with the information specified in Rule 14d-6. The largely overlapping schedules focus on the bidder's identity, source of funds, and plans for the target. Schedule 14D-1, however, also requires bidders who are not natural persons to furnish financial statements if the "bidder's financial condition is material" to the target shareholder's decision.

b. **Impact on investors: relevance and cost.** Why would shareholders ever want to have information about the bidder? Perhaps they would if they might remain minority shareholders—either because they so wished or because the bid encompassed only a portion of the target's shares. But most successful bidders merge out the minority shareholders within one to two years after the tender offer at a price that equals or exceeds the tender offer price. So this disclosure probably has no impact on shareholders' decisions to sell, but requiring it probably costs them by discouraging tender offers. The reason is that compliance with Schedule 14D-1 may be costly (although if the bidder is a "reporting company," the cost is merely that of including its previously prepared financial statement), and litigation about compliance even more so—not only in terms of out-of-pocket expenses, but delay as well.

c. **Must the bidder disclose information about the value of the target?** Most courts have found appraisals and the like too speculative or uncertain to require disclosure, thereby avoiding this issue. It is likely that such information will affect the market price and the bargaining among the bidder, the target, and possible white knights. But if courts required disclosure of such information, the bidder's incentive to search for it would decline dramatically. Moreover, a bidder could be caught in a "Catch 22" bind. If it overestimated the target's value, it might be liable to nontendering shareholders on the theory that they declined the offer (and the tender offer therefore failed) because they relied on the bidder's overly optimistic appraisal.

6. **Bidder Tactics and the Problem of Coercion.**

    a. **Economizing on the cost of acquisition.** The two most readily available methods are: (i) acquiring as much stock as possible prior to announcement—most commonly via open market purchasing, but often through private large block purchases from an institution or a former controlling shareholder; and (ii) pressuring target shareholders to tender—primarily by structuring the offer to penalize holdouts.

    b. **Pre-announcement stock acquisitions.** A typical bidder makes a rapid acquisition of just less than 5% of the target's stock, which avoids the need for filing Schedule 13D. Once across the 5% threshold, the bidder will customarily engage in massive purchasing during the next 10 days, at which time it must file Schedule 13D, disclosing its identity and plans. Of course, anxiety about either a rival bid or the prospect of becoming locked into an expensively obtained minority position (once a bidder obtains a 10% holding, section 16(b) may limit its ability to sell off its stock) may incline the bidder to make an early tender offer. (Before acquiring $15 million or 15% of the voting securities or assets of a substantial target, a bidder must file under the Hart-Scott-Rodino Act and refrain from purchasing additional securities until the expiration of the relevant waiting period.)

    c. **Pressuring shareholders to tender.**

1) **Why pressure?** Once a bid materializes, a bidder may reasonably expect that: (i) target shareholders may try to extract more for their shares by holding out; (ii) rivals, alerted by the bid that the target is a good buy, may make a competing bid; and (iii) target management may engage in efforts to protect their jobs or future financial health. Bidders try to reduce such behaviors by pressuring shareholders to tender. The traditional pressure takes the form of a "two-tier" or "front-loaded" tender. To illustrate: rather than offering $100 per share for all shares, a bidder may offer $125 per share for one-half of the target's shares while simultaneously announcing its intention to "merge out" the remaining one-half at $75 per share.

2) **Should the law regulate pressure tactics?** Some commentators answer "no" on the grounds that permitting such tactics maximizes the return on the bidder's search costs, which increases the number of bids, which promotes shareholders' interests. Commentators who answer "yes" disagree about the appropriate regulation. Some advocate a voting requirement under which shareholders could ***both*** tender and vote against the tender offer: a majority vote against would kill the offer; a majority vote in favor would keep the offer alive and permit those who voted against to tender their shares. Others advocate measures to promote auctions so that if a bid falls below what other informed bidders would pay, such bidders will have a chance and a reason to compete. Obviously, mandatory disclosure does not regulate pressure tactics.

G. FEDERAL REGULATION OF THE TARGET

1. **Mandatory Disclosure; Rule 14e-2: Position of Subject Company with Respect to a Tender Offer.** As a means reasonably designed to prevent fraudulent, deceptive, or manipulative acts or practices within the meaning of section 14(3) of the Act, the subject company, no later than 10 business days from the date the tender offer is first published or sent or given, shall publish, send, or give to security holders a statement disclosing that the subject company:

    a. Recommends acceptance or rejection of the bidder's tender offer;

    b. Expresses no opinion and is remaining neutral toward the bidder's tender offer; or

    c. Is unable to take a position with respect to the bidder's tender offer. Such statement shall also include the reason(s) for the position (including the inability to take a position) disclosed therein.

2. **Schedule 14D-9.** When target management makes the recommendation required by Rule 14e-2, it triggers the filing requirement of Rule 14d-9. Like Schedule 13D, Schedule 14D-9 requires disclosures about the filers' identity and back-

ground. The most significant disclosure, practically, is Item 7: "whether or not any negotiation is being undertaken or is underway by the subject company in response to the tender offer. . . ." But Schedule 14D-9 exempts some preliminary negotiations: "If no agreement in principle has yet been reached, the possible terms of any transaction or the parties thereto need not be disclosed if in the opinion of the Board of Directors of the subject company such disclosure would jeopardize continuation of such negotiations. . . ." Once Schedule 14D-9 is filed, target management must update any statements made in it, which can be problematic.

3. **Issuer Repurchases.** While a tender offer is pending, target management must make the disclosures required by rule 13e-1 (re: amount of securities to be bought and source of funds for the purchase) before purchasing any of its own shares. Before making a tender offer for its own securities, the target must make the disclosures required by rule 13e-4. These disclosures are similar to those required of the bidder under section 14(d) and (e).

H. FREEZE OUT MERGERS

1. **"Freeze Out" Mergers and the Appraisal Remedy.** Controlling shareholders may find it advantageous to "freeze out" minority holders through a merger in which these holders must accept cash for their shares. Most corporation statutes provide that holders who vote against a merger may insist that their corporation buy their shares at a price set by a court. (In most states, this same right belongs to shareholders who vote against the sale of all or substantially all of their corporation's assets, and in some states, it also belongs to shareholders who vote against certain important amendments to the articles of incorporation. Recently, many states have repealed the legislation granting such rights insofar as it applies to corporations with publicly traded shares, leaving shareholders in these corporations to the market.)

Minority holders have challenged the legality of freeze out mergers, putting into question whether "appraisal" is their exclusive remedy. In *Singer v. Magnavox*, 380 A.2d 969 (1977), the Delaware Supreme Court ruled that (i) a merger "for the sole purpose of freezing-out minority shareholders is an abuse of the corporate process" and (ii) even if the merger had a legitimate purpose, the controlling shareholders bore the burden to demonstrate its "entire fairness." The legitimate purpose requirement came to mean little because the Delaware Supreme Court held that a controlling shareholder's legitimate purpose would suffice. But "entire fairness" proved significant because it meant that the minority holder's lawyer could use the class action procedure (instead of the appraisal procedure, which required each shareholder to notify the corporation prior to the vote, cast a "no" vote, and petition the court for an appraisal) and perhaps obtain a more favorable measure of damages.

2. **"Entire Fairness"--**

Weinberger v. UOP, Inc., 457 A.2d 701 (Del. 1983).

Facts. In 1975, Signal Companies, Inc. ("Signal") proposed to acquire a controlling interest in UOP for $19 per share. UOP's shares were then trading on the NYSE for $14 per share. UOP's board sought $25 per share, but after arm's length bargaining, accepted $21 per share. At that price Signal acquired 50.5% of UOP, although many more shares were tendered. Signal nominated and elected six of UOP's 13 directors. When UOP's CEO retired later that year, Signal arranged to replace him with one of its longtime employees. This new CEO succeeded his predecessor on the UOP board and joined Signal's board, too.

In 1978, Signal's management directed two Signal officers to study the feasibility of acquiring the balance of UOP's outstanding shares. The two officers were also directors of both Signal and UOP. They concluded that the acquisition would be a good investment at any price up to $24 per share. At $24, the report projected a 15.5% return on investment. At $21—paying $17 million less—the report projected a 15.7% return. Neither the two officers nor anyone else ever disclosed this conclusion or their feasibility study to any non-Signal UOP director or shareholder.

At a meeting of Signal's executive committee on February 28, 1978, senior management proposed to offer $20 to $21 per share. UOP's CEO, who attended the meeting, labeled such an offer "generous." The executive committee authorized management to negotiate with UOP "with the intention of presenting a proposal to Signal's board . . . on March 6." Signal then issued a press release announcing its "negotiations for the acquisition for cash" of the UOP stock that it did not then own. The release noted that UOP shares had closed that day at $14.50. Two days later, Signal issued another press release referring to its earlier one about "negotiations" and stating that its management would recommend purchasing the minority interest in UOP for $20 to $21 per share.

Between February 28 and March 6, UOP's CEO consulted by phone with all of UOP's outside directors and retained Lehman Brothers to render a fairness opinion about the $20 to $21 price. He picked Lehman, the CEO testified, because, having served as UOP's investment banker for many years, it could best meet the deadline, then three business days away. UOP's CEO advised Signal's management that it should offer $21 per share in order to obtain the approval of UOP outside directors. Meanwhile, Lehman conducted a hurried and therefore "cursory" investigation and submitted a letter opining that a price in the $20 to $21 range would be "fair" to the minority shareholders.

On March 6, Signal's board proposed a cash-out merger at $21 per share, contingent on approval by a majority of the minority shares voted at a shareholder meeting ***provided that*** these minority shares plus Signal's shares equaled at least two-thirds of all of D's shares. UOP's board met simultaneously while telephonically linked to the other meeting. All board members had a copy of the proposal, UOP's most recent financial statements and financial data for 1974 to 1977, market price information, and Lehman's "fairness opinion letter." After presenting Signal's proposal and answering questions about it, directors affiliated with Signal, including UOP's CEO, left the meeting. The outside directors resolved to accept the offer.

UOP's management submitted the merger to the shareholders at the May 26 annual meeting. The proxy solicitation recommended approval. It stated: "The price was determined after *discussions* between James V. Crawford, a director of Signal and Chief Executive Officer of UOP, and officers of Signal which took place during meetings on February 28, 1978, and in the course of several subsequent telephone conversations" (emphasis added). (The proxy statement filed with the S.E.C. referred to "negotiations" rather than "discussions" but the wording changed after the S.E.C. asked for details about the "negotiations.") It also disclosed the Lehman "fairness opinion letter," but not the hurried nature of the investigation on which it was based. Minority shareholders cast more than enough votes for approval to make the merger effective.

Weinberger (P), a former shareholder of UOP, brought a class action suit against UOP and Signal, challenging the cash-out merger as unfair to the minority shareholders. A chartered investment analyst called by P testified that both a discounted cash flow analysis and a comparative analysis of the premium paid over market in 10 other tender offer-merger combinations showed that UOP's stock was worth $26 per share. The chancellor rejected this testimony as inconsistent with the "Delaware block" or weighted average method of valuation, which assigns a particular weight to assets, market price, earnings, and other "elements of value." The chancellor held that Signal had dealt fairly with UOP's minority shareholders and paid them a fair price, and so entered judgment against P. P appeals. The Delaware Supreme Court reheard the appeal en banc.

Issues.

(i)   Did Signal bear the burden of showing that the merger was "fair" to the minority shareholders?

(ii)   Did the evidence show that Signal dealt fairly with UOP's minority shareholders?

(iii) In evaluating the fairness of the price that Signal paid for UOP's shares, must the court use the so-called "Delaware block" method of valuation?

(iv)   Did the evidence show that Signal paid a fair price?

(v)   When minority shareholders challenge a freeze out merger, must the controlling shareholder(s) demonstrate that the merger serves a legitimate business purpose?

Held. (i) Yes. (ii) No. (iii) No. (iv) No. (v) No. Judgment reversed.

♦   Signal had to show that the transaction was "fair" to the minority shareholders—that they received what an independent board would have secured for them—because directors who sat on both company's boards participated in the UOP board's decisionmaking about the merger without disclosing all material information in their possession.

♦   Signal failed to show that it dealt fairly with the minority shareholders or that it paid them a fair price. With respect to its dealings, Signal failed to disclose: (i) the feasibility study, which was derived from UOP information, or that Signal considered a purchase at $24 per share a good investment; or (ii) the cursory nature of the Lehman investigation or the serious time constraints set by Signal that caused it to be cursory. The negotiations were modest at best. Crawford (UOP's CEO), Signal's man at UOP, never really talked price with Signal.

♦ In evaluating the "fairness" of the price, a court need not use the "Delaware block" method exclusively. A court may use any valuation technique generally acceptable in the financial community, otherwise admissible in court, and consistent with section 262(h) of the Delaware corporation code, which governs the appraisal remedy. Section 262(h) provides that, in ascertaining "fair" price, a court should consider "all relevant factors," excluding "[o]nly the speculative elements of value that may arise from the 'accomplishment or expectation' of the merger." This eliminates the use only of "pro forma" data and projections of a speculative variety, not elements of future value, including the nature of the enterprise, which are known or susceptible of proof as of the date of the merger, or damages resulting from the taking. The chancellor may grant other relief if this appraisal remedy proves inadequate because of fraud, misrepresentation, self-dealing, deliberate waste of corporate assets, or gross and palpable overreaching. Except for this case and other designated cases in which a plaintiff shareholder relied on the formerly prevailing interpretation of section 262(h), that section now governs the financial remedy available to minority shareholders in a cash-out merger.

♦ In evaluating the fairness of a nonfraudulent transaction, price may be the preponderant consideration. In light of the testimony of P's chartered investment analyst that UOP shares were worth at least $26 per share, Signal failed to show that it paid a fair price (particularly since paying UOP's minority shareholders $24 would have had relatively little long-term effect on Signal given that the returns projected by Signal's officers at $21 and $24 per share differed by only .2%).

♦ When minority shareholders challenge a freeze out merger, the controlling shareholder(s) need no longer demonstrate that the merger serves a legitimate business purpose. Requiring such a demonstration adds no meaningful protection now that the expanded appraisal remedy is available to shareholders and the chancellor has broad discretion to fashion such relief as the facts of a given case may dictate.

---

3.   "Fair Dealing"--

Kahn v. Lynch Communication Systems, Inc., 638 A.2d 1110 (Del. 1994).

Facts. In 1981, Alcatel U.S.A. Corporation ("Alcatel") acquired 30.6% of the stock of Lynch Communication Systems (D) pursuant to a stock purchase agreement. The agreement required that D amend its articles to bar any business combination unless approved in a shareholder vote by 80% of the shares voted. The agreement also gave Alcatel the right (i) to proportional representation on D's board (five of 11 during the relevant period, including two of three on the executive committee and two of four on the compensation committee) and (ii) to purchase 40% of any equity securities offered by D to others (as long as its holdings did not exceed 45% before October 1, 1986). Alcatel later increased its holdings to 43.3% of D's stock.

In spring 1986, D's management concluded that remaining competitive meant obtaining fiber optic technology. To obtain this technology, D's management targeted Telco Systems, Inc. ("Telco") for acquisition. Telco's management expressed interest, but Alcatel opposed the deal and proposed that D combine with an indirect subsidiary of Alcatel's parent, Celwave Systems, Inc. ("Celwave"), a maker of telephone wire, cable, and related products.

D's board heard a presentation about Alcatel's proposal at its August meeting. Several directors expressed interest in the Telco acquisition. One, Beringer, labeled Telco "an immediate fit"; another, D's CEO, agreed and opined that D would have no interest in Celwave if Alcatel did not own Celwave. The Alcatel directors vetoed the Telco acquisition. They also opposed renewal of the compensation contracts for D's top five managers, objecting that these managers were not following Alcatel directions. Management directors exited the meeting and the remaining board members voted against renewal. D's board appointed an independent committee of three directors unaffiliated with management or Alcatel to negotiate with Celwave.

Alcatel's investment advisor proposed exchanging a .95 share of Celwave for each share of D. The independent committee's investment advisors deemed the ratio inadequate and the committee recommended against the proposed merger. Alcatel withdrew the proposal and offered to acquire all of D shares that it did not already own for $14 cash per share.

D's board then authorized the independent committee to negotiate with Alcatel about a cash merger. The independent committee concluded that $14 per share was inadequate, and made a counteroffer of $17 per share. Alcatel then made offers of $15 and $15.25 per share, and the independent committee rejected them, too. Alcatel then offered $15.50 per share, and threatened that, if rejected, Alcatel would proceed with an unfriendly tender at a lower price. The independent committee concluded that all alternatives to a cash-out merger with Alcatel were impracticable: the "white knight" alternative because of the 80% "approval requirement," the repurchase and shareholder rights plan alternatives because of the resulting debt. The committee recommended approval of the $15.50 offer. D's board then approved the offer, with the Alcatel nominees abstaining. Kahn (P) sued to enjoin Alcatel's cash-out acquisition of D. The court of chancery denied his request for a preliminary injunction. He then amended his complaint to seek monetary damages in a class action on behalf of all of D's former shareholders. The court of chancery then found for D. P appeals.

Issues.

(i)   Did Alcatel exercise "control" over D so that it bore the fiduciary duty of a majority shareholder?

(ii)   If so, did Alcatel, as a controlling shareholder, discharge its burden of proving the "entire fairness" of the challenged transactions?

Held. (i) Yes. (ii) No. Judgment reversed.

♦   A shareholder owes a fiduciary duty to the other shareholders only if it owns a majority interest in, or **exercises control** over, a corporation. While Alcatel owned only 43% of D, the record supports the finding that the outside directors deferred to the Alcatel directors only because of Alcatel's stockholding. The outside directors' recommendation did not reflect their own business judgment, but Alcatel's threats.

♦   Because Alcatel was a controlling shareholder, it bore the burden of proving the "entire fairness" of the challenged transactions. That D's independent committee recommended approval does not shift the burden unless the committee had real bargaining power that it could exercise with Alcatel on an "arm's-length basis," and Alcatel could not dictate the terms of the merger. The record of this case demonstrates that the ability of the independent committee to negotiate at arm's-length with Alcatel was compromised by Alcatel's threat to proceed with a hostile tender offer if the $15.50 price was not accepted by D. Any semblance of arm's length bargaining ended when D's board surrendered to the ultimatum and agreed to a merger on Alcatel's terms.

---

4.   **Parent Corporation's Exchange Offer for Outstanding Shares of Controlled Subsidiary Can Be Structured to Avoid "Entire Fairness" Review--**

In re **Pure Resources, Inc. Shareholders Litigation**, 808 A.2d 421 (Del. Ch. 2002).

Facts. Unocal Corp. (D), owner of 65% of the shares of Pure Resources, Inc., made an exchange offer for the remaining 35%, a great deal of which was in the hands of institutional investors. D offered 0.6527 of a Unocal share for each Pure share, provided that (i) a majority of shares not owned by D were tendered (a non-waivable condition) and (ii) enough shares were tendered to enable D to own 90% of Pure and to effect a short-form merger under 8 Del.C. section 253 (a waivable condition). D promised that if it obtained 90%, it would consummate a short-form merger as soon as practicable at the same exchange ratio.

Pure's board empowered a special committee consisting of directors not representing D to retain independent advisors, take a position on whether the offer should be accepted, and to negotiate with D to see if it would increase its bid. The special committee sought the full authority of the board to respond to the offer, but D strongly opposed the delegation of such authority, and the matter was not pursued. The special committee did ask D to increase the exchange ratio, but D declined to do so, so the special committee voted not to recommend the offer.

Minority shareholders in Pure (P) sued to preliminarily enjoin D's exchange offer, claiming that D's offer was not "entirely fair" within the meaning of *Kahn v. Lynch Communication Systems, Inc.* (*supra*) and its progeny, which expressly govern negotiated mergers (and that D had made inadequate and misleading disclosure of the material facts necessary for Pure stockholders to make an informed decision whether to tender into the offer. D argued (i) that the "entire fairness" standard did not apply to an exchange offer when the offeror had not suggested explicitly or implicitly that holders who did not tender wold suffer as a result and had disclosed all material information; and (ii) that the offer fully met the applicable standard which was set forth in *Solomon v. Pathe Communications Corp.*, 672 A.2d 35 (Del. 1996), and similar cases.

Issue. Must a controlling stockholder demonstrate that its exchange offer for outstanding shares of a controlled subsidiary is "entirely fair?"

Held. No. Preliminary injunction issued until D amends its offer to condition it on approval of a majority of Pure's unaffiliated stockholders.

♦   Delaware law subjects a negotiated merger with a controlling stockholder to greater scrutiny (*Lynch*'s "entire fairness" standard, *supra*) than a tender offer from such a holder because in a negotiated merger the controlling stockholder is on both sides of the transaction.

♦   Many of the concerns that justify the *Lynch* standard are implicated by tender offers initiated by controlling stockholders. In some ways, the tender offer could pose a greater threat to minority holders than a negotiated merger when implemented with appropriate protective devices by an independent committee with the power to say no and conditioned on a majority of the minority vote. A tender offer from a controlling shareholder will reflect confidential information, and the offer will require disaggregated stockholders to decide whether to tender quickly, pressured by the risk of being squeezed out in a short-form merger at a different price later or being left as part of a much smaller public minority.

♦   Applying the *Lynch* "entire fairness" standard to tender offers from controlling shareholders, however, might reduce shareholder wealth because of over-deterrence and litigation costs. Especially in light of the increased activism of institutional investors and the greater information flows available to them, the *Solomon* standard should apply, modificd to take account of "inherent coercion" (fear of retribution if the merger is defeated) and "structural bias" (a wrongful threat that has the effect of forcing stockholders to tender at the wrong price to avoid an even worse fate later on). So, a tender offer by a controlling stockholder should qualify for scrutiny under the *Solomon* standard only when: (i) it is subject to a nonwaivable majority of the minority tender condition; (ii) the controlling stockholder promises to consummate a prompt section 253 merger at the same price if it obtains more than 90% of the shares; and (iii) the controlling stockholder has made no retributive threats. Moreover, to offset the informational and timing advantages possessed by controlling stockholders, the controlling stockholder must permit the independent directors on the target board both free rein and adequate time to react to the tender offer, by (at the very least) hiring their own advisors, providing the minority with a recommendation as to the advisability of the offer, and disclosing adequate information for the minority to make an informed judgment.

I. STATE TAKEOVER REGULATION

While Congress was considering the Williams Act, the states began regulating takeovers, always in a manner that favored target management. These statutes apparently reflected: (i) the political clout of target managements, especially in comparison to out-of-state bidders, and (ii) fear that a bidder might pursue efficiency, and thus shareholder welfare, by closing local plants or ordering layoffs. When the Supreme Court struck down Illinois's takeover statute in 1982 (in *Edgar v. MITE Corp.*, *infra*), many states passed "second generation" statutes. These statutes generally apply only to corporations incorporated within the state; they do not provide for a "fairness" review.

1. Five Kinds.

a. "Control share acquisition" statutes make "acquisition of control" subject to approval by a shareholder vote.

b. "Fair price" statutes. They regulate "second-step" mergers of two-tier takeovers. These statutes make mergers and similar business combinations between the corporation and an "interested shareholder" (defined to include holders of 10% or more of the corporation's shares) subject to approval by a supermajority of shares with one critical exception. No supermajority approval is required if the transaction meets statutory "fair price" standards. Although the definition of "fair price" varies among states, they all tend to assure nontendering holders bought out in a second-step merger or related transaction of a price at least as high as the highest paid for target shares by the "interested shareholder" over a recent period (typically, two years).

c. Moratorium statutes. They prohibit subject corporations from engaging in a "business combination" (including a merger, liquidation, or sale of substantial asset) for a specified period (five years in New York, which pioneered this type of statute; three years in Delaware) after any shareholder acquires more than a specified percentage of the corporation's shares (20% in New York, 15% in Delaware) unless the board gave advance approval of a larger acquisition.

    d.   **"Redemption rights" statutes.** These statutes essentially expand the traditional appraisal statute to cover "controlling share acquisitions" as well as mergers. Under the Pennsylvania statute, an acquisition of 30% of a firm's stock entitles other shareholders to receive, on demand, from the acquiror an amount in cash equal to the "fair value" of their stock in the target ("fair value" includes a pro rata share of the control premium paid for the first-step acquisition).

    e.   **"Constituency" statutes.** These statutes authorize or instruct directors to consider the interests of nonshareholder constituencies like employees, creditors, customers, and local communities.

2.   Federal Limitations on State Takeover Laws--

Edgar v. MITE Corp., 457 U.S. 624 (1982).

Facts. Edgar (D) was secretary of state of Illinois, which enacted a Business Takeover Act. The Act required that any takeover (tender) offer for shares of a target company be registered with the secretary of state. To accomplish this, the offeror was to notify the secretary of the proposal 20 business days before it was to become effective. The Act empowered the secretary to hold a hearing at any time during the waiting period on the substantive fairness of the offer, if the secretary believed it necessary to protect the shareholders' interests. A hearing would also be held if requested by a majority of the target's outside directors or by Illinois shareholders who owned 10% of the stock subject to the offer. If a hearing was held, the secretary could deny registration of a tender offer upon finding that it was inequitable or failed to provide full and fair disclosure of material information to the offerees.

MITE (P) initiated a tender offer of $28 per share for all outstanding shares of Chicago Rivet, whose shares were trading at about $24 each. P complied with the Williams Act, but not with the Illinois Act. It sought a temporary restraining order to enjoin D from enforcing the Illinois Act and sued for a declaratory judgment that the Act was preempted by the Williams Act and violated the Commerce Clause. D then moved to invoke the Illinois Act, but the district court issued a preliminary injunction prohibiting him from doing so. The district court ultimately entered final judgment in favor of P. The appellate court affirmed. D appeals.

Issues.

(i)   Does the Illinois Act substantially frustrate the objectives of the Williams Act?

(ii)   Does the Illinois Act violate the Commerce Clause by directly regulating interstate commerce?

Held. (i) Yes. (ii) Yes. Judgment affirmed.

♦ When Congress enacted the Williams Act, it did not explicitly prohibit states from regulating takeovers. However, a major goal of the Williams Act was to avoid favoring either the takeover bidder or the target's management. The purpose of this was to avoid discouraging takeover proposals, because they can provide a check on entrenched but inefficient management.

♦ The Illinois Act's precommencement notification requirement prohibits the offeror from communicating with the target's shareholders, but allows management to disseminate information about the offer to the shareholders. This gives management a powerful tool with which to fight the offer. Congress specifically sought to avoid this consequence, as it rejected such a requirement as part of the Williams Act several times. The notification provision is at odds with the Williams Act.

♦ Congress intended that the shareholders and the takeover offeror be free to go forward without unreasonable delay. The Illinois Act's hearing provisions introduce extended delay into the tender offer process, particularly by allowing management to insist on a hearing. The potential for delay upsets the balance that the Williams Act struck between management and the offeror.

♦ The Illinois Act is preempted by the Williams Act because Illinois allows the secretary of state to pass on the substantive fairness of the tender offer by denying registration if it is found that the offer is inequitable. Congress intended that shareholders be free to make their own decisions.

♦ The Commerce Clause permits only incidental regulation of interstate commerce by the states. The Illinois Act directly regulates transactions taking place across state lines. It could prevent those living in other states and having no connection with Illinois from doing business with P. The statute's sweeping effect is a direct restraint on interstate commerce, as it gives Illinois the power to determine whether a tender offer may proceed anywhere.

♦ The Illinois Act would be unconstitutional even if it only indirectly regulated interstate commerce, because the burden it imposes on interstate commerce far outweighs the local interests served by the law. The protections that the Act affords Illinois shareholders are mostly speculative, and the state has no legitimate interest in protecting nonresident shareholders. The Act also effectively allows Illinois to regulate the internal affairs of foreign corporations.

Concurrence (Powell, J.). The Williams Act assumes corporate entities of substantially equal resources. Its neutrality policy does not imply intent to prohibit state laws to assure greater protection for interests that may be broader than those of the target's management.

Concurrence (Stevens, J.). I do not join in the preemption holding. The congressional neutrality policy is not a prohibition against state legislation designed to provide special protection for incumbent management.

Concurrence (O'Connor, J.). I agree that portions of the Illinois Act are invalid under the Commerce Clause. It is therefore unnecessary to reach the preemption issues.

---

3. State Regulation--

CTS Corp. v. Dynamics Corp. of America, 481 U.S. 69 (1987).

Facts. Indiana passed a Control Shares Acquisitions Act ("CSAA") that applied to any business incorporated in Indiana that had: (i) 150 or more shareholders; (ii) its principal place of business, its principal office, or substantial assets within Indiana; and (iii) either: (a) more than 10% of its shareholders resident in Indiana, (b) more than 10% of its shares owned by Indiana residents, or (c) 10,000 shareholders resident in Indiana. An entity acquires "control shares" in such a corporation whenever it acquires voting power to or above 20%, 33.3%, or 50%. Voting power of these acquired shares is only granted on petition and approval of a majority vote of all disinterested shareholders of each class of stock. The acquiror can request a meeting for such vote within 50 days. If voting power is not granted, the corporation *may* buy back the stock, or if no petition calling for a vote is asked for, the corporation can buy back the stock.

Dynamics Corporation of America (D) owned 9.6% of CTS Corporation (P), an Indiana corporation. P elected to be governed by the new Act. D tendered one million shares of CTS, which would bring its interest to 27.5%. P sued, alleging that the Act violated the Commerce Clause and was preempted by the Williams Act. The district court agreed with P; the circuit court affirmed. D appeals.

Issues.

(i)   Does the federal Williams Act preempt Indiana's state law?

(ii)   Does the state law violate the Commerce Clause?

Held. (i) No. (ii) No. Judgment reversed.

♦   The state law is not preempted by the Williams Act.

> The state law is consistent with the intent of the Williams Act—it protects the shareholders against both management and the tender offeror. Neither contending party gets an advantage; it does not impose an indefinite delay on tender offers; it does not impose a government official's view of fairness on the buyer or the selling shareholders. The shareholders can evaluate the fairness of the proposed terms.

> If the tender offeror fears an adverse shareholder vote, it can make a conditional offer, accepting shares on condition that the shares receive the voting rights within a certain time period.

The Williams Act does not preempt all state regulation of tender offers, or state laws that limit or delay the free exercise of power after a tender offer (example: staggering the terms of the members of the board of directors).

J. PUBLIC POLICY AND CORPORATE CONTROL TRANSACTIONS: THE STAKEHOLDER DEBATE

Critics of takeovers have argued that:

1. **They Foster an Unhealthy Interest in What the Critics Call "Short-Term Profit Maximization."** (The critics have not enjoyed much success in reconciling this argument with the teachings of the Capital Asset Pricing Model.)

2. **They Prompt Undesirable Increases in Debt Financing, Thereby Posing the Threat of Too Many Bankruptcies.** The available empirical evidence does suggest that takeovers may coincide with notable increases in debt financing. The data do not suggest, however, a cause and effect relationship: within the same market, the financial structure of targets appears to be about the same as that of nontargets. Besides, the increase in debt financing may well benefit shareholders. It may reduce the expected costs of mistakes and misconduct by managements, and it may force managements to take business risks from which they would otherwise shy away, but that diversified shareholders would prefer.

3. **They Have an Adverse and "Unfair" Impact on Employees.** Some economists argue that, at least in some firms, managerial employees accept what would otherwise be below-market income in return for job security, thereby creating an implicit contract threatened by a hostile takeover. Moreover, firms may well defer payment of a considerable portion of managers' expected lifetime consideration until near the end of their careers. Deferral may provide managers with incentives to behave in ways that maximize share values, and it permits "ex post" review of a manager's performance. Some economists argue, therefore, that a takeover may frustrate managers' reasonable expectations about compensation.

NOTES

NOTES

NOTES

NOTES

NOTES

NOTES